REFLECTIONS ON LEADERSHIP

Edited by

Richard A. Couto

University Press of America,® Inc.
Lanham · Boulder · New York · Toronto · Plymouth, UK

Copyright © 2007 by
University Press of America,® Inc.
4501 Forbes Boulevard
Suite 200
Lanham, Maryland 20706
UPA Acquisitions Department (301) 459-3366

Estover Road
Plymouth PL6 7PY
United Kingdom

Library of Congress Control Number:
ISBN-13: 978-0-7618-3741-1 (paperback : alk. paper)
ISBN-10: 0-7618-3741-8 (paperback : alk. paper)

Table of Contents

List of Tables and Figures

FOREWORD
James MacGregor Burns

This book combines tribute with tribulation about my book *Leadership*. I like that. Whatever the tributes, I know there will always be tribulations. I will be crafty here though, and before others pick up the assault, I will launch a preemptive attack on my work.

As those of you who have read the book know, I treated leadership very extensively: revolutionary leadership, group leadership, intellectual leadership, and the like. I wrote a lot about transforming leadership, which I think is an exciting aspect of the study of leadership. I subsequently devoted an entire book (Burns 2003) just to the topic of transforming leadership and another book to the less visible forms of leadership that bring about social change (Burns 1990). However, I tried to do something much more than to place a label on one or another form of leadership. I hoped to reach a general theory of leadership; a theory that would encompass leadership at different times, different places, and in different cultures. Perhaps my effort was too general. Perhaps I tried to do too much. Nonetheless, I got a discussion going. From that discussion, I learned about three failings of my initial effort that I hope you will keep in mind as you read the following essays about my work, as you improve upon my investigation of leadership, and as you practice this incredibly puzzling phenomenon.

The Question of Power

I tried to do something on the question of power, but I did not do enough. I feel that power is really misunderstood in this country, and generally; we do not know as much about power as physicists know about energy. When I compare the two fields further, it is pitiful. Power is central to work in political science, but I do not think that political scientists know very much about it. We tend to take a quantitative approach to power: How many guns? How much money? Those sorts of questions do not ask enough about the recipients, the targets of power. What about the followers who are supposed to be led and manipulated, etc.? The most impressive or depressing lesson about power was Vietnam. We had the numbers, we had the guns, the planes, the tanks—the power of military arms. We completely misunderstood the psychology of the situation, however. I believe that happens repeatedly. I started placing the emphasis on followership, and not just on leadership, only recently because I realized that power is somewhere between and among followers and leaders.

Suppose, for example, I am on the way to a lovely lake on a beautiful campus on a bright fall morning. Suppose further that I have a suicidal impulse. I just lectured, and some students disagreed with me and did not take every word I said as absolute truth. Class had gone very poorly, I am upset, I am depressed, and I intend to jump in the lake to kill myself. On the way, somebody—a bad guy, a thief, and a murderer—says, "Your money or your life!" Well, being Scottish, that would give me reason to pause under any circumstance. After going through the usual Scottish inquiry— "What's really more important, my money or my life?"—and adding my depressed condition, I would look at my adversary and say, "Shoot me. That's fine. I'm just going down to kill myself, and you can take care of it for me, right here." In other words, he is not a threat to me and had no influence over me because he did not understand my situation, my wants and needs. He thought I valued my life.

That may be a feeble example, but it is the kind of interaction and relationship that I am interested in now and was not sufficiently interested in at the time I wrote *Leadership*. To put it very briefly, I think we have to link motivation with resources. The resources are generally clear—money and all that—but motivation among those we are trying to influence is the fascinating thing.

I got interested in leadership after doing some work in psychology. I would say, if my political science and history friends do not mind, I think psychology is the most important foundation for the further study of leadership. I think we have to study all fields, because leadership, above all, is a kind of a liberal arts education in itself. But we need better work on the nature of power and motivation. It is psychology that offers the keys to understanding them.

Reaching Generalizations

My book fails in a second way because it is difficult for the reader to generalize from it. I got into the serious study of leadership after doing a significant amount of research on Franklin Delano Roosevelt and on various members of the Kennedy family. I felt unsatisfied intellectually. Sure, I knew a lot about these people, but what did I know about leadership? What would I do if I were teaching Leadership 101? What could I say about leadership more than just talking about individual leaders?

The problem is even bigger. How do you generalize about leadership around the globe with its incredible variety of cultures and leaders, and, of course, leaderships—a very deliberate plural? I puzzled over that. Unfortunately, my book reflects my puzzlement rather than a resolution of how to reach safe generalizations about something similar in different times and places. I think my work is inadequate. I found the most help in the work of a psychologist, Abraham Maslow. His work offers a hierarchy of needs and develops the theories of others to explain that if you satisfy a need in another person or group, you do not go back to equilibrium necessarily. Instead, by satisfying some needs, you probably create new needs. I found his work very useful.

I tried to develop this idea into a broader hierarchy than Maslow's own hierarchy. I hypothesized that if you start to satisfy basic needs, food and shelter, then you go on psychologically to hope. If your hopes are more or less fulfilled, you move up the hierarchy into expectations. The interesting thing about this theory is that you get dynamics either way—expectations are fulfilled or they are blocked. If needs are satisfied, then people move on to new needs.

You also get dynamics, however, if needs are blocked. The frustrations of people when their expectations have been dashed or their needs have not been met create a dynamic that supports social change. Therefore, I finally elevated this into a point where someone going through this process or even masses of people going through this process, turns expectations into demands, and that is where the followers really take over. They *demand* the satisfaction of their needs; they are not just hoping any longer. They are not just wishing. They do not just need. They are demanding. And that is where the followers create and maintain leadership.

One thing I found lacking in Maslow's research was sufficient regard for what seems to me to be culturally-based needs. So, I experimented with a phenomenon that I think takes place before you get to the "need" level. I remain particularly entranced by this question because of its global implications. I asked, Is there any point where there is a common universal phenomenon underlying something that later becomes leadership? And my answer to this is summed up in the word *want*.

As you read about leadership, you learn how the terms *needs* and *wants* are treated loosely and interchangeably. I do not use them loosely. To me the most fundamental initial process or psychology or motivation is want. All people value security—they want it. I am not saying that a newborn baby is thinking security, but her parents are. The first thing needed for that baby is survival and the parents provide sustenance in different ways, in different cultures. The provision of sustenance and security, however different, seems to be a very common process, a universal process. If we could generalize over some process such as that, just at the start, then we would have a foundation to delve into the huge variety of needs and then the variety of hopes, expectations, and demands.

While I think this is still a pretty rough theory, it permits generalizations. What interests me as I read new material and re-read the familiar, particularly the classics, is the extent to which needs keep cropping up. Rousseau has some fascinating ideas about needs. He may be an excellent example of how a philosopher can have a profound social impact. I am afraid his was not a happy impact on the French Revolution. Tracing the connection between Rousseau's ideas about need and the violence of the French Revolution is work for students in the years ahead.

In the process of reaching for generalizations based on individual leaders, I realize now that I was writing about the forms of leadership that produce change, without putting them into the broadest context of social and historical causation.

We have too few historians in the field of leadership. Historians may offer us an overall theory of human change, of historical causation, social causation, and the like. We, of course, have the legacy of historical studies from the nineteenth century, the most preeminent of which is the work of Karl Marx. We can dispute Marx, but here was a man who tried to explain everything. There were others, particularly in that century, who thought, with the optimism of the Enlightenment perhaps, that we could really figure out the nature of change and direct it. Perhaps the way to make generalizations is to follow the approach of Marx and Carlyle. Begin with an overview of historical forces, of causation, and make generalizations from that vantage point rather than from my starting point with the study of individual leaders.

There Are More Than Two Parts to a Dichotomy

Third, and finally, I think my book is overly dichotomized. For example, I tried to present the conceptual frameworks of transforming leadership and transactional leadership as a contrast as though there is no connection between them. I now think that this is wrong. There is a stronger connection between transforming and transactional leadership than I led readers to believe. I think we have a spectrum. A few leaders operate wholly on the transactional side and a few leaders operate wholly on the transforming side, but most work on both sides of that spectrum and combine transforming and transactional leadership.

I do not know why I did not see the mixture there, because F.D.R., the man I studied most closely, was the lion and the fox. The very title of that book expresses the idea that politicians have to be powerful, like lions, and politicians have to be intelligent, like foxes. Of course, I stole that idea from Machiavelli. Tracing out how leaders select and use these tactics of transforming and transactional leadership fascinates me.

A Nonconclusive Peroration

I am not going to end with a great peroration. I hope only that I preempted the attacks of others. Nobody could be more critical of my book than I am, but wait, you will find out!

References

Burns, J. M. 1990. *Cobblestone Leadership: Majority Rule, Minority Power.* Norman, OK: University of Oklahoma Press.
———. 2003. *Transforming Leadership: The Pursuit of Happiness.* Boston: Atlantic Monthly Press.

INTRODUCTION
Richard A. Couto

Frequently, a study of leadership will reference James MacGregor Burns's remark "Leadership is one of the most observed and least understood phenomena on earth" (Burns 1978:2). The ubiquitous reference indicates the deference and tribute to his masterful and significant work *Leadership*. One might add, however, that *Leadership*, the book—a long and weighty book which may be more often cited than read—has informed the way we observe leadership, the practice. All of the contributors of this volume have read *Leadership* closely and most know its author personally. We follow in the pioneering footsteps that Burns's work has left.

Burns's work *Leadership* quickened the serious scholarly attention given to leadership and soon became a standard of excellence in the field. Others preceded Burns in their explicit and systematic attention to leadership, but he was among the first to produce an interdisciplinary synthesis of scholarship about, or related to, leadership within an explicit theoretical framework that incorporated the values of social needs and wants. The years since the publication of *Leadership* witnessed more scholarship on leadership and related topics. That scholarship inevitably takes cognizance of *Leadership* in terms of whether to defer or differ.

It is hard not to do both. The book's staggering sweep of world history and its analytical framework testify to rigorous, thoughtful, and imaginative scholarship. It is also dated. Those who have followed Burns and attempted to deal with a broad sweep of leadership (Bass 1985; Gardner and Laskin 1995; Heifetz 1994; Rost 1991; Wills 1995) have pointed out the gaps in *Leadership*. Indeed, Burns has done some critical reinterpretation of his own work with his efforts within *Cobblestone Leadership* (1990) and his most recent book, *Transforming Leadership* (2003). He has also staked out new directions for the field with the Kellogg Leadership Studies Project (www), the *Encyclopedia of Leadership* (Goethals, Sorenson, and Burns 2004), and a group that he gathered and cajoled to attempt an integrated theory of leadership (Goethals and Sorenson 2006). This book acknowledges the important contribution of *Leadership* and intends to continue the scholarship it stimulates.

The Jepson School of Leadership Studies at the University of Richmond and the Burns Academy of Leadership at the University of Maryland marked the scholarly contribution of *Leadership* at a one-day conference during which more than fifteen scholars examined Burns's work. Their presentations and those of a few people who were unable to attend make up the chapters of this book. Contributors reflect on their first introduction to *Leadership* and the importance of the book for them. Finally, each contributor builds on the work of *Leadership* to suggest new questions and challenges facing the field of leadership studies.

Burns's work provides a unifying thread for each chapter of this book. His work extends beyond the publication of words, however. Burns was determined to understand and to impart understanding about leadership in order to improve democratic practice and to promote social justice and equality. While we laud this work, we also join its ongoing challenge.

For Whom This Book Toils

James MacGregor Burns spent his professional career in undergraduate liberal arts programs. As he explains, "I got interested in leadership through the questions of my students while I taught an honors course at Williams." So, too, we intend this book to be an understanding of leadership that will enable the effective practice of and reflection on leadership, in the fundamental spirit of the liberal arts.

That spirit exceeds young undergraduates. It reaches anyone who ponders fundamental questions such as: What will we do? How do we intend to do it? What do we want from life? What do we want to give to others? Who are we? What do we stand for? What values will guide us? And how much responsibility will we take for others in our neighborhood, city, or town; company; church, temple, or mosque; state, region, country, or planet? These decisions have implications for the qualities and forms of leadership that we will choose and the manner in which we will practice the leadership that chooses us. Thus, this book toils for all of those who face those questions in hopes of supporting their search for answers.

The style of the book is mainly conversational. The combination of personal and scholarly hopefully reminds some of us and introduces others to the notion that scholars are people, and behind their printed words are experiences, wants, and needs that they transform and transact into scholarship. This book hopes to invite you, its readers, as the next generation of scholars and practitioners of leadership, into an ongoing reflection on leadership.

Plan of the Book

In the Foreword of this book, Burns offers a cogent and concise critique of his own work. He discusses the shortcoming of too many dichotomies in *Leadership*. He laments that others have understood transactional and transforming leadership, for example, as opposites rather than parts of a continuum. It is rare to find an author who speaks so frankly about the shortcomings of his own landmark study. It is typical of Burns to invite others to come forward and try as he did to further our understanding of a commonplace, and yet significant, phenomenon and to assume that perhaps others will do it better than he did. Without making the latter claim, contributors to this book are willing to come forward, explain what they have done, and suggest what remains to be done.

Section I provides background to James MacGregor Burns and his work *Leadership*. It explains the new standard that it set for the study of leadership as well as the problems it made for applying its concepts to the practice of leadership. Barbara Kellerman provides biographical and career information about Jim Burns. She also places Burns's work in its political and scholarly context and explains how she differs from Burns over a moral emphasis in discussions of leadership. Georgia Sorenson examines the role that Burns has played in mentoring the field of leadership studies. Ronald Heifetz, in Chapter 3, provides an understanding of the contribution of *Leadership* to his own work and to the field. He also tweaks the controversy over the moral dimensions of leadership to make them more applicable to practitioners. In the section's concluding chapter, Chapter 4, Adam Yarmolinsky—decidedly a practitioner as well as scholar of leadership—challenges Burns's treatment of change in *Leadership*. Yarmolinsky argues that change is a ubiquitous constant and leaders do little more than "mediate and adjust" institutions to adapt to some changes and to promote others.

Section II outlines some of the remaining challenges for the study of leadership in light of Burns's achievements and shortcomings. Two chapters place Burns's work in the context of organizational psychology. In Chapter 5, Edwin P. Hollander, a longtime friend and colleague of Burns, relates his theory of active followership to Burns's work on transforming and transactional leadership. Tiffany Hansbrough relates Burns's work to scholarship in organizational behavior in Chapter 6. Both chapters suggest how behavioral science contributes to the study of leadership and serves to critique Burns's work.

Philosophy and history also contribute insight into the remaining needs of the study of leadership. Terry Price presents some of the moral dimensions that determine the common good. He moves our considerations from the transactional/transforming dichotomy to a "transpositional" approach that injects moral discourse into leadership with an understanding of the need to address any leader's epistemological limits. Tom Wren fixes our attention on the unresolved paradox within Burns's work. How do you reconcile the exclusive nature of leadership with the inclusive nature of popular sovereignty? Laurien Alexandre explains both the shortcomings of Burns's work in dealing with gender and the shoring that it provides for more attention to it. She thus raises the general issue of increasing our critical historical awareness of overlooked elements in the study of leadership.

The final chapter suggests some avenues to theory building that move beyond *Leadership*. Margaret Wheatley borrows from the natural sciences in Chapter 10 to extol systems thinking as an approach to understand and exercise leadership in terms of patterns, processes, and relationships of mutual dependence.

Section III's chapters suggest new models for the study and practice of leadership. Gill Hickman holds out hope that formal organizations can provide moral, transforming leadership—a hope that Burns disavows in *Leadership* and that Adam Yarmolinsky discourages in Chapter 4. Larraine Matusak, in Chapter 12, rebuts Burns's lament of the passing and dearth of leadership by extolling the nature and character of the leadership of ordinary people taking extraordinary initiative for effective problem-solving action. Robin Gerber draws on her experience with organized labor to provide examples of the leadership of ordinary people as a challenge to civic and political leaders. Specifically, she asks that they no longer invest themselves in an inert citizenry. Of course, this requires that the rest of us stop our efforts to live down to some of our political leaders' expectations. Ronald Walters looks at the social movements of the 1960s for the civil rights of African-Americans to find leadership in the twenty-first century. Thus, he shares with the other contributors to this section hope for new and better leadership "from the bottom up." Chapter 15 offers a theory of effective narratives of adaptive work and uses it to synthesize the contributors' comments. It addresses the shortcomings of *Leadership* and proposes a means to address them while holding on to the essence of Burns's work.

Along the way throughout the book, introductions to each section will announce the themes in its chapters. The Conclusion deals with the limitations of *Leadership* as Burns enumerates and explains them in the Foreword. The Conclusion, just as the rest of the book, serves as a prologue to your efforts to advance the study and the practice of "good" and effective leadership.

Acknowledgments

Obviously, an edited book involves the work of many, and I owe more than ordinary thanks to the contributors. The press of other responsibilities and events kept pushing the completion of this work, and they were exceedingly patient with me. Maia Carter, Dominic Feriozzi, Jessica Horan, Kelly Pearce, and Rena Metzer assisted in organizing and conducting the conference "Leadership@20" that became this book. Emily Griffey and Leisel Mundth provided superb assistance and thus demonstrated again what extraordinary young women they are. Scott Allen helped with a close reading of Yarmolinsky's contribution. Marti Goetz provided an artist's eye for the cover. Rachel Petrella is an exceptionally fine editor and helped considerably in shaping the chapters. Barbara Couto Sipe and Nathan Craddock processed several manuscript drafts and scrutinized them for wayward syntax. All of my former colleagues at the Jepson School of Leadership Studies encouraged and assisted me, particularly John Rosenblum. The University of Richmond Faculty Research Committee's professional development funds and Antioch University's Ph.D. Program in Leadership and Change provided support for this work. Laurien Alexandre, my colleague at Antioch, was kind enough to offer to fill in the important gender gap in Burns's work and in this one. Both Peggy Lobb and Jacqueline Duresky provided invaluable copyediting assistance. Cassie King, despite her size, remains unparalleled in my experience in wrestling the English language into submission or at least my use of it.

I am also grateful to my students at Antioch. Their needs and those of all students of leadership studies challenged me to bring to them the thoughts of some of the best people in the field. Their questions and those to come indirectly led me to push forward on a theory of effective narratives of adaptive work. The embodied narratives of my colleagues at Antioch also contributed greatly to that part of the book. In particular, Deborah Baldwin stands out as the exemplar information guru for whom anyone engaged in research hopes.

Finally, of course, there would be no book without James MacGregor Burns. He remains a model of intellectual vigor, strong convictions, and supportive collegiality. This book is dedicated to him with deference and difference and as a tribute and a tribulation. It is unimaginable that he would have it any other way.

References

Bass, B. M. 1985. *Leadership and Performance Beyond Expectations.* New York: Free Press.

Burns, J. M. 1990. *Cobblestone Leadership: Majority Rule, Minority Power.* Norman, OK: University of Oklahoma Press.

———. 2003. *Transforming Leadership: The Pursuit of Happiness.* Boston: Atlantic Monthly Press.

Gardner, H., and E. Laskin. 1995. *Leading Minds: An Anatomy of Leadership.* New York: Basic Books.

Goethals, George R., Georgia J. Sorenson, and James MacGregor Burns, eds. 2004. *Encyclopedia of Leadership,* 4 vol. set. Thousand Oaks, CA: Sage Publications.

Goethals, George R., and Georgia L. J. Sorenson, eds. 2006. *The Quest for a General Theory of Leadership.* Northampton, MA: Edward Elgar.

Heifetz, R. A. 1994. *Leadership Without Easy Answers.* Cambridge, MA: Belknap Press.

Kellogg Leadership Studies Project Working Papers. www. http://www.academy.umd.edu/publications/klspdocs/. Retrieved February 20, 2006.

Rost, J. C. 1991. *Leadership for the Twenty-First Century.* New York: Praeger.

Wills, G. 1995. *Certain Trumpets: The Nature of Leadership.* New York: Simon & Schuster.

SECTION I
JAMES MACGREGOR BURNS AND *LEADERSHIP*

This Section introduces James MacGregor Burns and his work. Barbara Kellerman and Georgia Sorenson provide the most information about Jim Burns, the person and the professional. They explain the personal importance of his mentoring relationship with them as well as the importance of *Leadership* on the field of leadership studies. However, we are not engaged in creating a cult of personality or orthodoxy of thought. Indeed, as Ronald Heifetz points out, the genius of *Leadership* is to maintain doubt, to pose questions, and to deny all answers the status of being final. Just as we do not seek to create a cult, nor do we want to depose Burns from his deserved stature. He and his book offer important starting points from which to understand, study, and practice leadership.

Barbara Kellerman goes to the heart of an important issue that others will take up in this volume. Is leadership a moral exercise? For her, the focus should be on leaders' "ability to get others to follow where they lead." We shall come back to this issue of morality or effectiveness frequently in these pages. Kellerman raises it early and concisely for us.

Georgia Sorenson puts *Leadership* in the context of the scholarship on leadership. Where Kellerman gives us the mark of the man and his work, Sorenson provides a metric of the work and its time. Her work in Chapter 2 emphasizes the contribution of the book's interdisciplinary nature, its theoretical efforts, and the importance it places on values—especially broad moral ones. She describes Burns's work in Thomas Kuhn's terms of a paradigm shift and the development of a field of inquiry. She offers a succinct and important context of other studies and approaches with which to measure the significance of *Leadership*.

Ronald Heifetz, in Chapter 3, describes his effort to work with the frameworks that Burns provided. Heifetz, with deference, points out the deficiencies of Burns's work in assisting mid-career professionals to analyze their leadership experience. Indeed, Burns's Foreword contains some of the insufficiently developed areas that Heifetz discusses. Heifetz's discussion of leadership with and without authority, whether formal or informal, touches on another theme—the place of values in leadership—that we will revisit at several places in the book.

Adam Yarmolinsky develops the important question about a leader's capacity to conduct change. He, like Heifetz, scales back the degree of change that a transforming leader can initiate in a world in which change is the only constant. Leaders, Yarmolinsky suggests, have to catch up to a moving train. In this view, he anticipates the discussion of a new paradigm for leadership that Margaret Wheatley offers in Section II.

Yarmolinsky brings to his consideration the unique perspective of someone who spent years in the very highest ranks of the federal government and in large organizations. From that vantage point, he echoes Kellerman's and Heifetz's concerns that language about transforming leadership fuels unwarranted grandiosity about leaders and their capacities to bring about change, moral change in particular. Yarmolinsky, perhaps like Kellerman, sees effectiveness as a value and suggests, like Heifetz, that effective leaders combine change with continuity of values.

CHAPTER 1
JAMES MACGREGOR BURNS: LEO AS LEADER
Barbara Kellerman

> *As a not-so-young graduate student at Yale in the early 1970s, I came to seek out James MacGregor Burns. I was a Ph.D. candidate in the political science department. It was not then—nor is it now, for that matter— terribly hospitable to women, particularly those who lived off campus to pursue graduate work while simultaneously raising children, and most definitely not to those of us women who insisted on studying leadership. What has also become clear over time is that, my naiveté as a graduate student notwithstanding, I had hit pay dirt. My trip to Williamstown in the early 1970s to meet Burns turned out to be the professional equivalent of a pilgrimage to Mecca. For those of us who sought to make meaning of leadership before leadership was "in," Jim Burns was heaven sent.*

In the interest of full disclosure, I should mention that my graduate career was not exactly a model of convention and consistency. My master's degree was in Russian and East European studies, so my move into political science was pushed by my interests in power, authority, and influence—in the Soviet Union, in the United States, in China, and in Germany. In other words, my curiosities had definitely metamorphosed, converging finally on the abstraction some of us refer to fondly as "leadership." A Fulbright grant to work in Bonn closed the deal; my dissertation would be titled *Willy Brandt: Portrait of the Leader as a Young Politician.*

What to do? Where to turn? Who would be a mentor? One thing was certain at the time: there was absolutely no one in Yale's Political Science Department who was both equipped and inclined to legitimize my increasingly strong interest in how the few get the many to go along. Among other things, there was no field, or even subfield, called leadership studies. Until the 1980s, even so obvious a resting place as a department devoted to the study of politics was, in fact, hostile to the multidisciplinary approach that the study of leadership absolutely demands.

Jim and I

Enter Professor Burns. He was an eminent scholar and so, of course, I knew his work. In particular, I had long recalled his postscript of sorts to *Roosevelt: The Lion and the Fox*. It provided the excuse I needed to make contact. This postscript, "A Note on the Study of Political Leadership," was no more than a few pages long, but the fact that Burns decided to include it in the award-winning first volume of his two-volume biography of our thirty-second president sent me, then an embryonic scholar anxious for intellectual support, an all-important message. Leadership was respectable, and it was a legitimate area of intellectual inquiry. Burns was not, he wrote in the mid-1950s, out to "revive the discredited idea that great leaders can freely make history or refashion society." Rather, Burns thought, the leader brings about lasting change "only by altering, if he can, the channels in which the stream of events takes place" (Burns 1956:487).

Emboldened by that postscript, I wrote to Burns, briefly describing my growing interest in leadership and my plan to make it the theoretical focus of my doctoral dissertation. He answered promptly and politely. Actually, he was much more than prompt and polite. He was curious about my work, interested in how I intended to use leadership theory in my thesis on Brandt, and willing to lend support in any way he could. His attention and courtesy were unlike anything I, the political scientist as *mensch,* had encountered to that point. So began a conversation that has continued in one fashion or another for thirty years. It may or may not be accurate to say that *Leadership* played a central role in that conversation. In either case, it is true that the writing and publication of *Leadership* coincided with my own birth as a scholar of the subject and that the tie between Burns and me has turned out to be a tie that binds.

I completed my dissertation in 1975. In 1977, Glenn Paige published *The Scientific Study of Political Leadership*. Then *Leadership* came out in 1978. It is, I think, no accident that the books by Paige and Burns, which together gave leadership a modest place at the political science table, came out within a year of each other, or that they both appeared in the late 1970s. The fact of the matter is that they mirrored the mood of the time.

This is not to say that for either Paige or Burns the study of leadership was a departure. Paige had previously edited a collection of readings on the subject and, as indicated above, Burns had testified to his interest in leadership, as opposed to an interest simply in leaders, two decades earlier. Rather, it is to suggest that, for American scholars in particular, the time was right.

It was apparent by the mid-1970s that political leadership in America was at a turning point. President John Kennedy had been murdered in 1963, Malcolm X in 1965, then Robert Kennedy and Martin Luther King Jr. in 1968. Also in 1968, President Lyndon Johnson was drummed out of the White House. Vice President Spiro Agnew was forced from office in 1973, and President Richard Nixon was, in effect, sacked in 1974. So, in just more than ten years, three chief executives and four other leading Americans had been eliminated in one manner or another.

However, the crises of leadership were not confined to the top. Two changes, in particular, proved as enduring as they were significant. First, the

modern civil rights and women's movements, both in their heyday in the 1960s
and 1970s, challenged established patterns of power and authority with vigor
and tenacity. Second, the Vietnam War and the Watergate scandal cloaked the
American electorate in a mantle of cynicism and doubt that remains in place to
this day. In these last three decades, we have witnessed a decline in our faith in
government that is tangible and apparently permanent.

Small wonder, then, that social scientists finally began to acknowledge the
obvious: Leadership or the lack thereof, matters. The reaction was predictable—
an explosion of books and articles about a subject that had previously been side-
lined. I do not claim that all of a sudden there was sweetness and light in the
leadership field. Joseph Rost counted no fewer than 110 definitions of leadership
in the 312 books, chapters, and articles that represented leadership literature for
the 1980s (Rost 1991:70). And even today there remains scant agreement as to
what exactly leadership is. But, what is clear is that the study of leadership increasingly came to be viewed as important during the Reagan years and that no
single work did as much to legitimize the field as Burns's *Leadership*.

Leadership and I

To my mind, the whole of *Leadership* matters more than its parts. Unlike many
of my colleagues, whose work has been powerfully influenced in specific ways
by the distinction between transactional and transforming leadership, I have
chosen to tread a path that does not directly intersect with Burns's seminal work.
This said, and my early proclivity for the study of leadership having been docu-
mented, I still wonder whether the work I have done in my guise as scholar
would have been possible without Burns and his big book. I have already al-
luded to Jim as mentor, but his role as colleague has been no less important. As I
graduated from student to professor, both literally and metaphorically, Burns
remained steadfast—always available, always curious, always challenging, and
always, in the end, supportive. Clearly, no single individual has played as large a
part or as positive a role in my professional life as James MacGregor Burns.

What *Leadership* did, as a by-product, was to bestow credibility on my own
work. Burns was hardly a kid when he wrote the book. In fact, he was already an
esteemed scholar with a sterling track record and a shelf full of prizes, including
a Pulitzer and a National Book Award. Ipso facto, by writing about leadership at
such length and in such depth, Burns bestowed on the subject the academic
equivalent of the *Good Housekeeping* Seal of Approval. It is not too much to say
that his work encouraged me to continue my own work in the field. By giving
leadership studies even a small place in the academic sun, *Leadership* paved my
way. Among other things, it was really quite easy for me to find good publishers
for a series of books that otherwise might well have been orphaned.

Who in the mid-1970s would have guessed that by the mid-1980s there
would be considerable interest in a collection of original essays on leadership,
complied and edited by scholars from different disciplines, all of whom had
thought a good deal about how their fields of study approach leadership issues?
And who in the mid-1980s would have imagined that by the mid-1990s these

essays would still be selling at a modest, but nevertheless consistent, clip? I should add, too, that *Leadership: Multidisciplinary Perspectives,* a book I edited, benefited considerably from the short, strong foreword written by Burns. In his usual mince-no-words style, Burns wrote, "The problem is that no field of study calls for a more difficult and daring crossing of disciplinary borders than does the study of leadership, and no field suffers more from narrow specialization" (Kellerman 1984: vii).

Political Leadership: A Source Book was, at least in part, a response to the need to know more about leadership that Burns had identified in *Leadership*. In its prologue, Burns had argued that "the crisis of leadership" in the 1970s was mediocrity and that, in turn, the "fundamental crisis underlying mediocrity is intellectual" (Burns 1978:1). He pointed out that leadership had not always been such a neglected field of study. For at least two millennia, "Leaders of thought did grapple with the vexing problems of the rulers vs. the ruled," but later, for reasons Burns was too much of a gentleman to identify outright, "The study of rulership and leadership ran into serious intellectual difficulties." The fact was that mid-twentieth-century social science had not done the subject justice. Indeed, as we have seen, Burns's own disciplinary base, political science, was especially culpable. For most of their modern history, departments of political science, or government, or politics have remained immune to the siren songs both of leaders as individuals and of leadership as an interactive process. *Political Leadership* was intended as something of a corrective to what a few of us considered at least a sad state of affairs. Among other things, it was conceived so as to clarify that, fashion notwithstanding, there was indeed "a critical mass of literature on political leadership that testified to the significant work already accomplished" (Kellerman 1986: xiv).

I have written two other books that owe a debt to the work of Burns. While it is clear in both cases that I generally followed where Burns led, it should be made equally clear that in one key respect we parted company: I was not then, nor am I now, particularly interested in leadership as a moral exercise. Rather I have a Machiavellian approach, if you will. I want to know what works. As far as my exploration of the books I have mentioned was concerned, I wanted to explore why some obviously clever men, such as Jimmy Carter, were not as effective in the White House as their obviously less clever counterparts, such as Ronald Reagan. In *The Political Presidency,* I wrote, "I am not asking if the [president's] leadership was, for example, courageous, wise or moral, or if it led the country down the proper path. I am asking only if it was effective in the sense that [he] was able to accomplish what he wanted to accomplish. Thus, the key questions in evaluating an administration will be: Was the president able to get his way when he wanted to? If so, how did he do it? And if not, why not?" (Kellerman 1991: x). Similarly, in *The President as World Leader,* Barilleaux and I noted that for us, "The issue is not whether our presidents are wise, clever, or just. Rather, the focus is on their ability to get others to follow where they lead" (Kellerman and Barilleaux 1990: vii).

On one level, this parting of the ways would seem to be no more than a matter of choice. Some scholars equate leadership with morality, while others do not. In fact, this issue divides the community of leadership scholars, at times fractiously. Burns made his position perfectly clear. According to him, someone like Hitler, to take perhaps the most egregious example, is not a leader. Burns calls him a "power wielder." In other words, as anyone who has ever read *Leadership* will tell you, Burns distinguishes between leaders and power wielders by saying, "Power wielders may treat people as things. Leaders may not" (Burns 1978:19). He does this so as to exclude from the distinction "leader" all those who do not seek to realize goals held by those with whom they interact. According to Burns, leaders engage followers, whereas power wielders inflict themselves on respondents. Again, this is not a position or a definition to which I adhere. In fact, I would go so far as to argue that the field of leadership studies has been hurt rather than helped because, along with Burns, the majority of leadership scholars are mesmerized by this ideal of moral leadership. In my recent book, *Bad Leadership: What It Is, How It Happens, Why It Matters,* I tackle these issues head on.

This having been said, *Leadership*'s elevation of followers, which drew attention to the role they did, after all, play in the leadership process, provided the field with a much needed corrective. Up to then, work on leadership, within political science, for example, had focused on either leaders, as individuals or as members of an elite, or on the led, as the mass, the people, or the electorate. Among the many successes of *Leadership* was Burns's emphasis on the importance of the interaction between the leader and those led. He reminded us once again that in the area of leadership, as in so many other areas of human endeavor, it takes two to tango.

A final note in this regard: *The Political Presidency* (1991) was about leadership in domestic affairs, and *The President as World Leader* (1990) was about leadership in foreign affairs, precisely because there is an important distinction to be made between the two. The former is generally about leaders leading followers, and the latter is generally about leaders leading other leaders. When a president talks to members of his Cabinet, the dynamic is different from when he talks to other heads of state. In *Leadership,* Burns heightened our collective awareness of leadership, however defined, as an interactive process. My point is that this interaction can take place between leaders and followers or between leaders and other leaders.

Leo as Leader

Burns was born in Melrose, Massachusetts, on August 3, 1918. That makes him a Leo, as the *Astrology Encyclopedia* describes those born under the fifth sign of the Zodiac. Leo is a "positive masculine sign," symbolized by the lion. Leos are supposed to be, among other things, challenging, bold, commanding, ambitious, and inspirational. The fact of the matter is that Burns is what he so eloquently describes in *Leadership,* an intellectual leader. So, let us stop for a moment and consider the concept to which his sixth chapter is dedicated, "Intellectual Leadership: Ideas as Moral Power." For certain, and in keeping with the point I made earlier, I do not subscribe to the subtitle. Sometimes ideas that persuade are immoral. The point is that leadership can be a product of the life of the mind. It is a distinction as appealing as it is persuasive, especially, perhaps, to women. Because women have historically been denied access to the so-called corridors of power, they have, relatively often, used pens to make points. Think of Harriet Beecher Stowe and *Uncle Tom's Cabin* or Betty Friedan and *The Feminine Mystique.*

Of course, as Burns makes perfectly clear, to think great thoughts is in and of itself not enough. Intellectual leadership demands that the idea be communicated and carried out into the world in which it is necessarily embedded. "However transcendent their theories and values," Burns writes, "intellectual leaders are not detached from their social milieus; typically they seek to change it" (Burns 1978:142). It is this amalgam of intellectual work and social and political activism that so deftly characterizes Burns himself.

It should be added that, as Burns describes them, intellectual leaders are inveterate optimists. The great eighteenth-century French thinkers of whom he writes had few illusions about humans but had hopes about humans as high as they could be (Burns 1978:143). Thus, by extension, Burns's own lifelong involvement with the world around him is fueled by the conviction that changes for the better are possible. Broadly conceived, this conviction has created change in four areas.

Scholarship. Burns has been a professor of political science at Williams College in Massachusetts for just about half a century. But if Williamstown has been home, it has neither defined nor confined him. Throughout a long life characterized as much by prodigious energy and hard work as by a creative and crafty mind, Burns has been one of only a handful of twentieth-century scholars who may fairly be called outstanding. His writings traverse the field from an introductory text—*Government by the People,* that is legendary both for its various incarnations and huge sales—through biographies that, in addition to those on Roosevelt, tracked lives that loomed large in twentieth-century American politics (including those of John and Edward Kennedy) and onto scholarly tomes that have lingered for decades, such as *The Deadlock of Democracy* and historical chronicles that coursed the nation's history, three volumes, for instance, of *The American Experiment.* Then, of course, there is this work that gave birth to a field, *Leadership.*

It is not often that a book becomes the basis for an area of study or that a man creates a field of inquiry. Even so, the suggestion that without *Leadership* and Burns's subsequent initiatives, leadership studies as we now know it would not exist is no exaggeration. *Leadership* was important to the social sciences for two reasons: the need for a book on the subject was so great, and the book itself is so good. In one fell swoop, *Leadership* put leadership on the map by providing an unparalleled resource for anyone, in any field, interested in the subject. In fact, although Burns wrote primarily about the political universe, the concepts of transactional and transforming leadership have had more of an impact on those studying private-sector leaders than on those studying their public-sector counterparts.

In Search of Change. Burns never really pretended that objectivity is supposed to be the social scientific ideal. From the start, he was a curious mix, a political scientist who wore his heart on his sleeve. Of course, it has been precisely his passions—for the United States of America, for the Roosevelts and the Kennedys, for the wheeling and dealing and horse-trading that is American politics, and for great deeds done by great men and sometimes women—that have made Burns an intellectual leader. Clearly, the professor wrote for many reasons. Among them was the desire to create change.

Academic Activist. Sure, Burns wrote about politics. It is, after all, his line of work. But did it suffice for him to observe from a distance? Not on your life. Burns is a congenital activist. He is, to resurrect a quaint phrase, a liberal democrat demanding to be heard. In fact, for a chap with a rather soft voice and a manner best described as Yankee gentleman, Burns has an amazing capacity for cutting through the din.

Burns has never been content to stay in place. The life of the mind may be enough for others, but in and of itself it is not sufficient for Burns. Throughout his career he has sought to have an impact on political science, in particular, and more generally on the academy. As Burns matured, his leadership roles became formal—president of the New England Political Science Association, of the American Political Science Association, and of the International Society for Political Psychology. Formal titles such as these were not about appearances, nor about the garlands of office. They were about using authority and influence to effect change for the benefit of the whole.

After graduating from Williams, Burns went to work in Washington, D.C. A few years later he was a combat historian in Guam, Saipan, and Okinawa. In 1958, he ran unsuccessfully for Congress. In 1976, he initiated the ambitious Project '87 to commemorate the two-hundredth anniversary of the Constitution. Some years later, he served as member of the Massachusetts Democratic Party Charter Commission. Soon after, and fortunately for those of us in leadership studies, he took on higher education in America and helped start programs of leadership studies at the University of Maryland, the University of Richmond, and Williams College.

L'Hômme Engagé. It is arguably Burns's actions even more than his words that best explain how one man was able to do so much. Once *Leadership* was published, Burns was in unremitting pursuit of additional scholarship on leadership. Like the proverbial terrier with the pant leg in his teeth, Burns would not let go. He would not rest and has not rested in his quest to legitimize leadership studies. He pushed organizations such as the American Political Science Association, the International Society for Political Psychology, and most recently, the International Leadership Association to sponsor panels and roundtables on leadership. He pushed schools and institutions, particularly the University of Maryland and the University of Richmond, to accept leadership studies as a legitimate area of academic inquiry. He pushed some of the nation's most distinguished foundations to provide support for the study of leadership. And he pushed academics, journalists, elected officials, and community activists to devote more of their time to writing and thinking about the interaction between leaders, followers, and the various contexts within which they are embedded.

I do not believe that Burns actually had a particular plan in the late 1970s. Rather, I think that in the time that has lapsed since *Leadership* was published, a mission has evolved to put leadership studies on the map and then do everything possible to keep it there. Burns is a scholar, and he is also, like the eighteenth-century French philosophers he so vividly describes, *l'hômme engagé*. In *Leadership* he writes, "The conflicts within [the French philosophers] conjoined with the intellectual and social conflicts around them to draw them into the tension points of their time and place" (Burns 1978:145).

Leadership Reconsidered

We are in a world of a hundred "posts"—post-modern, post-industrial, post-Cold War, and, of course, post-*Leadership*—but let the message not be garbled. Burns's work now behind him, he continues to break new ground. For example, deconstructing the conventional leader-follower divide, as he did in "Empowerment for Change," a 1996 paper written for the Kellogg Leadership Studies Project, Burns compels us to think thoroughly and ever more precisely of exactly who plays what role in the leadership game.

Thus, although we focus on *Leadership*, we need to look forward rather than backward. A plethora of programs at higher institutions of education testifies to the maturation of leadership studies and to the remarkable array of activities associated with the field—in education, service, and scholarship. The public, private, and nonprofit sectors are increasingly aware of leadership as a universal phenomenon of enormous political, social, and economic consequence—no negligible legacies for a man who boasts only that the strawberries he grows are the best in the world and will offer you his preserves as proof.

References

Burns, J. M. 1956. *Roosevelt: The Lion and the Fox.* New York: Harcourt & Brace.
————. 1978. *Leadership.* New York: Harper & Row.
————. 1996. "Empowerment for Change." In *Rethinking Leadership,* eds. Bruce Adams and Scott W. Webster. College Park, MD: Academy of Leadership Press.
————. J. W. Peltason, T. E. Cronin, D. B. Magleby, D. M. O'Brien. 2001. *Government by the People,* 19th ed. New York: Prentice Hall.
Kellerman, B. 1984. *Leadership: Multidisciplinary Perspectives.* Englewood Cliffs, NJ: Prentice Hall.
————.. 1986. *Political Leadership: A Source Book.* Pittsburgh, PA: University of Pittsburgh Press.
————.. 1991. *The Political Presidency: Practice of Leadership.* New York: St. Martin's Press.
————.. 2004. *Bad Leadership: What It Is, How It Happens, Why It Matters.* Cambridge, MA: Harvard Business School Press.

———— and R. J. Barilleaux. 1990. *President as World Leader.* New York: St. Martin's Press.

Paige, G. D. 1977. *The Scientific Study of Political Leadership.* New York: Simon & Schuster.

Rost, J. 1991. *Leadership for the Twenty-First Century.* New York: Praeger.

CHAPTER 2
AN INTELLECTUAL HISTORY OF LEADERSHIP STUDIES: THE ROLE OF JAMES MACGREGOR BURNS
Georgia Sorenson

Thomas Kuhn, in *The Structure of Scientific Revolutions,* discusses the use of the history of the research activity itself, rather than the constellation of facts, data, laws, and achievements, as a means of producing a "decisive transformation in the emergence of a new kind of science" (Kuhn 1962:1). This science would not be "who discovered what, when," but rather a more nuanced and interpenetrating view of the creative and scientific process. Utilizing Kuhn's approach, I will focus on the role of Jim Burns in the development of leadership theory and leadership studies, and although it has some "who" and "when," the story cannot be told without a view of Jim Burns's central contribution. It is a part of a larger effort to examine the intellectual history of leadership studies, building upon the earlier and excellent work of Joseph Rost (1991) and Bernard Bass (1990).

> *I regard James MacGregor Burns as my friend, colleague, collaborator, and co-conspirator. He served on my dissertation committee and has been a significant mentor since then. On November 6, 1997, in the Great Hall of the Library of Congress, we named the Academy of Leadership at the University of Maryland for him. Over the years, we have been together at Williams, the Academy of Leadership, Jepson, back to the Academy, and recently at the Army War College.*

Leadership and Leadership

Human beings have always been keenly interested in leaders and in leadership. Confucius sought laws of order between leaders and subordinates. Plato described an ideal republic with philosopher-kings providing wise and judicious leadership. Later, Plato and his colleagues established the *Paideia,* a school for leadership in early Greece. In the sixteenth century, the Italian Niccolo Machiavelli illuminated another side of leadership—some say the more practical side. Jim Burns's *Leadership* was a truly interdisciplinary examination of leadership.

It offered a considered theory of leadership and spawned the field of leadership studies, or at least provided the field a common ground.

The word *leader* first appeared in the English language in the 1300s; it stems from the root *leden* meaning "to travel" or "show the way" (Rost 1991:38-44). The term *leadership* followed some five centuries later. Indeed, the scientific study of leadership, as opposed to the study of leaders, has arisen primarily in the United States and almost exclusively since the turn of the twentieth century. Fields as divergent as political science, psychology, education, history, agriculture, public administration, management, anthropology, biology, military sciences, philosophy, and sociology have all contributed to an understanding of leadership, and many of them have even established subfields in leadership.

The heightened interest in leadership by academics has also brought the rise of leadership studies in academe. There were nearly six hundred leadership-development programs at American post-secondary institutions in 2000, more than double the number in 1996 (Schwartz 2000). The efforts range from single leadership resource centers to graduate degree programs in leadership studies (*Philanthropy Digest* 1998:1). While certainly not its sole architect, perhaps no other individual has energized leadership research and influenced the emergence of leadership studies as an academic discipline to the extent that James MacGregor Burns has.

Many people credit *Leadership* with the surging interest in both leadership research and leadership studies. Researchers at the Center for Creative Leadership surveying the field of leadership education on college campuses cited *Leadership* for the growth of empirical studies of attributes and behaviors, literature on charisma, and measurement scales for transformational leadership, as well as the enormous growth of leadership studies, research, training programs, and publications (Schwartz, Axtman, and Freeman 1998). Bernard Bass, a distinguished leadership researcher, dedicated his important book, *Leadership and Performance Beyond Expectations*, to Jim Burns and reported, "After I read [*Leadership*, I was] never the same again" (Bass 1995:466).

What is so special about this book? It is beautifully written, researched, and edited to be sure. But its uniqueness, I would argue, is threefold: First, it was a truly interdisciplinary examination of leadership. Second, it offered a considered theory of leadership. And third, it spawned the field of leadership studies.

An Interdisciplinary Approach to Leadership
A Walk across the Campus Green

As a scholar, Jim Burns has pursued a somewhat unorthodox career. He received his Ph.D. from Harvard in government, and for many years taught the standard political science courses at Williams, his alma mater. But he also was keenly interested in history and biography and branched off from political science to write a two-volume biography of Franklin D. Roosevelt, the second of which, *Roosevelt: The Soldier of Freedom,* won both the Pulitzer Prize and the National Book Award. As a political scientist, he co-authored, with Tom Cronin and Jack

W. Peltason, what became the most widely used text in American government, *Government by the People.*

He felt that political science was somewhat too concentrated on conventional subjects like interest groups, power, and institutions. At the same time, he felt that biography was too narrowly focused on individual leaders. So, in mid-career, he branched out from the disciplines of history and political science to a "non-discipline" now called *leadership studies.* After writing a short book titled *Uncommon Sense,* and later *Edward Kennedy and the Camelot Legacy,* in 1976, he took on a massive self-assignment to write a comprehensive study of leadership, published simply as *Leadership.* Burns writes:

> After my books on Roosevelt, JFK, Ted Kennedy and while working on *The Vineyard of Liberty,* I reflected on what I had learned. I felt I learned a lot about leaders but not much about leadership. So I went about a conscious study of leadership. I began to look in history, sociology, and political science. I didn't think political scientists had much to say about leadership. We often have viewed leadership as power. I felt that economics, history and political science all took a quantitative approach to power: the more guns—the more money leaders have—the more powerful they are. I didn't think we, as political scientists, were particularly interested in power recipients or followers.
>
> I thought that the field of psychology might offer some a useful framework for understanding leadership. I knew about this young psychology professor at Williams College, Al Goethals, though I don't think I had met him before. I walked over from Stetson Hall to the psychology department and introduced myself and we talked. He was very responsive, made some reading suggestions—including the work of Abraham Maslow—as I recall. I went to the psychology library, and there found the work of Maslow, Hollander, Kohlberg, and others. I found psychology had a lot more to say about the universals of leadership [than political science] (Burns 2000).

Al Goethals became the architect of the new leadership program at Williams College, Jim's long-time dream. At the time of first encounter, however, he was a young psychologist who had admired Burns from afar. He writes:

> I will never forget the day. I had read Burns in my undergraduate days. I knew that presidential leadership fascinated us both. Jim was 13 when FDR was elected, and I was 15 when JFK came into power. I was elated when we became colleagues at Williams, though of such different generations we rarely even saw each other across the green.
>
> One day he walked over from Stetson Hall, the political science department, and knocked on my door, saying simply: "I'm writing a book on leadership and I think psychology is important. I know David Barber's work, Fred Greenstein, the work on political socialization, and the presidency. I'm interested in motivation and self-esteem among other things. Can you recommend some readings in psychology?" (Goethals 2000).

This framework, the use of psychology, philosophy, psychoanalysis, history, political science, biography, and sociology—enriched with case studies—would become the backbone of *Leadership.* Later, other scholars would also take an interdisciplinary approach (Maccoby 1983; Gardner and Laskin 1995; Rosenbach and Taylor 1984); other efforts were contemporary (Paige 1977;

McCall and Lombardo 1978). However, none of these works compared to the scope and depth of Burns's first effort (Rost 1991:2).

A subsequent developer of a vast research agenda utilizing the concept of transformational leadership, Bernard Bass, described the immediate impact of *Leadership*. "Burns's concept of transforming leadership opened the door to making use of sociological, political, and psychoanalytic understandings of leadership—the leadership of social movements, of political parties, of bureaucracies, and so forth" (Bass 1993:375). It was truly a radical, if not revolutionary, approach.

A Theory of Leadership

Shortly before the publication of *Leadership*, psychologist James Hunt lamented: "What is missing, in addition to quantity of theoretical formulations or models, is a grand or generalized theory of leader-subordinate relationships—if indeed, such a theoretical development is possible" (Hunt and Larson 1977). It would appear not. In 1974, Stogdill's *Handbook of Leadership* listed 4,725 studies of leadership and 189 pages of references. He concluded, however, "the endless accumulation of empirical data has not produced an integrated understanding of leadership" (Stogdill 1974: vii).

It might be useful to look back to the 1970s and examine the context and frustration that produced Hunt's lament. Researchers, not theorists, dominated the study of leadership in the twentieth century. These researchers—usually in the fields of social, behavioral, or experimental psychology—were involved in inductive theory building, with gradual but limited success.

Within that tradition, the analytical dimensions are undefined, and the researcher creates a set of measures that reflect implicit analytical dimensions. After conducting empirical studies, an assessment is made of what measures group together using statistical methods, factor analysis or discriminate analysis. Then the clusters are given names, tested for reliability, refined, and used to do subsequent empirical research (Melcher 1977:96).

Factors such as leader intelligence, educational level of followers, dominance, affiliation, achievement orientation, formal and informal leadership, consideration, initiating structure, and every other conceivable variable were tested in self-reports, experimental groups, field studies, and organizations.

In an important early essay on the topic, however, Arlun Melcher decries inductive theory construction, because "principal attention is given to the reliability of measures and little or no attention to the logical adequacy of the underlying model" (Melcher 1977:96). Too often, the early research yielded models that suggested a set of relationships between variables without offering meaningful explanations of them. Burns's theory brought into focus two vastly important dimensions of leadership—that leadership was relational and that the motivations of leaders and followers were keys to understanding leadership and change.

One of the central problems of the inductive approach in constructing a universal leadership theory is the post hoc manner in which it has been developed.

That is, "The same studies [are] used to construct it and to provide empirical support for it. This inductive method, in which the theory is being shaped to fit known results ...[makes it] impossible for it to conflict with these results" (Melcher 1977:96). Much of the leadership research in the present and immediate past demonstrates the limitations of the inductive method.

What then is good theory? Filley, House, and Kerr suggest,

A theory should first have internal consistency; that is, its propositions should be free from contradiction. Second, a theory should have external consistency; that is, it should be consistent with observations. Third, it must be stated so that its predictions can be verified. Fourth, a theory should have the characteristic of generality. Finally, a practical theory should have the attribute of scientific parsimony (cited in Schriesheim and Kerr 1977:9).

How does Burns's theory measure up? I would argue that Burns developed the first comprehensive theory of leadership for modern scholars, utilizing the more abstract, deductive method. He drew upon his vast experience of leaders and leadership, his studies of presidents and movement leaders, and upon an array of disciplines, both his own and those new to him. On the third point of good theory—the verifiability of predictions—Burns has been criticized for his lack of operationalization of key variables and the abstractness of his constructs. However, he was looking for universals not particulars—the "grand or generalized" grail sought by Hunt and others.

A Relational Approach to Leadership

Burns challenged researchers to abandon the leader-focused model and to take up the study of leadership aimed at "realizing goals mutually held by both leaders and followers." To do so, he suggested, involves greater attention to the role of followers, as well as the motivations of potential opponents and competition from other actors. Burns speaks of "the reciprocal process of mobilizing, by persons with certain motives and values, various economic, political, and other resources, in a context of competition and conflict, in order to realize goals independently or mutually held by both leaders and followers" (Burns 1978:425). In short, in the terms of Edwin P. Hollander, Burns characterized leadership as a process, not as a person. What strikes us as obvious has not always been so, especially before 1978.

For the most part, leadership research of the first five decades of this century focused on leaders themselves and has come to be called the era of the "Great Man Theories." These were essentially the study of individual leaders—"leaderships" rather than "leadership," to paraphrase Burns. Hollander, one of the few contemporary researchers who focused on the role of followers in the leadership process, describes this period as the search for traits of good leaders. Hereditary properties such as intelligence, height, and self-confidence appeared to be distinguishing characteristics. Whether idealistic or normative, leadership research sought to identify traits or abilities that set leaders apart from non-leaders. However, research failed to produce a set of traits that leaders must possess to be effective (Melcher 1977:94).

As the notion of inherited or inherent leadership was dispelled, social scientists of the American behaviorist movement measured behavior of leaders in an attempt to deconstruct leadership. In effect, their operating hypothesis was that the behaviors of effective leaders differed from those of ineffective leaders. Psychologists at Ohio State and the University of Michigan contributed pioneering research in the behavioral understanding of leadership. The Ohio State studies profiled leaders, but after years of study of "consideration" and "initiating structure" and other two-dimensional variables, they failed to explain or predict leader behavior (Rost 1991; Melcher 1977:95).

Unknown to Burns, but working at the same time and in a parallel fashion, was another important cadre of social scientists who were generating empirical research findings that would support his reciprocal-relationship concept. The Southern Illinois University Leadership Symposia, originating in 1971, produced four important volumes: *Current Developments in the Study of Leadership* (1973), *Contingency Approaches to Leadership* (1974), *Leadership Frontiers* (1975), and *Leadership: The Cutting Edge* (1977). Working with the U.S. Army, an early pioneer in leadership research, Owen Jacobs of the Army Research Institute and Gerry Hunt of Southern Illinois produced a research agenda which culminated in the symposia. This work paid particular attention to the relationship between leaders and the group and managerial implications in the workplace. There were twinned variables, "consideration" and "task performance," but the behavior was much more interpenetrating and complex than it appeared.

The key, Burns felt, was in the hypersensitive force field of motivation. "Leaders must assess collective motivation—the hierarchies of motivations in both leaders and followers—as studiously as they analyze the power bases of potential followers and rival leaders" (Burns 1978:435). "To perceive the working of leadership in social causation as motivational and volitional rather than simply as 'economic' or 'ideological' or 'institutional' is to perceive not a lineal sequence of stimulus-response 'sets' or 'stages,' not even a network of sequential and cross-cutting forces, but a rich and pulsating *stream* of leadership-followership forces flowing through the whole social process" (Burns 1978:437).

This relational approach to leadership—"a rich and pulsating" process held together by the glue of motivations, both hidden and apparent—yielded an exquisite internal and external consistency. It was obvious. It was parsimonious. And it was certainly generalizable across sectors of identity, community, and place. So much so that I discovered on a recent consultation trip to China, that the dean of a government school of leadership asked me to convey to Jim Burns that he was the only Western scholar "who understood the Chinese Cultural Revolution and had captured Mao's motives perfectly."

Values-Added Leadership

Burns's theory had a second powerful component, what I like to call a "values-added" dimension. Until Burns's book, the goal of good leadership was seen as "effectiveness," a goal that Kellerman espoused in Chapter 1. Burns transformed our view of leadership by insisting that great leadership had moral dimensions. "Moral" to Burns did not mean just the everyday virtues or daily ethical dimensions, but adherence to the great public values such as liberty, justice, and equality. Moral leadership was the purview of great leadership. He thus made a distinction between two different but compatible leadership behaviors—transactional and transforming. He defined transactional leadership as everyday brokerage, "the process whereby one person takes the initiative in making contact with others for the purpose of an exchange of valued things" (Burns 1978:19).

So much has been written about transforming leadership, I thought I would share a more personal account of these two concepts. In describing his parents, Burns gives us a glimpse of the antecedents of transforming and transactional leadership.

> My father was the general vice president for sales of a large milk company located in nearby Charlestown, Massachusetts. He was, in a way, the consummate salesman, a very pleasant personality that served him in that post in a company that had small units all through eastern Massachusetts and, indeed, eastern New England. My mother did not have formal paid work until her children were grown up. She was a very strong-minded woman. My parents were divorced when I was about eight, and my mother, brothers, and I moved to Burlington, Massachusetts. At that time, it was a small, undeveloped rural town that had no high school. We lived in a remote part of the town...
>
> I think that my parents influenced me in that my father was a great role model for how to approach, deal with, compromise with, and bargain with people, whereas my mother took very strong moral positions. I guess that some of my belief in moral leadership and moral convictions stems from her (Bailey 2001:115).

The hallmark of fine theory is that eventually it becomes obvious to all. But those of us in the leadership field know our debt to Jim Burns. He pushed us from leaders to leadership, defined leadership as a process between the leaders and the led and put motivation at the core of the leadership process. Leadership scholar emeritus Joseph Rost dedicated his *Leadership for the Twenty-First Century* "to James MacGregor Burns, who changed my whole way of thinking about leadership" (Rost 1991); so true for so many of us.

The Birth of Leadership Studies in Academia

Leadership studies is an emerging field of study in academia. For many years, concepts such as *headship* in anthropology, *roles* in psychology, *power* in political science, and *management* in business were explored in a single disciplinary fashion. While subfields within disciplines, such as educational leadership or political leadership, are still apparent and multidisciplinary research is quite prevalent, the field of leadership studies has become increasingly interdisciplinary since Burns produced *Leadership*. Schools such as the Academy of Leadership at the University of Maryland, the Jepson School of Leadership at the University of Richmond, and the Antioch Ph.D. Leadership and Change program are home to scholars and faculty from across the disciplinary spectrum. In 1994, the Jepson School, where Burns was a founding scholar for three years, offered the first major in leadership studies. Today, there are more than a hundred such programs, leadership minors, certificates, graduate degrees, and Ph.D.s. in leadership studies. "Leadership programs are now embedded in every imaginable discipline," says Mary K. Schwartz, co-editor of *Leadership Education* (Schwartz et al. 1998), the premier compendium on educational leadership efforts. There is tremendous growth in attention to leadership in liberal arts, in particular, history, literature, and philosophy, as well as the original base of business and social sciences (Schwartz 2000).

In a telling analysis of the disciplinary base of leadership faculty, the behavioral and social sciences, together with business management, seem to drive most leadership coursework in America (Howe 1997:286). In Howe's analysis across courses, "Moral and ethical leadership is emphasized in 44 percent of the coursework sample, and 23 percent focus on transformational leadership." Five courses studied by Howe curiously focused on transactional leadership. I should add that schools for leadership are emerging all over the world: in China, in England, in Japan, and in Tanzania, to name a few. It is clearly a worldwide phenomenon that Burns envisioned so long ago.

Criticism of Leadership Studies

Leadership studies has not been without its critics in the public, private, and political spheres. An opinion editorial in the *New York Times*, written by a special education teacher, touched upon some of the valiancy the term *leadership* carries. She worried that the explosion of leadership institutes and curriculum across the country might leave some people behind. The fact that leadership studies has been seen as "focusing on elites, fostering dissolution of traditional academic disciplines, and soaking up federal funds for the few as opposed to the many" remains an issue (Morrice 1998). Benjamin DeMott (1993) described funding given by the now defunct U.S. Department of Education's Eisenhower Leadership Program to academic leadership programs as "academic pork."

The politics on campuses can be fierce when it comes to new disciplines and leadership studies has generated its share of controversy. The president of the University of Richmond, home to the Jepson School of Leadership Studies, has decried the value of leadership studies in the press. Harvard University has refused tenure to its only leadership faculty member in the Kennedy School. The new principal of Kennedy High School in Maryland attempted to dismantle the school's nationally recognized federally funded leadership program. The University of Maryland has been slow to accept the notion of a leadership major.

There is no question that the very word *leadership* stirs up conflicting feelings. However, some of the critics who claim that leadership studies is not a rigorous discipline with a coherent theoretical base have only to look at the evolution of other disciplines in academia to see that leadership studies is far from unique in these matters. From the time of Bacon down to the present day, intellectuals have attempted to classify the sciences to parcel out the world of fact into its natural divisions. Thomas Jefferson parsed the world, and his library, into Memory, Reason, and Imagination. J. A. Thomson, who writes about the history of science, asserts that science is not defined "by its subject matter, but by its point of view, the particular kind of question it asks" (cited in Titchener 1929). There is no question on which leadership studies has a unique viewpoint. The same group activity, for example, will be looked at differently by a sociologist, a political scientist, or a biologist. A leadership scholar would have a distinct point of view as well, and the questions asked would be quite different.

Amedeo Giorgi refutes critics who complain that leadership studies lacks coherence and rigor. He points out that many other fields lacked the same qualities when they started. "Psychology did not have an early or adequate coherence that we lost over time; we were never coherent in the mature sense of the term. While from time to time there has been agreement with respect to a label—the study of the mind, consciousness, psyche, experience, or behavior—a common in-depth knowledge of each of the terms was never achieved" (Giorgi 1985:48).

The field of psychology grew out of the field of philosophy. The first "psychologists" were in philosophy departments. When these scholars formed the new field of psychology in 1892, they had forty-two members (Koch and Leary 1985:21). Even Titchener, one of the founders of the new discipline, did not claim that psychology had a distinct and peculiar subject matter. He explained that "the difference between physiology and psychology lies simply in our point of view" (Titchener 1929:19). In a field of study that embraces behaviorism, psychoanalysis, and Gestalt therapy, psychology's subfields point to the lack of a comprehensive central perspective that could clarify the meaning of psychology and provide the basis for unifying apparently disparate subfields. Instead, psychology is left with gaps. What is the relationship between psychophysics and psychotherapy? Giorgi asks (Giorgi 1985:49).

In short, the field of leadership studies per se is no more or no less coherent than other disciplines. Indeed, coherence itself may be undesirable, as the disciplines themselves are approaching each other's boundaries at breakneck speed. Pearsona, for example, warns us that, however ingeniously we may map out the territory of knowledge, "every branch of science passes, at one or more points, not only into the domain of adjacent, but even of distinct branches" (cited in Koch and Leary 1985:514). Social psychology, the nether region between sociology and psychology, has long been an established subfield. But even newer enterprises, such as neurobiology, environmental psychology, and political psychology, demonstrate that the twenty-first century will see more interdisciplinary searches for truth. In fact, multi- and interdisciplinary studies are among the fastest growing sectors of academic life (National Center for Educational Statistics www).

Conclusion

A century from now, observers and scholars will probably see the last half of the twentieth century as an epochal time in the evolution of leadership theory and practice. Burns has his own hopes. "I have become even more impressed by the role of values in the study and exercise of leadership; more impressed by the role of conflict, which tends to be down-played in much of the literature by people who are more interested in consensus; and more interested in creativity, in leaders as creative persons" (Bailey 2001:126).

Since *Leadership* was published, the study of leadership has spawned thousands of publications across numerous disciplines. Forty-four professional journals, such as *Leadership Quarterly* and *The Journal of Leadership Studies*, have been established and are devoted exclusively to the study of leadership. More than 570 dissertations utilize the concept of transforming leadership. More than 900 academic leadership programs in the United States have been created, many offering majors, minors, and graduate degrees in leadership studies. Professional associations, the International Leadership Association, and the Leadership Learning Community bring together scholars, activists, and leaders from all over the United States and the world.

To end at the beginning and to return to Thomas Kuhn, *Leadership* joins the world of scientific revolutions. It produced "a consequent shift in the problems available for scientific scrutiny," and like other revolutions, "transformed the scientific imagination in ways that we shall ultimately need to describe as a transformation of the world within which scientific work is done. Its assimilation requires the reconstruction of proper theory and the re-evaluation of prior fact, an intrinsically revolutionary process" (Kuhn 1962:6-7). Kuhn cautions that such a transformation seldom happens because of a single person and never overnight. Still, it was James MacGregor Burns who showed us the way.

References

Bailey, J., and R. Axelrod. 2001. "Leadership Lessons from Mount Rushmore: An Interview with James MacGregor Burns." *Leadership Quarterly* 12, 113-127.

Bass, B. M. 1993. "A Seminal Shift: The Impact of James Burns's Leadership." *Leadership Quarterly: Special Issue—Charismatic Leadership: Neo-Weberian Perspectives* 4(3/4), 375-377.

———. 1985. *Leadership and Performance Beyond Expectations*. New York: Free Press.

———. 1990. *Bass & Stogdill's Handbook of Leadership*, 3rd ed. New York: Free Press.

———. 1995. "Theory of Transformational Leadership Redux." *Leadership Quarterly* 6(4), 463-478.

Burns, James MacGregor. 1978. *Leadership*. New York: Harper & Row.

———. 2000. Personal interview. August 12.

DeMott, B. 1993. "Choice Pork: Inside the Leadership Studies Racket." *Harper's Magazine* (Dec.), 61-77.

Freeman, F., et al. 1997. *Leadership Education, A Source Book, 1996-1997 Volume 2*, 6th ed. Greensboro, NC: Center for Creative Leadership.

Gardner, H., and E. Laskin. 1995. *Leading Minds: An Anatomy of Leadership*. New York: Basic Books.

Giorgi, A. 1985. "Toward the Articulation of Psychology as a Coherent Discipline." In Sigmund Koch and David Leary (Eds.), *A Century of Psychology as a Science* (pp. 46-59). New York: McGraw Hill..

Goethals, A. 2000. Personal interview. August 11.

Howe, W. 1997. "Leadership Education: A Look Across the Courses." In *Leadership Education, A Source Book, 1996-1997 Volume 2,* 6th ed. Greensboro, NC: Center for Creative Leadership.

Hunt, J., and L. L. Larson. 1977. *Leadership: The Cutting Edge.* Carbondale, IL: Southern Illinois University Press.

Koch, S., and D. Leary. 1985. *A Century of Psychology as a Science.* New York: McGraw Hill.

Kuhn, T. 1962. *The Structure of Scientific Revolutions.* Chicago: University of Chicago Press.

Maccoby, M. 1983. *The Leader: A New Face for American Management.* New York: Ballantine Books.

McCall, L., and M. M. Lombardo. 1988. *Leadership: Where Else Can We Go?* Durham, NC: Duke University Press.

Melcher, A. 1977. "Leadership: A Functional Analysis." In J. G. Hunt and L. L. Larson (Eds), *Leadership: The Cutting Edge* (pp. 94-108).. Carbondale, IL: Southern Illinois University Press.

Morrice, P. 1998. "Leaders, Leaders Everywhere." *New York Times,* August 3, p. A19.

Paige, Glenn D. 1977. *The Scientific Study of Political Leadership.* New York: Free Press.

National Center for Educational Statistics. www.nces.ed.gov.pubs 91/91396.pdf

Philanthropy Digest. 1998. "Leadership Programs Grow Increasingly Popular on College Campuses," 4:45.

Rosenbach, William E., and Robert L. Taylor, eds. 1984. *Contemporary Issues in Leadership.* Boulder, CO: Westview Press.

Rost, J. 1991. *Leadership for the Twenty-First Century.* Westport, CT: Praeger.

Schwartz, M. 2000 (August). Personal interview.

Schwartz, M. K., K. M. Axtman, and F. H. Freeman, eds. 1998. *Leadership Education: A Source Book of Courses and Programs,* 7th ed. Greensboro, NC: Center for Creative Leadership.

Schriesheim, C., and S. Kerr. 1977. "Theories and Measures of Leadership: A Critical Appraisal of Current and Future Directions." In J. G. Hunt and L. L. Larson (Eds). *Leadership: The Cutting Edge..* Carbondale, IL: Southern Illinois University Press.

Stodgill, R. 1974. *Handbook of Leadership.* New York: Free Press.

Titchener, E. 1929. *Systematic Psychology.* Ithaca, NY: Cornell University Press.

CHAPTER 3
THE SCHOLARLY/PRACTICAL CHALLENGE OF
LEADERSHIP
Ronald A. Heifetz

Clearly, the audiences for whom authors write and teach shape significantly our content. So, before moving to an analysis of the some of the key ideas in *Leadership*, it is important to say that Jim Burns was, I think, writing for a different audience than the audience for whom I write and teach. When we speak to intellectuals, thinkers, or scholars, we ask questions and analyze issues differently than when we write for activists, managers, and politicians in the trenches who have to find ways to raise challenging issues in organizations and politics and still stay alive in the process. My sense is that Jim wrote primarily for the former audience, and I the latter. I think and write primarily for the mid-career and executive practitioners who come through my courses and consulting work.

Burns's undertaking was extraordinary. You cannot help but notice when you read Jim's book that a lot of spirit, soul, and heart went into that book. In important ways, the book sounds Biblical in its repetitious cadence. One senses that Jim struck chords repeatedly, not only because they needed to be revisited from an analytical perspective, but also because there was a spirit in those messages that he had not yet finished working through either in the book or in his own system of thought.

Through themes such as the relationship between power and purpose and assertions that power lacking purpose is bankrupt and meaningless, we watch Burns struggle with a moral conception of leadership. His struggle stands out against the overwhelming pressures in the social sciences to render leadership a value-free subject of conversation and study. That is, perhaps, the most important legacy of the book, even beyond the important distinctions he makes and his analysis of history. It's the soul of the work, along with the heart and the passion that make their way through the usual filters of scholarship. This essential normative challenge has inspired a generation of students as well as a generation of scholars.

Many of these practitioners have already accumulated scars on their backs from the times when they raised tough questions that few wanted to address, or represented a perspective that others preferred to avoid. It has been my task as a teacher and thinker to discover how to get them back into the field operating more wisely in spite of the dangers and difficulties. I consider it successful when they describe their readiness to go back into the fray. They know they are going to get knocked off balance, but they have some lessons for walking the razor's edge. They seem better prepared and more willing to bear the risks and pains of leadership (Parks 2005).

Many of the difficulties I have found in assigning Burns's *Leadership* to practitioner-students and working with it for decades have come from the need to find ways to apply his perspectives, his passion and his normative intuitions in practical language and practical insights. What follows is a brief discussion of some of the key ideas from his book that I think have required translation and further work in order to render them applicable to an audience of practitioners.

Authority, Leadership, and Their Units of Analysis

Burns had a powerful intuition about the distinction between leadership and power—that somehow the unit of analysis for analyzing leadership ought to be different from the units of analysis for analyzing power. I do not think he wrestled that insight all the way to the mat, but the insight, I believe, becomes crucial when we do. It shifts the ground of leadership studies.

I have learned from my practitioner-students that developing this insight fully requires two steps. First, we have to distinguish between two kinds of authority. And second, we have to distinguish leadership from authority and identify a unit of analysis for leadership distinct from the unit of analysis used for authority.

Our leadership literature has tried to distinguish leadership from authority for a long time. Anthropologists have routinely distinguished head-ship from leadership, for example. But to my mind, scholars in their efforts so far have not distinguished authority from leadership; they have distinguished between two forms of authority: formal and informal. Formal authority is the authority one gets because of election or selection to a position; in a sense, any job description is a formal authorization. Yet, as we know, and as Richard Neustadt wrote in *Presidential Power* in 1960 and Joseph Nye more recently in *Soft Power*, a critical source of anyone's power does not come from the powers granted through formal authorization. It comes from the power of one's informal authority: the degree to which people look to someone with trust, with admiration, and with respect to represent a value or point of view held dear. For example, the formal powers of the President of the United States rarely change during a four-year term, but the real power to govern fluctuates weekly as the President's informal authority—approval rating, professional respect, moral standing—waxes and wanes.

Both formal and informal authority relationships have the same basic structure. The social contract is identical: Party A entrusts Party B with power in exchange for services. Sometimes this contract is formalized in a job description or an authorization establishing a task force, organizational unit, government agency, or organizational mission. Sometimes the contract is left implicit, particularly with subordinates and lateral colleagues, who may to varying degrees trust, respect, and admire someone, and therefore give that person the key power resource of their attention. However, all authority relationships, both formal and informal, appear to fit the same basic definitional pattern: power entrusted for service. "I look to you to serve a set of aspirations I hold dear."

Our literature on leadership often implicitly defines leadership as the capacity to gain respect and admiration in order to influence people in informal ways without having to use the coercive mechanisms of formal authority. In our current culture, people often say, "That's leadership" when they refer to someone whom others admire and see in an influential light, someone who gains a following through persuasion and inspiration. This view, that leadership is the same as informal authority, is an attractive one, particularly in our day and age when the uses of coercive power seem less and less legitimate. But most would also agree, for example, that Abraham Lincoln exercised extraordinary leadership in going to war against the "insurgency" of the Confederate South, though he clearly used coercion in doing so. To equate leadership, then, with only the power of persuasion *sans* any background threat or application of force seems to make little sense when we test it against our historical understanding or daily lives, however much we might *like* to generate more leadership like that.

Moreover, many people have had a great deal of informal authority gained through inspiration and persuasion without then using those resources in the exercise of leadership. The world seems to have an abundance of charlatans. One can have a considerable "following" and not lead. A "following" correlates with a group giving informal authority to someone, but whether one leads with that influence may be another matter. The implication of this reasoning is the counter-intuitive assertion that "followers do not define leadership," they define one half of an authority relationship: Party A.

To determine whether Party B exercises any leadership requires that we distinguish leadership from both forms of authority and their power resources. Burns's radical intuition suggests that our conception of leadership should not use authority, and its forms of power, as its unit of analysis, but should instead use the quality of one's impact on the lives of people and polities—the transformative effect.

The benefits of these distinctions are profound. Here are four of them. First, distinguishing leadership from authority enables us to engage in the critically important work in our age of distrust of "recovering our capacity for authority"—to renew our ability to form relationships of power and trust. Teresa Monroe at the University of San Diego designed a course, "Exercising Authority: Power, Strategy, and Voice", that we co-taught at Harvard from 1992-1995 in which these concepts were central.

Second, we can draw more usefully on decades of research, spurred by the work of Chester Barnard's *The Functions of the Executive* and advanced in the curricular materials from the Department of Behavioral Science and Leadership at the United States Military Academy at West Point, analyzing the uses of the powers of formal authority, and distinguishing them from the persuasive and soft power of informal authority (Neustadt 1991; Nye 2004).

Third, these distinctions enable us to analyze the resources and constraints of formal and informal authority on the practice of leadership and to examine why so many people with authority do not exercise leadership. We can then begin to answer the question: Why do authorities routinely squander their power and popularity?

And fourth, these distinctions enable us to celebrate, learn from, and affirm the vital practice of leadership without and beyond one's authority. They enable us to generate ideas for practitioners to draw on the strategic differences between leading with authority, leading without authority, and leading beyond one's authority. All three of these basic situational variables for leadership require somewhat different tactics and, to some degree, a different application of diagnostic and action principles.

Burns's intuition then takes us to the logical conclusion that the unit of analysis for analyzing formal and informal authority is the power formally conferred through institutional procedures, and the power informally conferred by followers. Moreover, these positional and relational correlates of power do not suffice as a way to analyze leadership.

To what unit of analysis, then, should we anchor a conception of leadership? Burns, as well as my colleagues and I, have worked on this normative question, and we have generated somewhat different answers to it. In our "shop," we define leadership as the activity of mobilizing progress, and we define progress as the work of mobilizing people's adaptive capacity to tackle tough problems and thrive (Heifetz and Sinder 1988; Heifetz 1994; Heifetz and Linsky 2002; Williams 2005). The unit of analysis we have found most useful for leadership is progress in meeting adaptive challenges, or *adaptive work*.

The concept of "thriving" is a metaphor drawn from the concept of adaptation in evolutionary biology in which a successful adaptation accomplishes three tasks (Mayr 1988; Kirschner and Gerhart 2005):

- it preserves essential DNA—the accumulated wisdom of generations;
- it re-arranges, re-regulates, or discards the DNA that no longer serves the current need;
- and it innovates to develop capacity that enables the organism to thrive in new ways and in challenging environments

A successful adaptation enables a living system to take the best from its history into the future. It is conservative as well as progressive.

Anchoring a conception of leadership in the work of progress—resolving contradictions within our cultural DNA to clarify the values in thriving or between our cultural DNA and the demands of our environment to realize those values—enables us to view authority and various forms of power as a set of tools and constraints, rather than as ends. They do not define leadership, though they are often central to its practice.

By using different units of analysis for leadership and authority, i.e., work and power, and thereby uncoupling them, we can then analyze what we commonly observe: that people lead—i.e., mobilize progress on challenges demanding new adaptations for the social system to thrive—both with and without authority at the same time. Moreover, the various forms of power, from coercive to inspirational, remain useful in various contexts in the practice of leadership.

Leading With and Without Authority

Understood this way, nearly all leadership requires operating across boundaries of authority, laterally and upward, as well as among those with whom one has direct authority. This is because adaptive challenges rarely fall neatly within current organizational structures since those structures were yesterday's design solutions to yesterday's adaptive challenges now rendered routine or technical. Even presidents of companies over which they may have extraordinary formal authority frequently have to exercise leadership among people on Wall Street, as well as shareholders, customers, or people controlling public opinion. Obviously, as Larraine Matusak (1997) has passionately written, the growth and development of our organizations and polities need people to exercise leadership from roles of citizenship without any authority, without waiting for the coach's call—and we need that in democracy every day.

Let me try to illustrate the practice of leadership beyond and without authority with two quick stories. The first is well known. The Rev. Martin Luther King Jr. had formal authority over a very small group of people in a small organization, the Southern Christian Leadership Conference. Yet, he had a great deal of informal authority among a much larger group of people, Americans of many persuasions who looked to him to champion and represent their values. They entrusted him with various resources of power, including attention, funds, and public support, because he had moral authority in their eyes. But King's most important target audience consisted of all those Americans who paid him no mind, who trusted him not in the least, or worse, might have hated him, disliked him, or held him in contempt. To mobilize this set of constituencies was the most critical task of his leadership.

So, in essence, King's essential leadership challenge was to lead without any authority—somehow to mobilize, stimulate, and provoke *those* people across the country to reevaluate their priorities, to look at the gap between the values they said they stood for and the reality of the way they were living. In Jim Burns's terms, which borrow from psychoanalytic practice, leadership required surfacing and illustrating the internal contradictions within America, which then would generate conflicts between and among factions in the nation which, if orchestrated properly, would produce progress toward narrowing that gap and more closely realizing those values.

Here's another story of a person leading without any authority for what must have seemed in interminable time. Sousan Abadian found this story while doing her doctoral research on Native American poverty in British Columbia in 1995. While trying to understand why some tribal bands had gone from nearly 100 percent alcoholism to 95 percent sobriety, she met an extraordinary woman, whom we shall call Maggie, who had exercised leadership during the previous ten years in turning her band around. In their conversation, Abadian asked Maggie, How did you come to think that it would be possible to heal your tribe, when so many around you were drinking? How did you step out of the box? And Maggie told her the following story.

Many years ago I used to baby-sit for Lois, who lived in a neighboring band within our tribe. Once a week I'd go the few miles to her community and take care of Lois's little ones. But after two months, I started to wonder, "What could Lois possibly be doing every Tuesday night? There's not much to do around here." So one evening after Lois left to go to the meeting lodge, I packed up the children and went over there. We looked through a window into the lodge and saw a big circle of chairs, all neatly set in place, with Lois sitting in a chair all by herself. The chairs in the circle were empty.

I was really curious, you know, so when Lois came home that evening, I asked her, "Lois, what are you doing every Tuesday night?" And she said, "I thought I told you weeks ago, I've been holding AA (Alcoholics Anonymous) meetings." So I asked her again, "What do you mean you're holding meetings? I went over there tonight with the children and we looked through the window. We watched you sitting there in a circle of chairs, all alone." Lois got quiet—"I wasn't alone," she said. "I was there with the spirits and the ancestors; and one day, our people will come."

Every week Lois set up those chairs neatly in a circle, and for two hours, she just sat there. No one came to those meetings for a long time, and even after three years, there were only a few people in the room. But ten years later, the room was filled with people. The community began turning around. People began ridding themselves of alcohol. I felt so inspired by Lois that I couldn't sit still watching us poison ourselves.

In their leadership, the two women were initially mocked and marginalized. They acted before they had any collaborators or so-called followers; for stretches of time, they had none. No one was looking to them, no one asked them and no one followed them for a very long time. They spent years feeling out of place in their own communities, unwelcome at parties and gatherings where alcohol flowed. Indeed, they spent weekends off the reservation to find people with whom they could talk. They had put themselves, as well as significant relationships with neighbors, friends, and family at risk. They led without authority and, eventually, they succeeded. But for a long time, they did not know success (Abadian 1999).

The world is full of people like Maggie and Lois. And I expect that many readers will recognize themselves and others in stories like theirs. Jane Mansbridge, in her current research on "everyday feminism," is showing us that the world is full of women who have exercised leadership, sometimes only at key moments, and sometimes in sustained efforts, but quietly without notice, until they happened to bump into an Abadian or Mansbridge and their notebooks. So to equate leadership with authority not only ignores a widespread and critically important social phenomenon, but also does injustice to all of these heroic people practicing necessary everyday leadership.

If the health of a society requires enlightened leadership only from the people at the top of organizations, or at the top of our political apparatus, we are in trouble. We are then in what Dr. Seuss (1990) describes as, "The Waiting Room," waiting for the occasional philosopher-queen or philosopher-king who can pull rabbits out of the hat. That mode of dependency and waiting is dangerous. Adaptability requires variability, because you never know who, in a changing environment, has the capacity to take us into the future. In many businesses, for example, the chief bottlenecks to growth and adaptability are the quality and distribution of leadership. Our organizations and communities need distributed leadership, with and without authority.

We need, therefore, to study and analyze strategies of leadership with authority and we need to help people develop strategies of leadership without authority and beyond their authority, as well. By distinguishing leadership from power, Burns pointed the way. By unfastening leadership from its traditional moorings of formal and informal authority relationships—and the study of those power dynamics—Burns provided a basis for placing leadership studies on the footing of the "work" of leadership—the processes by which communities and organizations develop and clarify their values and change themselves to live up to those values.

Leadership and Values

In a sense, Burns said, Look, it isn't right for us to be defining leadership in a value-free way; we've got to tackle the values inherent in a concept of leadership. In this and other books, we see Burns at work to develop a normative framework.

When I began teaching leadership in 1983, I was not convinced that we needed a value-laden definition of leadership. I leaned in that direction, but was not persuaded. Moreover, I found the normative dilemma perplexing. Yet I have found that few, if any, of my practitioner-students view leadership in a value-free sense. Only scholars seem to view it consistently that way. Although students may say in one breath that leadership is a value-neutral term, when I ask them, "Would you rather be a leader or a manager, a leader or a follower, a leader or an authority?" nearly all of them immediately respond, "I'd rather be a leader." Consequently, I came early to believe that, in operation, the word "leader" is inherently value-laden, i.e., in its common usage, desirable values are attached to it.

For example, six weeks into an executive program in the spring of 1984 for senior officials from the U.S. Department of Defense, a colonel in the Air Force came into the seminar room looking crestfallen. When I asked him what was wrong, he said, "You know, when I was commissioned an officer, they told me I was a leader and now twenty years later I realize, 'My God, all I've been is an authority figure. Maybe, I have not exercised any leadership at all.'" That depressed him because he held the self-image of "leader" close to his heart. It was not a value-neutral term like chair or electron—it was like the word good or hero, representing attributes he wanted. After further reflection, the colonel came in a week later looking cheerful. I again asked him, why? "Now I see options for leadership I never saw before."

When politicians run for office, they put bumper stickers on their car. The stickers do not read: "Paul Adams for good leadership." They announce, "Paul Adams for Leadership." The assumption is that leadership is something voters should want. I have found that also to hold true in my teaching and travels around the world. The desired form of leadership may change considerably in different cultural and organizational contexts, but people generally view leadership as valuable, even when they may not see themselves as "leaders." The term is commonly used with a positive valence.

Thus, if we talk about leadership in a value-neutral sense, as simply the capacity to gain a following, or a high position of authority, and to motivate people to realize one's vision—very common conceptions of leadership—then students who passionately want to see themselves as leaders will walk away reinforced in having as their guiding star, "I want to excel at getting people to do what I think is the right thing to do. Now I have to learn more about motivation, influence, how to gain authority, and the power of persuasion." Yet, is that the mode of leadership we thinkers and educators want to promote?

In my experience as a teacher and consultant, people just don't take the term "leadership" lightly. And perhaps we have to contend with that empirical observation with more intellectual courage. We have to face the likely fact that whatever we teach, our concept is going to have an impact on the assumptions and choice of values our students use to develop further for themselves the self-image and ability to practice leadership.

Normative Frameworks for Values Analysis

Burns had the courage not to beg this normative issue. Like him, we have to confront the cultural artifact that "leadership" may be an inherently normative term in common usage. Of course, how we do that remains an open question.

Burns tests three normative frameworks, to varying degrees. First, he argues, "The goals of a leader and follower have to be mutual." Yet, I think he knows intuitively that this criterion is insufficient, because history is replete with examples in which leaders and followers quite mutually went over a cliff together. Indeed, the primary reason why we see so little leadership from people in authority is, I believe, because constituents frequently beg for easy answers and reward our politicians for giving them just that: pandering and not leadership.

For example, down the road from where I live, an old-anti-war activist from the 1960s, Sam Gejdenson, had represented New London, Connecticut in Congress since 1981. During the 1990s, his heart was still not particularly hawkish, but when the Cold War ended and nearly all military and policy experts agreed that the United States no longer needed Electric Boat in New London to continue making additional nuclear submarines, Congressman Gejdenson couldn't just come out and say, "Good news, folks we did it. The Cold War is over!" Why? That reality meant it was time to leave one's job, up-root one's family, to sustain a traumatic disorientation, collectively for an economy quite dependent on Electric Boat and personally for thousands of workers. He couldn't come home and say, "Good news..." because by and large people in his district were looking to him to keep the ship-building plant open. So, Gejdenson did his best to protect those jobs. He gave speeches in Congress, wrote pieces in the *New York Times,* and argued that the country needed its submarine production capability for future contingencies and should keep the factory open. Policymakers continued to disagree, but displaying the right fighting spirit gained him re-election, once by one vote. Still, his district saw the train coming, and Gejdenson left office in 2000. He was unable to protect them entirely from the changes demanded by the times.

It is very hard to win people's favor when you are telling them tough messages or bad news. So, it isn't enough that a leader's goal be mutual with the constituency because constituents, or followers if you prefer, often do not want to face up to painful trade-offs. Adaptive challenges often demand costly adjustments that involve learning new ways of supporting and arranging our lives, and taking responsibility for challenges beyond what we expect to do, or feel accustomed to handle. All too frequently, people don't authorize leadership; they authorize protection.

Burns's "mutuality" framework is a leap forward from the traditional conception of leadership—a leader has the vision, and the rest is a sales problem, i.e., to inspire, motivate, or persuade followers to realize one's own vision. The mutuality framework at least compels our students to ask, "What collective value shall we pursue?"

Burns's second normative framework has gained the most attention of the three models: transforming leadership not only meets the needs of followers, but also elevates them to a higher level of moral functioning. Working with Maslow's hierarchy of human needs, Burns posits that people begin with the need for survival and security. When those basic needs are fulfilled, we concern ourselves with "higher" needs like affection, belonging, the common good, and serving others.

This framework has the benefit of provoking us to think about how to construct a hierarchy of values, and, as Burns subsequently has argued, to differentiate between various kinds of values— instrumental, modal, and end values—as we evaluate qualities of leadership performance. However, several problems emerge in the application of this framework to practice as it unfolds in real time. First, I have not been able to find the right level of abstraction for a hierarchy of values that would apply across cultures and organizational settings without either being so general as to lose all traction, or so specific as to be culturally imperialistic in its application. For example, within any organization or society, there will be competing views of the common good, with highly moral people representing these differences. Who is right? Should leadership theorists come up with a framework to evaluate the sincerity of intentions, or the moral legitimacy of these competing claims? Even if we could do so for one culture, would

it apply somewhere else? Perhaps these questions can be answered with historical perspective, but I believe we get lost in a conceptual maze when we move
from retrospective analysis to prescriptive analysis and application.

Second, Burns's application of Maslow might be called transforming leadership because it inspires and elevates followers, but, in my terms, it may propa-
gate massive societal work avoidance. For example, countless thousands of
soldiers die in wars having elevated their orienting values from self-protection to
the common good, and millions have done so in vain, swept away in tragically
common trends in which domestic constituencies opt for technical solutions and
easier answers as a way out of major challenges to their ways of thinking and
acting at home.

The values that should orient leadership practice must orient day to day
action, and at the same time be sufficiently spacious to honor the different normative frames of reference operating in different cultures and societies. Some
operational values can serve this purpose, for example, a commitment to reality-
testing from multiple points of view.

Finally, I think the notion, "I'm going to elevate you," runs against the grain
of Burns's first framework, which hinges on a mutuality of needs between
leader and follower. It is, in some ways, a regression to a more archaic view of
leadership—the leader has the vision, and the rest is a motivational issue. In
doing so, I think Burns gets himself entangled conceptually. He creates a laby-
rinth from which I do not believe he, or anyone since, has found a way out.

Still, the achievement remains. The important question is not, "Did Burns
solve the normative problem?" The achievement is that he raised the issue so
powerfully that it set in motion a continuing dialogue on the question, "What
normative basis are we going to use to conceptualize the practice of leadership?"

Leadership and Value Conflicts—A Third Normative Framework

Burns provides a third way to confront this issue that comes closer, in my experience, to being helpful conceptually and applicable to practice. As I have
applied it, his third normative framework holds that the task of leadership is to
mobilize people to face the internal contradictions in their own values, or in the
discrepancy between their values and their practice. Sometimes these internal
contradictions are generated endogenously by internal forces of dissent; and
sometimes these contradictions are generated exogenously by new challenges in
the environment that then provoke internal debate about strategic priorities and
practices. Now, this is not the framework that Burns develops fully in his volume, but the basic element is there, quite loud and clear. I find it enormously
useful because from it one can generate a rich set of guidelines for diagnosis and
action, as I have tried to do in my teaching and writing. For example, how does
one assess, among the many ways an "internal contradiction" manifests itself in
a complex social system, what the underlying tensions are really about, how to
parse them and then sequence the issues emanating from them in a strategic
manner? How should one orchestrate multi-party conflict, and what are the contextual variables? Internal contradictions rarely manifest with only two sides to

the issues. How do you reality-test competing perspectives to avoid illusions and partial diagnoses? How should one regulate disorder to keep it within a range of productive disequilibrium so that difficult conversations between factions in a community or organization can be rendered productive? Clearly, King and his colleagues in the Civil Rights Movement galvanized attention to one of our major internal contradictions as a nation. Indeed, his dream was "deeply rooted in the American dream," which gave it purchase in the hearts and minds of Americans across the country.

Burns's third way is more a suggestive direction than a developed framework like the transforming model. In this third way, one of the central tasks of leadership is to build containing vessels, structures and processes, for orchestrating different voices—holding environments in which those pressures can be harnessed. The differences generate not only conflict but also creativity, because people don't learn by staring in the mirror, they learn by engaging differences. I think Burns's "conflict model" points us in this direction, and I believe a great deal more thought should be given to it.

Taking Issue with "Followers"

These reflections on normative frameworks lead me to two more thoughts. Burns talks about elevating followers. I think this was both right and wrong. I believe it is right in the sense that he, in essence, is talking about developing citizenship, developing citizenship beyond followership—developing an active citizenry in which people are willing to take responsibility for their communities in the original spirit of democracy. In the Jeffersonian sense, citizenship development remains a central task and challenge for the democracies. I share Burns's passion for leadership that develops citizenship, and I place it squarely in the center of the model I develop in my writing.

But I believe it is more than a semantic disagreement to take issue with the term "follower." I take issue on three counts. First, I consider the term an archaic throwback to our primal yearning for charismatic authorities who "know the way." That yearning may always be with us, particularly in times of crisis and distress, at least in some form, but the language construct, leader/follower, reinforces the tendency toward a social contract of inappropriate dependency among citizens of organizations and societies. In my work with practitioners, this dyadic construct bolsters a set of imbedded assumptions about organizational problem-solving and processes of social progress—look to authority for answers, find somebody to follow.

Second, the term "follower" does not capture the *experience* of being stimulated to take action, responsibility, or make changes in one's life. For example, the black and white people mobilized by the Civil Rights Movement in the 1960s felt mobilized to take responsibility for the challenges of their communities; some of them were mobilized to exercise leadership themselves; and most became engaged citizens. Few, if any, had an experience of "followership." In short, the term inaccurately describes a leadership that mobilizes responsibility-taking and generates more leadership. It is limiting because in a democracy, we need active citizens, not followers, and we need people who take on leadership without much, if any, authority.

Third, embedded in this construct is perhaps the central source of confusion in the leadership field, the conflation of leadership with formal or informal authority, and the formal powers and informal influence that come with them. As I have suggested, any follower is someone who confers power, often informally, to a person or institution in exchange for a service. This is a definition of authority relationships; but this relationship does not define leadership. The point is that our language can entrap us in a set of confusing, imprecise, and counterproductive assumptions about how problems are solved and challenges are met in public and organizational life. As human beings, our default setting when facing times of distress seems to be to overly vest authorities with solutions to our collective challenges of direction, protection, and order, i.e., to treat adaptive challenges as if they were technical problems, and then to draw on a more regressive social contract embodied in the dyad, leader/follower.

I appreciate the efforts made by many of our colleagues, like Robert Kelley (1992), and now Barbara Kellerman (forthcoming), to transform our sense of the term "followership," but I think, as an empirical matter, this is hopeless. The construct brings with it too much baggage in terms of reinforcing both dependency assumptions in our social contracts and the misconception that leadership is the same as the capacity to gain formal or informal authority. Indeed, I think in Burns's writing, there are clear hints of these two questionable assumptions at work, and I believe they need to be surfaced, and perhaps changed as we build on his efforts.

What terms to use instead? I have found it useful, as have many others, to use terms like citizens, constituents, members, senior or lateral colleagues, or subordinates depending on the context to denote the people whom one mobilizes in efforts to lead. Indeed, in two books so far, I have found it quite easy to avoid using the term "follower" altogether.

Taking Issue with "Transforming"

I would take issue for two reasons with Burns's word "transforming." Perhaps because we come from different assumptions here and speak to concerns of different audiences, I am less worried that my practitioner-students, even those who are deeply scarred from their experience, may fail to have high goals and high aspirations. In my experience, people know how to dream. One may need to peel away a few layers of scar tissue causing cynicism and resignation, but the dream-generator is often there to be primed again.

I am more concerned with the potential for grandiosity, because when you become a leader to people, particularly with formal and informal authority, and people begin to look to you as a repository of hope and aspiration, as well as their pains, pretty soon you can be tempted to begin to believe that you really have got the answers that people yearn to believe you might have. People look to you to know and maybe, maybe you have succeeded in pulling the rabbit out of the hat two or three times. But then you are even more likely to fall into the trap of becoming an "idolized hero." The danger emerges because when people really begin to think you know what you're doing, it's very easy to believe that they are right—that you do. I see that among politicians, top business management, policy experts, and even Harvard faculty all the time!

I believe we need leaders to develop immunity to grandiosity, immunized against the temptations of their constituents who all too often seek clarity and certainty. We need leaders who can live with what General Giuseppe Cucchi, a former student from Italy, called "the doubt," even when everyone around wants to believe your press releases, and you do, too.

Thus, I am concerned about using words like transforming leadership because I fear that it fuels grandiosity, rather than rigorous reality-testing and a public honesty that mobilizes people in polities and organizations to tolerate uncertainty, ambiguity, and often the need to take responsibility for tough trade-offs in their lives. We need leaders who dream well, but who also plant their feet in reality, and test reality daily for new information that demands mid-course correction, and sometimes a revision of the overall mission and strategy. Maggie, in addressing the challenge of alcoholism in her community in British Columbia did not think of herself as transforming the community. Indeed, one doesn't transform a community; at best I think one engages the community in an ongoing process of adaptive work that probably will never end because the environment or endogenous realities within the community itself will continue throwing at it new and difficulty challenges. In her community's case, strip away alcoholism, and people have then to contend with the problems left underneath the anesthesia: sexual abuse, child abuse, poverty, unemployment, and a host of adaptive challenges to indigenous cultures generated by a history of trauma that has yet to be integrated in more successfully adaptive forms (Abadian 1999).

To create a normative ideal of transforming leadership risks the danger of reinforcing the grandiose mindset, "I'm going to transform my organization or society." Indeed, between the conflicting images of leadership within Burns's volume of the advocate for democracy and citizen leadership and the advocate for larger than life transformative heroes, many of whom like Mao do great damage, I side squarely with the former. The latter, I believe is simply the wrong mindset for developing the leadership capacity we need to meet the needs this new century has already brought to us.

Second, the word transforming connotes a fairly sharp discontinuity from the past, and suggests that such discontinuities are good and desirable. I think this is problematic. In my reading of history in politics and business, most significant and sustainable change builds largely on the past. The degree of change actually pales if one were to take into account all that is also conserved in the know-how and culture of the polity or organization. As in biological evolution, where most of the DNA remains unchanged, and most core processes are left untouched, sustainable progress that enables an organization to thrive in new ways and in new environments roots itself and innovates in ways that take the best from its history into the future. Hence, I prefer the term adaptation, even though it appears less ambitious. Indeed, as I have suggested before, the grandiosity invited by terms like "transformative" carries great risks. Mao, Lenin, religious missionaries, colonial "do-gooders," of which there have been many, at times the "Washington Consensus" of development economists, "democratizers" of the world, have done and are continuing to do extraordinary damage engaged in transformational efforts that attempt to radically depart, rather than change-by-building-from the virtues of the culture that preceded them. Transformational thinking is too prone, in my experience, to being ahistorical, as if history is to be discounted rather than valued for the constructs of culture that should endure.

An Enduring Contribution

Clearly, Burns's contribution endures. Jim Burns had the insight and courage to challenge both the scholarly community and our general culture to distinguish leadership from power and engage in developing a normative theory of leadership. His subsequent writing and his prodigious organizing efforts to mobilize scholars and practitioners have produced the beginnings of major advances in our conceptualization and general practice of this essential art. My colleagues and I stand on his shoulders.

References

Abadian, Sousan. 1999. *From Wasteland to Homeland: Trauma and the Renewal of Indigenous Communities in North America.* Doctoral dissertation, Harvard University. See also Heifetz and Linsky, *Leadership on the Line*, pp. 9-11.

Heifetz, Ronald A., 1994. *Leadership Without Easy Answers.* Cambridge: Belknap/Harvard University Press.

------ and Donald Laurie. 1997. "The Work of Leadership." *Harvard Business Review* (January-February).

------ and Marty Linsky. 2002. *Leadership on the Line: Staying Alive through the Dangers of Leading.* Boston: Harvard Business School Press.

------ and Riley Sinder, 19880. "Political Leadership: Mobilizing the Public's Problem-Solving." In Robert Reich (Ed.) *The Power of Public Ideas.* Cambridge: Harvard University Press, pp. 179-204.

Kirschner, Marc W. and John C. Gerhart, 2005. *The Plausibility of Life: Resolving Darwin's Dilemma.* New Haven: Yale University Press.

Matusak, Larraine. 1997. *Finding Your Voice: Learning to Lead... Anywhere You Want to Make a Difference.* San Francisco: Jossey-Bass.

Mayr, Ernst. 1988. *Toward a New Philosophy of Biology: Observations of an Evolutionist.* Cambridge: Belknap/Harvard University Press, pp. 95-115.

Neustadt, Richard E. 1991. *Presidential Power and the Modern Presidents 3rd ed.* New York: The Free Press.

Nye, Jr., Joseph S. 2004. *Soft Power: The Means to Succeed in World Politics.* New York: Perseus BBS Public Affairs.

Parks, Sharon Daloz . 2005. *Leadership Can be Taught: A Bold Approach for a Complex World.* Boston: Harvard Business School Press.

Seuss, Dr. 1990. *Oh, the Places You'll Go!* New York: Random House.

Williams, Dean. 2002. *Real Leadership.* San Francisco: Barrett/Kohler.

CHAPTER 4
THE CHALLENGE OF CHANGE IN *LEADERSHIP*
Adam Yarmolinsky

It is a bit of a shock to realize that I have been active in anything, let alone public service, for more than fifty years. But, in 1998, I had been involved in public affairs for one-half century. That experience and my reflection on it led me to challenge the arguments of James MacGregor Burns. His paper (Burns 1996) leads me to make this elaborate rebuttal. Burns described the world as static, except when leaders intervene; that is not the world that I know. I learned in high school physics that even an apparently stable desktop consists of a mass of whirling subatomic particles. So, yes, in the face of change, leaders make a difference, but it is a difference in reconciling change and stability.

Leadership as Mediating Change

I propose to challenge Jim Burns's formulation of leadership as change agent. This may seem foolhardy in light of great leaders such as Martin Luther King Jr., Gandhi, Rosa Parks, Abraham Lincoln, Franklin Delano Roosevelt, and Lyndon Baines Johnson, all of whom we associate with change. You do not need a leader to precipitate change, however. Even in the most traditional societies, change clearly is the law of life; when the weather changes, people must adapt. This is true of physical weather. It is true of social, political, and economic weather. When the soil is exhausted, when the rains fail, when there is no more "gold in them dar hills," society has to change. When technology makes some forms of human labor obsolete, as in the cotton fields of the South immediately before and after World War II, people have to change. When technological improvements in transportation and communications make supplies of labor available and economical where they were not available and economical before, then production centers change, such as the Nike factories in

> Burns is, of course, one of the great leaders in the field of leadership. I have had kind of a running argument with him for the last two or three years: whether leaders should be regarded primarily as change agents, as he contends, or whether they should be regarded as mediators between what change is necessary and what change is possible, as I contend.

Indonesia. Changes like these cascade through the system like water cascading down a Versailles fountain.

Leadership, it seems to me, is irrelevant to these facts of change. Changes happen without leadership. A system that is apparently stagnant is, I suspect, not stagnant any more than a dead body is stagnant. It is suffering from entropy. It is falling apart. It is losing energy. Moreover, what the leader does is to find ways to re-energize the system by helping people to recognize that is has to change. It is not that the leader is changing it, but that the leader is helping the system to recover.

You may say, "It takes leadership to recognize these changes." I would argue that it does not. To recognize the beginnings of change is the role of the scientist, the philosopher, and perhaps the artist. Even to consider how best to respond to the change we recognize does not reach the essence of the leadership role. Rather, the leader must mediate between the facts and circumstances of change and the resistance of society to change. Every institution is in the business of resisting change. It is too busy, it is too set in its ways, and it does not have time. I always enjoy the variant of the joke about changing a light bulb. For example, "How many faculty members does it take to change a light bulb?" To which the response is, "Change?" One of the things that leaders or potential leaders discover is that people who work for them are not going to do what they are told to do automatically, immediately, or wholeheartedly; mostly because they are too busy with things that they were already doing.

The Engine of Change—Mediation

I like to make the argument that operating at any reasonably high level in any organization, public or private, is really like being in charge of an engine. Let us say it is the engine on a moving vehicle that operates at a high speed. It usually is about to run out of fuel and has to be oiled continuously to prevent it from seizing up. So, between keeping the machine from running down for lack of fuel or seizing up for lack of oil, there is seldom, if ever, a time to think about where it is going. In order to effect desirable change in the institution, a leader must take into account that the institution itself is not standing still. It is changing and maybe in good and bad ways. This is where relativity comes in. You have to jump on the train while the train is moving, and you have to figure out which way it is moving. It may be moving backwards with respect to what you want but forward with what else is happening in the world. No matter the direction, it is moving when you get on board. It comes as an unpleasant surprise to people fresh in leadership positions to discover that they cannot give orders and expect them to be obeyed. Not because of rebellion in the ranks, but because people are too busy, and perhaps too set in their ways of fueling and oiling the institutional engine. They will get to new ideas when they can, if they can.

The dilemma is that leadership is a joint enterprise. One cannot lead without the cooperation of others. Otherwise, you may be a particularly distinguished, competent, or unusual performer, but you are not a leader. Lao Tzu says the ideal ruler is one, who rather than being recognized when he acts, leaves the impression among the people that they did it themselves. I think that it is more than just prestidigitation. Walt Whitman said, "Great artists need great audiences." I am not sure they do. Many artists find audiences only after their deaths. We recognize them as great posthumously, which is nice for the audience, mainly, but it a little late in the day for the artist. Leaders are different from artists, and Whitman adage is more applicable to leaders than artists. The test of leadership is the audience, but an audience that participates in the act rather than watching it. The art of leaders is active followers.

The leader is a mediator, a moderator, someone who adjusts the facts of change and the intransigent facts of organizations and institutions. A few examples, going back a hundred years to Abraham Lincoln, illustrate my point. Abraham Lincoln did not achieve his greatness as a leader by ending slavery. I would argue that he achieved his greatness by mediating between what he recognized as the terrible crime, sin, I suppose he would have said, of slavery and the preservation of the Constitution and the country that it governed. In addition, you remember Lincoln said, "If I could save the Constitution by eliminating slavery, I would do it. If I could save the Constitution by preserving slavery, I would do that." Well, that was perhaps an overly dramatic way of making his point.

He was making the point that there was a contradiction in the fact, the need, or the requirement that slavery be abolished and that was the intransigent resistance to that change. Slavery was abolished in most civilized countries decades before it was abolished in the United States. It was not abolished in the United States until after Lincoln's assassination. The Emancipation Proclamation simply freed slaves in areas where they were already free because these were areas occupied by U.S. troops. Lincoln recognized that he had to square the circle. He had to reconcile the irreconcilable, and he did it by steering a very cautious course indeed. That seems to me the oldest example that I can think of in relatively recent times of the exercise of leadership as mediation between change and institutional intransigence. You can say Lincoln is a change agent, but I would rather say he was an adjusting agent. The change was bound to happen. The question was *how* it was going to happen.

I am puzzled about the abolitionists, in contrast. I do not know that the abolitionists were admirable people—admirable as individuals perhaps, but not as leaders. It is not clear to me, as I think about it, that the abolitionists accelerated the abolition of slavery. For one thing, abolitionism certainly hardened the resistance of the South. Think about current analogies. I feel very strongly about the need to curb proliferation of nuclear weapons. In order to do that we have to make it clear to the non-nuclear world that nuclear weapons are of no use and that we do not value our nuclear weapons. The only use they have is to prevent other people from using nuclear weapons. However, I think those who say we must proceed immediately and, take steps directly, to abolish nuclear weapons are probably doing more to harden the resistance of people who do not want to take sensible steps—such as a no-first-use agreement, taking weapons off alert, deeper cuts, and all the rest of it. Demands for immediate change may do more harm than good. They may take the fuel or oil from the engine.

Now, let me offer another example, an obvious one perhaps—F.D.R. and World War II. F.D.R. went to the most extraordinary lengths to find ways to save the Allies. Indeed, if he had not worked out the Lend-Lease deal, the destroyer deal, then Germany would have had a much greater chance to win the war. We like to think that the Allies would have won the war anyway. I think an examination of the course of events will tell you that they came very near to losing it. Therefore, what F.D.R. did was to recognize that it was necessary for the United States to get involved; but it was not something that he could make happen without dealing with intransigence and inertia. He had to find ways to accommodate the nature of institutions that he governed which, for one thing, postponed our involvement, indeed our assistance, of the Allies for so long that we might have failed. Again, F.D.R. had to focus on the *how* as much as the *what.*

Similarly, I would argue that Lyndon Johnson mediated and adjusted in the civil rights struggle and the related development of the War on Poverty. The latter includes Medicare and Medicaid, which were not formally included in the War on Poverty, but which had a much more profound impact than anything done within the formal four corners of the Economic Opportunity Act. Lyndon Johnson never decided on where he was going until he figured out how to get there. If that sounds like opportunism, so much the better for opportunism; I think it is a necessary characteristic of an effective political leader. There is a wonderful novel about Lyndon Johnson. The protagonist is the governor of a large southern state, but it is evident from the first page that it really is a fictional version of Johnson's career. At one point, the narrator, who is a journalist who is working in the statehouse, says to the governor apropos of some program the governor is trying to put across, "You mean you would settle for half a loaf?" The Lyndon Johnson character says, "Half a loaf, half a loaf...it's a goddamn slice of bread." That is a form of leadership that makes change possible, certainly not only by directing change, but by making continuity possible as well. Maybe the American presidency is too easy an example of leadership as mediation to serve as a case.

You Win by Not Having to Fight a Battle

Military leaders may offer better examples. We think of the military as command and control with no apparent need for mediation or adjustment. Richard Neustadt in his book on the presidency (1991) quotes Harry Truman about his successor, General Eisenhower. "Poor Ike," [Truman] says, "he will get in the White House, and he will say, 'Do this. Do that.' and nothing will happen. He will discover that it's not like it is in the army." Well, it is not that way in the army, either.

Anyone who is in high office in the uniformed military discovers very soon that there are very few things you can do by giving direct orders. Somebody said the only thing you cannot do with a bayonet is sit on it. If you look at the classic figures in military history, you do not find command and control. Sun Tzu (1963 rpt.) wrote a classic of Chinese military theory. Writing before what in the

Western world is the pre-Christian era, Sun Tzu has a series of precepts that reinforce a fundamental principle: you do not win a war by winning battles. You win a war by putting the enemy in a situation where he will not fight and where you triumph. You win by not having to fight a battle. Sun Tzu's little book has been a vita maker for military leaders through the centuries. It is required reading at all military schools in the United States and Europe. General Sherman probably read the book. He fought one battle during his celebrated march through Georgia. He fought it because he said, "I don't want to give the enemy the impression that I have any standard way of proceeding. So just to throw them off balance, we are going to have a battle." That was the only battle he fought. He did not do it because he felt the need to win that battle. Even in the military, leaders mediate between the facts of military power and intransigent resistance of an enemy to change.

Leadership without Power

Now, what about other categories of leaders? I am thinking of leaders without the panoply of power. Martin Luther King Jr., in his last months before he was assassinated, was waging a losing struggle against the forces in the civil rights movement that wanted to use violence. He was lending, I think, almost all of his energies to mediate between the needs of the movement and the needs of African-Americans. He was also concerned with the need to maintain a peaceful transition to an integrated world—change and continuity.

Let us think about leaders in community action. Saul Alinsky was a wonderful community action organizer, and he wrote several books (Alinsky 1989; 1991). *Reveille for Radicals* is probably the best known one. Again, I think it ought to be one of the basic texts that people preparing for leadership should carry in their knapsacks. But what Saul Alinsky said over and over again is that community organizers cannot tell the community what to do. They have to position the community and position themselves so the community develops its own leaders. The community comes up with its own answers to its problems, and all that the community organizer can do is nudge, kind of the way you nudge a pinball machine. If you nudge it too much, a sign is going to light up and say "tilt," and you have to go back and start all over again. So even among leaders who cannot depend on being in a designated leadership position, effective organizers achieve their ends by understanding the situation and finding ingenious ways to mediate between what is needed—whether it is decent jobs or decent housing or getting the streets paved or more streetlights or police—and the resistance of both government and the community to participating in change.

Yes! Communities resist change. Because it is poor and powerless, a community may think that it is always going to be poor and powerless. The leader is a change agent, but not in the way that anyone would think you go about trying to achieve change. You have got to sneak around the back of the barn and all the other outbuildings before you come out achieving anything. Moreover, the achievement is not your achievement. It is somehow the achievement of all the institutions that you are insidiously working with or in which you are sneaking around.

Now, almost as a postscript to my categorization of kinds of leadership, I ask myself—what about intellectual leadership? Einstein, Galileo, Madam Curie—were they leaders? I would say not. If they were leaders, it was a lonely kind of leadership. Nobody followed them. Their ideas were picked up and embraced. They gained recognition. They became famous. But people were not persuaded to join in a movement which they led. It is a contradiction in terms to talk about intellectual leadership when we are talking about forms of leadership. I do not think what they did, though monumental, is what changed our society. They pulled aside the curtain and revealed facts about the world that we had not seen. That is not leadership anymore than the Wizard of Oz pulling aside his curtain is leadership. It is what we *do* with that new view that is leadership. Intellectual leadership notices that things are happening that nobody else notices. It is an observer's function, not a leader's function.

Revolution and the Failure of Change

I went through the Depression as a small child. Although I was perhaps insulated, I did see men selling apples on street corners. I saw the shantytowns. Of course, we have homeless people today, but not in the great of numbers we did then. If Hoover had been reelected, we could well have had a revolution in the United States. Who would have put it down? Would we then have had a kind of totalitarian or authoritarian state? These might-have-beens are not very productive speculations for historians. Neither a revolution nor its suppression happened. F.D.R. chose to use his enormous energies and imagination to work within the system. If you do not mind having a revolution, you may be able to be a change agent without reference to continuing the existing institutions. F.D.R. worked for change and continuity.

It is a good thing that he did, because revolutions are not the best possible way to achieve change. Too often the pendulum swings over to the other extreme, and you are as badly off after the revolution as you were when you started. Look at the examples from the Soviet Union to Iran. If the Shah of Iran, just to pluck an example out of the Middle East, had been an effective leader, there would not have been a revolution in Iran. Iran would have changed, but it would not have changed into an oppressive theocracy.

The nature and the source of change always offer difficult questions. But starting with an assumption that leaders only mediate change also provides new insights, even into the old saw, Was Hitler a leader? You need to separate yourself from the pervasive sense of evil and yet recognize that you cannot talk about Hitler without talking about the problem of evil. Hitler helped to free up the worst instincts of the worst of the German people. He could not have done it if those instincts and those people were not there, if those tendencies were not there waiting to emerge. He did not change them; he made it possible for them to behave the way they did.

Leadership, Change, and the "Institutionalization" of Followership

There is a great line in Gilbert and Sullivan's *The Gondoliers*. The story revolves around a mythical Italian principality in which the gondoliers revolt. They are promptly put down and when they are, somebody disparages the revolt's intent by saying, "If everybody is somebody, then nobody is anybody." Well, that strikes us as a horribly undemocratic sentiment completely inconsistent with our principles. However, successful leaders recognize the proposition that nobody by themselves is anybody, except as he or she can mobilize and organize the community to make changes take place. Moreover, you do not mobilize it by pulling out your sword and saying, "Forward! Charge!" Sometimes you have to say, "Around end!"

Change happens constantly, unchangingly; but leadership to mediate that change is a sometime thing. Leadership is much more complicated than people who have not had the experience of leadership can take in. Leadership involves subordinating oneself to the institutionalized creation of what we probably wrongly refer to as followers. Leaders, or successful leaders, are good at dealing with the institutionalization of followership.

Maybe transforming leadership is the equivalent of the kind of mediating role in a changing world which I am describing, in lieu of being a change agent in an unchanging world. Maybe I am only quibbling. But if change is central to leadership, maybe I am touching on a central question for the study and practice of leadership. If you start with a world of change that a leader joins, instead of starting with a world of stasis that a leader moves, I think your analysis works a little differently. Was Pandora a change agent? Was she a leader?

References

Alinsky, S. 1989 rpt. *Rules for Radicals: A Practical Primer for Realistic Radicals.* New York: Vintage Books.

———. 1991 rpt. *Reveille for Radicals.* New York: Vintage Books.

Burns, J. M. 1996. "Empowerment for Change." In B. Adams and S. Webster (Eds.) *Rethinking Leadership: Working Papers.* College Park, MD: University of Maryland, Burns Academy of Leadership.

http://www.academy.umd.edu/publications/klspdocs/jburn_p1.htm.

Neustadt, R. E. 1991. *Presidential Power and the Modern Presidents: The Politics of Leadership from Roosevelt to Reagan.* New York: Free Press.

Sun Tzu. 1963 rpt. *The Art of War.* New York: Oxford University Press.

SECTION II
UNDERSTANDING *LEADERSHIP*

Section I provided an introduction to James MacGregor Burns and *Leadership*. Section II will build a bridge from *Leadership* to the continuing study of leadership. We begin by switching attention from the leader to interaction between and among people. Edwin Hollander, in Chapter 5, underscores the leader-follower relationship that is central to his ideas. This early and pioneering scholar recounts and extends his concept of "idiosyncrasy credit." He leads us from the leader-centric model to understand different ways in which leaders may relate to followers and how that relationship affects leadership. He comes down on the side of support and delegation as leaders' actions that foster and represent greater interaction. He finds less distinction between transactional and transforming leadership than a dichotomy suggests. Both forms of leadership share similar characteristics grounded in leader-follower relations that include attributions that followers make toward leaders. Thus, Hollander broadens the applicability of Burns's essential contribution to formal organizations and deepens it by explaining its antecedents in other scholarship.

Tiffany Hansbrough, in Chapter 6, does more to relate transactional and transforming leadership. She suggests that if we take any interaction of leader and follower and freeze it, like a photograph, we may examine it for its details. In particular, Hansbrough suggests there are levels of analysis for any particular leader-follower interaction. Using the familiar example of grades and an imaginative example of a frog pond, she explores how Burns's theory of group action, implicit in his work, leaves important gaps for practice, such as those that Heifetz found in trying to teach from *Leadership* to mid-career professionals. She brings to the forefront the theories, neglected in Burns's work, that deal with differences within a group. She points out that we need more theory to understand leadership as making a group different than it was before or different from another group. Such change is not possible without understanding how differences develop within a group and how they may be overcome, as obstacles to common purpose, with modal values. This work is, in itself, transforming leadership shared by a group and perhaps a key to understanding day-to-day leadership practice.

Terry Price, in Chapter 7, takes us back to the roots of values and leadership and explains the implications of Burns's assumption that leadership implies values. As a philosopher and ethicist, Price helps us wrestle the question of values to the mat, a struggle that Burns undertook as Heifetz depicted. By examining conceptions of the "common good," Price brings us to exacting distinctions between transactional and transforming leadership, renews the need for leaders to forge agreement among their members, and ratchets up the demand of transforming leadership to include the values of other groups as well as one's own, even when engaged in transforming change. He also qualifies Hansbrough's outline for leadership. Rather than offering a formulation to aggregate disparate elements within a group, Price offers the more difficult formulation of aggregating the valid disagreements over values and motivations between contending groups. He leaves us to ponder the irony that the common good may require that we forego any insistence on epistemic certainty about any other common good.

In Chapter 8, Thomas Wren takes up the challenge of the "common good" and other values—equality, order, and individual liberty—in real historical terms. How do we reconcile them within a regime of popular sovereignty? He traces for us Burns's discussion of intellectual history and the efforts of James Madison, a primary intellectual leader on this topic, to reconstruct authority in a popular sovereignty. Madison had three different resolutions as conditions changed, underscoring Wren's point of the importance of history to establish the context of leadership. Interestingly, Wren uses a metaphor of "the flywheel of history," suggesting the engine metaphor of Yarmolinsky. Indeed, Madison seems to bring change because of the changes he faces and seems less a prisoner of the engine than Yarmolinsky's metaphor might have suggested. But then, Madison is no ordinary leader, as Wren makes clear. Wren illustrates the uses of history to inform leadership studies and provides us a framework for continued work.

In Chapter 9, Laurien Alexandre reminds us of the intellectual ferment of the 1960s that set a foundation for momentous and paradigmatic new work in feminist scholarship. She looks in vain within the covers of *Leadership* for reference to women's place in history, including their place in historical change. She holds Burns accountable for the omission of women in his discussion of leadership. She is just as straightforward in her praise for the theoretical elements of his work that permit an engendered analysis of leadership. Ironically, although Wren reports being put off initially by Burns's use of psychobiography, Alexandre is reassured by it. She also invites us to push the boundaries of psychology and to look at human development, including the role of the family, for its relationship to leadership.

Margaret Wheatley also invites us to a different image of leadership, a systems perspective borrowed from her background in biological science. In Chapter 10, she suggests that we move from the psychological approach to understanding leadership—Burns's continued preference—to look at leadership through the lens of living systems—somewhat akin to Alexandre's proposal to move to a perspective of human development. Yet Wheatley offers a broader perspective on leadership: the lens of ecosystems, living systems built around dependence and relationship. She leaves leadership and leader behind to promote the principles of life as the starting place of leadership studies. Thus, the principles of effective organizations have more to do with how we choose to structure our social organizations and cognitions. In regard to the latter, we may infer Wren's concerns for the context that history provides us but applied to an awareness of the here and now. Creative life in organizations and groups requires participation, learning, agency, and self-organizing systems. Wheatley offers a starkly contrasting view of organizational leadership than Yarmolinsky did.

Taken together, the chapters of Section II provide insight into the complexity of the study of leadership. Our contributors—psychologists, a natural scientist turned organizational consultant, a philosopher, historians, and a lawyer and biographer—suggest that any element of leadership, for example, values, however complicated in itself, becomes more complex when seen, as it is, an interaction between leaders and followers. That interaction has meaning because of messages each group and the individuals within them acquire over time. Moreover, any message from any time may have several different meanings. Some may see confusion here. Others may understand that this complexity extends the tribulation of an exciting intellectual challenge. How do we understand small parts of leadership with knowledge of the large system of which it is a part? How do we assemble an interdisciplinary synthesis of many parts of leadership within that large system to explain the individual small parts?

CHAPTER 5
RELATING *LEADERSHIP* TO ACTIVE FOLLOWERSHIP
Edwin P. Hollander

The range and astuteness of analyses and insights of *Leadership* are indeed impressive. They especially resonate with my long-held views that leadership is not just about the leader and that studying leadership involves more than leaders and their power (Hollander & Webb 1955). Early in this landmark book, Burns defines leadership as a *relationship* between leaders and a multitude of followers. "Leadership, unlike naked power-wielding, is thus inseparable from followers' needs and goals" (Burns 1978:19). My inclination, from the outset, takes this relationship to mean involving followers actively in desired mutual pursuits. This kind of leader-follower relationship is basic to what I call "inclusive leadership," most particularly in encouraging practices that yield bonding elements such as loyalty and trust (Hollander 1958; 1978 a, b; 1992 a, b; 1995; 2006). With this as background, we can now consider basic factors in understanding and practicing inclusive leadership (Hollander 2006).

Jim and I discovered the mutuality of our views at a succession of meetings at annual conferences of the International Society of Political Psychology (ISPP), in which we were both active. It was at an ISPP conference early in the 1990s that I gladly arranged a session on leadership-followership, at Jim's suggestion and with his participation. Later he suggested this topic as the focus for a study group for the Kellogg Leadership Studies Project (KLSP 1997). Soon after, I took on the new role of convener for the KLSP focus group to study this topic, with Lynn Offermann succeeding me in that role. The group's efforts ultimately led to the KLSP publication *The Balance of Leadership and Followership* (Hollander and Offermann 1997) as well as presentations at professional meetings.

Leaders, Leadership, and Followership

Traditionally, the leader is seen as the main actor in decision making. My emphasis, by contrast, favors a balance toward the participation of followers in shared decision-making processes. Their increased participation has merit on the grounds of values such as respect, democratic practice, and likely follow-through. Mostly, research findings show better quality and implementation of decisions when participation is present (Hollander and Offermann 1990).

This view departs from the long-standing tradition of relying heavily on the leader's qualities, instead of the relationship of these to followers, and how followers perceive and respond to the leader. Leader-centrism is quite common, and indeed, is part of the emphasis on an active conception of a dominant leader, at least in directing others' activity (Hollander 1985). Though we have progressed, "leader-centrism" continues to hold a powerful allure. Even the "great man" theory remains alive in such guises as "corporate savior" and, of course, "charismatic leader."

The qualities of leaders are obviously important, but Robert Reich makes the equally important point that "we need to honor our teams more, our aggressive leaders and maverick geniuses less" (Reich 1987). In particular, leaders need the skills to engage followers in productive and satisfying mutual pursuits. However, this view presents a departure from the usual way of seeing leaders' qualities as possessions, rather than as interpersonal links to others involved in shared activities.

Leaders and leadership both depend upon followership. Despite this interdependence, comparatively little attention has been given to followers, who accord or withdraw support to leaders, compared to the effects of the leader on followers (Hollander 1992a; 1992b). Furthermore, this imbalance also neglects the important role of followers in defining and shaping the latitudes of a leader's action. A view of followership as both active and critical (Kelley 1992) presents a considerable contrast to the more frequent focus on the leader as the center of attention and power, as with the sun in our solar system.

Ironically, the relationship of leaders and followers has a small but enduring place in the study of leadership. Chester Barnard's (1938) "acceptance theory of authority" exemplified this process. It centered on the follower's pivotal role in judging whether an order is authoritative. Followers, Barnard suggested, make this judgment according to whether or not they understand the order, believe it is not inconsistent with organizational or personal goals, have the ability to comply with it, and see more rewards than costs in complying and remaining with the organization or group (Hollander 1978a·47). Mary Parker Follett in the 1920s and 1930s proposed similarly that attention be paid to who gives orders and how they are received by the persons to whom they are directed (Graham 1995). This call for attention to followership is more than episodic.

Leadership and followership exist in a relationship built over time. Effective leaders bolster that relationship by providing for followers' needs, not only in tangible ways but also through such intangible rewards as support, fairness, and trust. As part of good business practice, Fayol (1916) long ago advocated attention to worker well-being, in addition to satisfying remuneration, bonuses, and profit sharing. Yet, the focus on such tangible rewards left a significant gap in understanding the role of intangible rewards in leadership (Hollander et al. 1996). To enrich this conception, we need to turn to the actual experiences of followers with leaders.

A body of research shows how inattention to leader-follower relations can produce dysfunctional outcomes from what Drucker (1988) has called "misleaders." For instance, Hogan, Raskin, and Fazzini (1990) found that organizational climate studies from the mid-1950s onward showed 60 percent to 75 percent of organizational respondents reported their immediate supervisor as the worst or most stressful aspect of their job. Indeed, from his ten-year literature review, DeVries (1992) reported a base rate of at least 50 percent for executive incompetence. Lord and Maher (1991) say that follower perceptions are checked against prototypes held by them and their related expectations of how leaders should perform, or "implicit leadership theories" (ILTs).

Followership thereby provides the key to charismatic leadership, as well as to its loss. Max Weber originated the concept of the charismatic leader, who is distinguished by a strong personal appeal and extraordinary determination, especially in time of crisis. However, Weber also recognized that if "leadership fails to benefit followers, it is likely that ... charisma will disappear" (Weber 1946 rpt:360). In short, followers accord this quality. Weber does not suggest the leader possesses charisma independently of followers, as others too often portray it. Willner (1984) and Hollander and Offermann (1990) are among those studying charisma as an attribution dependent upon relational qualities in the leader-follower bond. "It is not what the leader is but what people see the leader as that counts in generating the charismatic relationship" (Willner 1984:14). From her study, she goes on to note that variations in their personalities do not permit any generalization about a single charismatic leadership type, nor did a crisis serve as a necessary or sufficient cause for their emergence (Willner 1984:60).

Such findings highlight the importance of followers as perceivers with expectations of, and attributions about, leader performance and values. These points underscore the vital nature of the interdependence of leader and follower on a wide range of matters, including the morality of leadership (Hollander 1992a; 1992b; 1995).

Leader-follower relations are basic to significant leadership events and outcomes, good or bad. Burns's work deals explicitly with the moral dimension in leadership. He even defines leadership as "a process of morality to the extent that leaders engage with followers on the basis of shared motives and values and goals" (Burns 1987:36). In more specific terms, Howard Gardner observed, "[Leaders are] persons who, by word and/or personal example, markedly influence the behaviors, thoughts, and/or feelings of a significant number of their fellow human beings" (Gardner 1995:8).

The Attributional Perceptual Approach

This phenomenon of leaders-followers interaction is seen also in a perceptual pattern that involves follower attributions about a leader's intentions, values, and performance. One aspect of this has been termed the "romance of leadership" (Meindl, Ehrlich, and Dukerich 1987). They found that in perceiving group and organizational performance, positive or negative outcomes are more likely to be attributed as effects of the leader's actions than to other factors. Because leaders are symbols, Pfeffer (1977) says that if something goes wrong, the whole staff or entire team cannot be fired, but firing the manager can convey a sense of rooting out the problem's source.

A consequence of the attributional approach is to make more explicit the significance of followers' and others' perceptions of the leader, not least regarding expectations about leader competence and motivation. Realistically, imagery and self-presentation may still obscure the truth about the leader's intentions and dealings, yet there remains the basic question of the degree to which followers are able to evaluate the leader in regard to each of these matters.

Nevertheless, the usefulness of the follower's perspective as an avenue to understanding leadership is illustrated by the work on "derailment" (McCall, Lombardo, and Morrison 1988). The study involved four hundred promising managers, who appeared to be on a fast track. Those failing to reach their expected potential were found to show various kinds of inconsiderate behavior toward others but rarely to lack technical skills. With a sample of 2,600 top-level managers, Kouzes and Posner (1987) looked at qualities these managers admired in their leaders. Among the most frequently chosen qualities were honesty and inspiration, in addition to competence and the abilitly to be forward-looking. Here again the interpersonal or relational arena was seen as playing a major role.

In our own research, my colleagues and I have used a mode of event analysis called "critical incidents," with rating scales of the leader described in the event, plus other evaluations. Our sample of 293 organizationally based respondents was found to distinguish good from bad leadership mostly by relational qualities. Reports of positive rewards of sensitivity to followers, support, and praise dominated good leadership but were absent or negative in bad leadership. The four relational qualities that most frequently differentiated the two were scales of perceptiveness, involvement, trustworthiness, and rewardingness (Hollander and Kelly 1992; Hollander et al. 1996).

A significant percentage of the respondents mentioned *support* as the *intangible reward* provided by the good leader in the critical-incident situations. Respondents illustrated the relational reward of support with examples of the following practices: "Provided a clear message which helped me interact more effectively" (communicating); "gave recognition to whoever provided the input" (fairness); "problems were handled quickly, promptly, and effectively" (action-oriented behavior) and naturally, "backed up his staff" (support).

Conversely, in the bad condition, respondents described a *lack of sensitivity and support* as the two unrewarding behaviors displayed by the leader. However, other behavior categories occurred. They involved unfairness ("rules do not go for everyone"); unsupportive actions ("never made her thoughts clear"); or anger/harshness ("constantly sought to demean me"). In addition, untruthful/deceptive behavior was associated with bad leadership.

In response to the leader's behavior and obtaining rewards respondents in the good condition indicated increasing participation/followership. This response was most strongly associated with behavior categories involving communication and delegation/empowerment, at 50 percent of each, indicating that benefits resulting from good leadership may occur more often when certain behaviors are displayed.

Respondents in each of the critical-incident categories in the bad condition (except poor communication) indicated passivity/withholding as their reaction to bad leadership. Behaviors involving a lack of support were associated with the clearest effects. Approximately 30 percent of these respondents also mentioned expressing thoughts or feelings to the superior and discouragement/disappointment in response to the leader's actions. In each of the categories in the good condition, respondents reported that the leader's behavior developed/strengthened the relationship as the effect of the incident. The effects of the critical incident on the leader-follower relationship in the bad condition parallels those found in the good condition. In the bad condition, about 30 percent of the respondents, across critical behavior categories, mentioned weakened relationship, with the exception of poor communication, which apparently could not get much worse. A similar percentage indicated a loss of respect of the superior, which may reduce the legitimacy of the leader and his or her ability to take action. Finally, incidents involving unfairness were associated with an avoidance of the superior or job termination.

Moreover, there are differences of relational rewards within the good condition. The traditional behaviors of communicating and taking needed action are primarily leader-centric. The more modern leadership approaches of delegating and support are representative of greater follower interaction. Specifically, delegating exemplifies the belief that leaders should relinquish some of their power to facilitate growth in their subordinates. Supportive behavior is related to this development because it provided the encouragement, both personally and professionally, which is necessary for followers to develop the desire and ability to accept these leadership challenges. Though all of the behavioral categories indicated by respondents represent examples of effective leadership behavior, the modern approaches result in even more favorable outcomes for the leader, follower, and leader-follower relationship. The patterns of rewards and outcomes associated with these behavior categories, absent or negative in the bad condition, justify the essential point of relational approaches to good leadership, viewing leadership as a mutual process involving intangible as well as tangible rewards.

Transactional Leadership and the Idiosyncrasy Credit Model

This recent critical-incident research reinforces the importance of leader-follower relations in leadership outcomes, as proposed in the Idiosyncrasy Credit Model that deals with the latitude followers provide leaders for their action (Hollander 1958; 1964). The essential formulation in the model is that *credits are earned over time in the perceptions of others as a sign of loyalty by competence in helping to achieve the group's task goals and conformity to the group's norms.* Credits may then be drawn on to take innovative actions in line with expectations associated with the leader's role. Therefore, *early signs of competence and conformity can permit toleration of nonconformity, in the form of innovations, later.* Various experiments with groups, including a group-decision task, tested the model initially. Later research at Harvard by Estrada et al. (1995) also supported the model with work-group studies longitudinally.

Underlying the Idiosyncrasy Credit Model is recognition that a process of attributions made by followers is significant to accepting influence. The same behavior seen to be nonconforming if shown by one group member may not be so perceived when displayed by another. In short, nonconformity is defined within a group context, and the particular actor perceived within it, especially regarding his or her status (Hollander 1958; 1961). In addition, nonconformity can be viewed with regard to the common expectancies applied generally as a norm for group members and the particular expectancies applied to a high-status member. Accordingly, leaders may initiate change, perhaps in seemingly nonconforming ways, but be fulfilling in an accepted innovative role. While there may be greater tolerance of nonconformity for the high-status member in some ways, there are restrictions imposed regarding particular expectancies, which can be thought of as role behaviors.

Because the Idiosyncrasy Credit Model deals with a perceptual process in which followers accord or withdraw credits for a leader, it serves as an essential paradigm of a transactional process, but one with wider consequences. Having been granted credit by followers, it is then more likely for a leader to have them accept and follow innovative actions otherwise seen as unacceptable. This goes to the heart of the attributions that underlie the development of follower loyalty and trust in the leader. That was the theme of an analysis of the so-called crisis of leadership (Hollander 1978b). The essential point of giving attention to the followers' place in the leader-follower relationship was evident in the Human Relations Movement (See e.g., McGregor 1960; Likert 1961) with its emphasis on engaging followers in leadership; the roots of this movement were seen even earlier in Barnard's (1938) and Follett's (Graham 1966) conceptions, as noted above.

Transactional leadership has long referred to a fair exchange in which the leader gives something to followers and receives esteem and latitude for action in return (Homans 1961). The essence of the transactional form of leadership is to consider it not so much as a thing that a leader possesses, but as a *process* involving followers in a specific context with particular transactional requirements (Hollander and Webb 1955). Furthermore, it places weight on *relational* factors, processed by follower perceptions of a leader's legitimacy, values, intentions, and competence, among other attributes (Hollander and Julian 1969). Finally, this attributional process extends as well to the factors that make for transforming leadership (Hollander 1993).

Despite its relational elements, transactional leadership has been distorted to mean "management" and to refer to very different processes, such as "management by exception" (Bass 1985). This is a mistakenly imported conception that has not been part of usual transactional thinking, such as the reciprocity norm (Gouldner 1950). It also makes a too literal carryover from the *political* realm, i.e., doing favors to "buy votes" from constituents, to the *work* realm. Consequently, such generally approved leadership practices as intellectual stimulation and individual attention to followers, which provide obvious rewards to them, have been appropriated wholly into transforming leadership. However, these practices have long been valued as good leadership, especially in the transactional emphasis on the two-way leader-follower relationship.

Transactional and Transforming Leadership

Burns considers the transforming phenomenon to involve a more intense leader-follower relationship, though its origin rests in the same interdependence and identification (Hollander 1992a) that supports transactional leadership. Regarding the distinction between transactional and transforming leadership, Ehrlich and his colleagues assert that "conceptually, the basis for either form of leadership is a relational and perceptual exchange developed between a leader and his or her subordinates" (Ehrlich et al. 1990:231). But the actuality of this transaction between leader and followers is usually obscured in accounting for the transforming phenomenon. Instead there is an insistence on a firm dichotomy between transactional and transforming leadership by considering only tangible rewards and failing to acknowledge the intangible ones followers receive from transforming as well as transactional leaders. In this respect, Chemers contends that intrinsic rewards of "self-esteem, a sense of purpose, or salvation . . . become highly attractive and supremely motivating" when followers' needs are intense enough. "Under such circumstances, charismatic or transformational leadership may be seen as a special, elevated case of the more mundane transactional exchange processes that are the basis for all, person-to-person, team leadership" (Chemers 1993:312).

Accordingly, transforming leaders do provide rewards to followers, as Bass (1985) notes in listing those of personal attention and intellectual stimulation. However, the followers' reciprocation to the leader is usually unacknowledged, since that would support the view that a transaction has occurred. This would breach the artificial separation of measures that is maintained by Bass (1985), through the labeling of transactional leadership in a different way from its original, and much richer, conception. Curphy (1993), for example, found that transforming and transactional leadership were not independent, but were highly related in ratings given by cadets to their officers at the U.S. Air Force Academy.

Furthermore, would-be transforming leaders appear to need transactional qualities to establish the basis for a relationship with followers, at least initially. In that vein, Bensimon (1993) found that new college presidents who were successful had adapted by displaying both kinds of qualities as appropriate. Wallace (1996) showed a similar mixed pattern of accommodation in her study of corporate executives considered to be effective.

Implications and Conclusions

As various studies noted here indicate, relational factors hold a special place in maintaining a leader-follower bond. Indeed, whether leaders are called transforming or transactional, the common element that unites them is attention to followers' needs. In this respect, regarding the political arena at least, Burns says that "only the followers themselves can ultimately define their own true needs. And they can do so only when they. . . can make an informed choice among competing 'prescriptions'" (Burns 1978:36). Both intangible as well as tangible rewards are found to be essential, however, to the motivation to follow.

The present era clearly necessitates alternatives to the traditional power conception of leadership and followership. In organizations, such developments as a team emphasis, delegation, and participative decision making are harbingers of what Burns asserts by stating that ultimately the moral legitimacy of both transformational and transactional leadership is grounded in followers having *conscious choice among real alternatives* (Burns 1978:36). However labeled, good leadership assuredly demands no less, in consonance with the admirable values Burns espouses.

References

Barnard, C. I. 1938. *The Functions of the Executive.* Cambridge, MA: Harvard University Press.

Bass, B. M. 1985. *Leadership and Performance Beyond Expectations.* New York: Free Press.

Bensimon, E. M. 1993. "New Presidents' Initial Actions: Transactional and Transformational Leadership." *Journal for Higher Education Management* 8(2), 5-17.

Burns, J. M. 1978. *Leadership.* New York: Harper & Row.

Chemers, M. M. 1993. "An Integrative Theory of Leadership." In M. M. Chemers and R. Ayman (Eds.), *Leadership Theory and Research: Perspectives and Directions*, pp. 293-319... San Diego, CA: Academic Press.

Curphy, G. J. 1993. "An Empirical Investigation of the Effects of Transformational and Transactional Leadership on Organizational Climate, Attrition, and Performance." In K. E. Clark, M. B. Clark, and D. P. Campbell (Eds.), *Impact of Leadership*, pp. 177-188. Greensboro, NC: Center for Creative Leadership.

DeVries, D. L. 1992. "Executive Selection: Advances But No Progress." *Center for Creative Leadership: Issues and Observations* 12, 1-5.

Drucker, P. F. 1988. "Leadership: More Doing than Dash." *Wall Street Journal*, Jan. 6:14.

Ehrlich, S. B., J. R. Meindl, and B.Viellieu. 1990. "The Charismatic Appeal of a Transformational Leader: An Empirical Case Study of a Small, High Technology Contractor." *Leadership Quarterly* 1(4), 229-247.

Estrada, M., J. Brown, and F. Lee. 1995. "Who Gets the Credit? Perceptions of Idiosyncrasy Credit in Work Groups." *Small Group Research*, 26, 56-76.

Fayol, H. 1949. *General and Industrial Management.* (trans.) Constance Storrs, London: Pitman Publishing.. (Original work published in French, 1916.)

Gardner, H. 1995. *Leading Minds: An Anatomy of Leadership.* New York: Basic Books.

Gouldner, A. W. 1950. "The Norm of Reciprocity: A Preliminary Statement." *American Sociological Review* 25, 161-179.

Graham, P. 1995. *Mary Parker Follett: Prophet of Management.* Boston: Harvard Business School Press.

Hogan, R., R. Raskin, and D. Fazzini. 1990. "The Dark Side of Charisma." In K. E. Clark and M. Clark (Eds.), *Measures of Leadership.* pp. 343-354.   West Orange, NJ: Leadership Library of America.

Hollander, E. P. 1958. "Conformity, Status, and Idiosyncrasy Credit." *Psychological Review* 65, 117-127.

----. 1960. "Competence and Conformity in the Acceptance of Influence." *Journal of Abnormal and Social Psychology* 61, 361-65.

----. 1961. "Some Effects of Perceived Status on Responses to Innovative Behavior." *Journal of Abnormal and Social Psychology* 49, 247-50.

----. 1964. *Leaders, Groups, and Influence.* New York: Oxford University Press.

----. 1978a. *Leadership Dynamics: A Practical Guide to Effective Relationships.* New York: Free Press/Macmillan.

----. 1978b. "What Is the Crisis of Leadership?" *Humanitas* 14(3), 285-296.

----. 1985. "Leadership and Power." In G. Lindzey and E. Aronson (Eds.),*The Handbook of Social Psychology, Vol. II,* 3rd ed., pp. 485-537. New York: Random House.

----. 1992a. "The Essential Interdependence of Leadership and Followership." *Current Directions in Psychological Science* 1(2), 71-75.

----. 1992b. "Leadership, Followership, Self, and Others." *Leadership Quarterly* 3(1), 43-54.

----. 1993. "Legitimacy, Power, and Influence: A Perspective on Relational Features of Leadership." In M. M. Chemers and R. Ayman (Eds.), *Leadership Theory and Research: Perspectives and Directions,* pp. 29-47.. San Diego, CA: Academic Press.

----. 1995. "Ethical Challenges in the Leader-Follower Relationship." *Business Ethics Quarterly* 5(1), 55-65.

----. 2006. "Influence Processes in Leadership-Followership: Inclusion and the Idiosyncrasy Credit Model." In D. A. Hantula (Ed.), *Advances in Social and Organizational Psychology: A Tribute to Rosnow,* need page numbers.,. Mahwah, NJ: Erlbaum.

----, and J. W. Julian. 1978. "A Further Look at Leader Legitimacy, Influence, and Innovation." In L. Berkowitz (Ed.) *Group Processes,* pp. 153-165. New York: Academic Press.

----, and D. R. Kelly. 1992. "Appraising Relational Qualities of Leadership and Followership." Paper presented at the 25th International Congress of Psychology, Brussels, Belgium (July 24).

----, and L. R. Offermann. 1990. "Power and Leadership in Organizations: Relationships in Transition." *American Psychologist* 45:179-189.

----, and L. R. Offermann. 1997. "Introduction." *The Balance of Leadership and Followership.* College Park, MD: University of Maryland, Burns Academy of Leadership.

----, and W. B. Webb. 1955. "Leadership, Followership, and Friendship: An Analysis of Peer Nominations." *Journal of Abnormal and Social Psychology* 50, 163-167.

----, E. Schwager, K. Russeva, and F. Nassauer. 1996. "Intangible Rewards Contributing to Leader-Follower Relations." Paper presented at the 26th International Congress of Psychology, Montreal, Canada (August 17).

Homans, G. C. 1961. *Social Behavior: Its Elementary Forms.* New York: Harcourt, Brace, and World.

Kelley, R. E. 1992. *The Power of Followership.* New York: Doubleday.

Kellogg Leadership Studies Project (KLSP) 1997. *The Balance of Leadership and Followership.* College Park, MD: University of Maryland, Burns Academy of Leadership.

Kouzes, J. M., and B. Z. Posner. 1987. *The Leadership Challenge: How to Get Extraordinary Things Done in Organizations.* San Francisco: Jossey-Bass.

Likert, R. 1961. *New Patterns of Management.* New York: McGraw-Hill.

Lord, R. G., and K. J. Maher. 1990. "Leadership Perceptions and Leadership Performance: Two Distinct but Interdependent Processes." In J. Carroll (Ed.), *Advances in Applied Social Psychology: Business Settings, Vol. 4,.* pp. 129-154. Hillsdale, NJ: Erlbaum.

McCall, L., and M. M. Lombardo (Eds.). 1988. *Leadership: Where Else Can We Go?* Durham, NC: Duke University Press.

McGregor, D. 1960. *The Human Side of Enterprise.* New York: McGraw-Hill.

Meindl, J. R., S. B. Ehrlich, and J. M. Dukerich. 1985. "The Romance of Leadership." *Administrative Science Quarterly* 30, 78-102.

Pfeffer, J. 1977. "The Ambiguity of Leadership." In M. W. McCall Jr. and M. M. Lombardo (Eds.), *Leadership: Where Else Can We Go?* pp. 13-34.. Durham, NC: Duke University Press.

Reich, R. B. 1987. "Entrepreneurship Reconsidered: The Team as Hero." *Harvard Business Review* 65(3), 77-83.

Wallace, J. L. 1996. "An Examination of Comparable Behavioral and Motivational Features of Transactional and Transformational Leadership as Regards Effectiveness and Follower Satisfaction." Doctoral Dissertation in Industrial/Organizational Psychology, Baruch College and Graduate Center, City University of New York.

Weber, M. 1946 rpt. "The Sociology of Charismatic Authority." In H. H. Gerth and C. W. Mills (Trans. and Eds.), *From Max Weber: Essays in Sociology,* pp. 245-252. New York: Oxford University Press. Original essay in German, 1921.

Willner, A. R. 1984. *The Spellbinders: Charismatic Political Leadership.* New Haven, CT: Yale University Press.

CHAPTER 6
JUMPING FROGS AND THE MULTI-LEVEL ANALYSIS OF *LEADERSHIP*
Tiffany Hansbrough

One day in graduate school, I saw *Leadership* on my office mate's desk. My initial reaction was that this one was one of the many "leadership how-to" manuals that pervade the business section in bookstores. Therefore, the book held little appeal for me. Later, upon becoming more familiar with the leadership literature, I made an unusual discovery—it was a book that detailed leadership theory not written for academics! Due to its choice of a broad audience, the book has been widely read but is not required reading for graduate students, such as I was, in organizational behavior.

> Unlike other authors in this volume, I cannot speak of a lengthy influence of *Leadership* on my work. When Burns's book was published in 1978, I was in sixth grade. At that point in my life, my biggest concern was my family's upcoming move to California. Therefore, unlike some of the other contributors, Burns's book did not make an impression upon me at the time of its publication. In this way I resemble most of the readers of this book.

I came to Burns's book with a specific focus of level-of-analysis issues. Applying this framework to Burns's theory suggests its conceptual confusion. In specifying a level of analysis for a theory, a researcher is making a prediction that the relationships are a consequence of differences between groups, within groups, or between members independent of groups (Dansereau, Alutto, and Yammarino 1984). Traditionally, theories examine leadership at one of three levels—between or among groups, within groups, or apart from groups. Here, I will examine different levels of analysis and explain that the meaning of Burns's theory shifts depending on the level of analysis.

Why Levels of Analyses Are Important

Some theories elect to evade the level-of-analysis issue and do not specify a hypothesized level. However, failure to stipulate a level of analysis renders theories imprecise, open to misinterpretation, and ripe for controversy (Klein, Dansereau, and Hall 1994). Consider the following possible cases of students' grades and the levels of analysis we can use to interpret them.

1. Every student gets either an A or a C. We may hypothesize the professor gave her favorite students As and the rest received Cs. Here, the professor's actions suggest there is a difference among the students of the same group, a class, based on some criteria other than the students' work.

2. Students get a wide range of grades from A to F. We may hypothesize that the professor assigned grades based on some reasonable assessment of the individual achievement of each student. Again, the professor's actions suggest that there are differences among the students, but the criteria shift to a focus on the students' work and from the professor's personal preferences, which of course may not be exclusive categories.

3. Students get either very high grades or very low ones depending on which professor they have. We may hypothesize that one professor gives grades with reference to some hypothetical standard outside of the class. In this case, the professor may hypothesize that all college students have too much stress in their lives and that she will not add to it; thus everyone gets an A. On the other hand, another professor may decide that students just don't care about personal responsibility and that she will demonstrate the consequences of that attitude by making it extremely difficult to get a grade higher than a C. Thus, the grades don't really tell us anything about student ability; rather they tell us about the professor since everyone gets pretty much the same grade.

Granted there are differences among the students, as indicated by their grades. Where do the differences come from—a professor's likes and dislikes, some criteria internal to the group and applied evenly, or some external criteria? Levels of analysis, thus, offer explanations that may vary widely and offer very diverse interpretations of an event. For example, straight-A students are unlikely to explain to the admission committee of law school that they took courses with professors in the first hypothesis and in the stress-reduction mode of the third hypothesis. A student on the verge of failing out of college is likely to invoke the first hypothesis and the unreasonably harsh grading standard of the third. Those designated as superior seek a level of analysis related to their achievement, and those relegated to lower ranks are more likely to look for some other element of explanation of the differences within and among group members. Similarly, the level of analysis has important implications for a leadership theory. Depending upon the hypotheses of group formation, the entire relationship of and followers, as well as their individual achievement, can change and take on a new meaning.

Leadership at the Dyad Level of Analysis: An Exchange

Many theories describe leadership as an exchange that transpires between leaders and followers. Typically, leaders give benefits to followers, who in turn reciprocate with increased responsiveness toward leaders (Hollander 1978). Homans (1974) notes that an individual in an exchange relationship with another has two expectations: 1) that the rewards of each will be proportional to the costs of each and 2) that the net rewards of each will be proportional to the investments. In this direct relationship, the relevant question for each individual is whether the reward received from the other, less the cost in getting it, was as much as expected and, therefore, as much as the individual deserved. Consequently, in exchange relationships, each individual serves as a standard for the other (Cohen and Greenberg 1982).

Unlike simple economic exchange, social exchange is not an explicit, contractually based arrangement. Rather, social-exchange relationships are based on trust. An individual gives to another, trusting that the other party will reciprocate. Further, as each individual is capable of destroying the dyad, trust serves as the cornerstone for the relationship. The dyad is typically asserted as the level of analysis, since exchange theory describes a transaction between two actors. It should be noted that the work group still remains relevant, as these relationships do not take place in a vacuum. If a dyadic view of leadership is endorsed, three distinct analytical alternatives are possible: 1) dyads based on differences within groups (assign grades based on favored status); 2) dyads independent of groups (assign grades based on individual performance); and 3) dyads based on differences between groups (assign exceedingly high or low grades). A range of leadership theories cluster at each of these levels of analysis.

Theories of Differences within a Group Based on Leader Behavior. Some theories describe leadership as two qualitative relationships, or exchanges, that develop with followers. Superiors make comparisons among subordinates that subsequently determine work-group status (Graen and Cashman 1975). Thus, followers become "in-group" members by virtue of comparison to other members. In other words, the composition of the group influences whether one is considered an "in-group" or an "out-group" member.

A frog pond provides a useful example of this phenomenon. Assume for a moment that we want to select the best possible frogs in a pond. We are selecting frogs for a jumping contest, so "best" implies a jumping ability. We have no information to judge what makes some frogs jump further than others in competition, nor the time to develop them. We may devise criteria such as size of webs, length of legs, character, and personality, but time prohibits using them on a case-by-case basis. Thus, assuming that authority works in a similar manner, some followers will always be selected into the in-group because they have the characteristics that the "frog hunter" prefers, which in this case is some reasonable semblance to the criteria, and, of course, proximity sufficient to catch them. Like the frog hunter, the professor develops in- and out-groups depending on criteria other than a particular task.

Vertical Dyad Linkage (VDL) theory (Dansereau, Graen, and Haga 1975) is an example of a theory that makes these comparative predictions. According to VDL, time constraints prohibit superiors from developing high-quality relationships with all members (Bass 1990). Therefore, superiors effectively "divide and conquer" forming high-quality relationships with only a select group of employees—the in-group. The dyadic relationships that transpire among subordinates are of two natures: superiors enact leadership roles with in-group members and supervisory roles with out-group members (Dansereau, Graen, and Haga 1975).

In-group members receive greater amounts of latitude, attention, and support from superiors. In exchange, in-group members provide superiors with greater amounts of time and energy on tasks, volunteer for special assignments, and offer increased loyalty. Conversely, the exchange involving out-group members is based on the employment contract. Out-group members receive paychecks for completing jobs in accordance with the job description. Since group members experience vastly different relationships with superiors based on in- or out-group status, variation between in- and out-groups is predicted to be greater than the variation of individuals within the entire group. Subsequently, relationships are impacted by differences within groups.

Theories of Differences Independent of Subgroups. In contrast to a VDL perspective, other dyad explanations of differences posit that neither leader characteristics nor the composition of the group impacts superior/subordinate relationships. Instead, the linkages with others are uncoupled, and an interaction with one individual has no bearing on subsequent interactions with other individuals (Dansereau et al. 1995).

For example, superiors evaluate each subordinate independently, as unique individuals, in terms of the provision of satisfying performance. Subordinates providing satisfying performance are accorded support for self-worth from superiors. Since superiors and subordinates interact independently of others in the unit, the relationship that transpires is independent of groups. Thus, it is possible that all, some, or none of the followers may enter into such an exchange with the leader, depending upon whether they provide the leader with satisfying performance. To revisit our frog pond, objective data would be used to determine the fit of any particular frog for our jumping contest. Therefore, the frogs do not compete with each other in order to be selected. Likewise, in terms of grades, each student's grade is determined on an individual basis.

Theories of Differences among Groups Based on Leadership Behavior. Other theories of difference assume that it flows primarily from some characteristic of a leader. Differences in grades are based on differences in professors, rather than how students compare to one another or how they perform as individuals. The level of analysis here switches focus from a relationship of leaders and followers to the traits of a person in authority or leadership. Thus, all frogs may be selected for our jumping contest because the leader is very inclusive and wants no frog to feel excluded or, perhaps, no frogs will be selected because, in the mind of the frog hunter, none are qualified to compete with a hypothetical set of contestants. Accordingly, the relationships that transpire between the leader and followers are of a similar nature. Greater variation of grades is expected between groups or among classes, but not within them because followers' outcomes are a function of leadership behavior rooted in personality characteristics.

In the case of the charismatic leader, followers view the leader as a role model. As such, the receipt of accorded esteem from the leader serves as a desirable reward for followers. If followers desire the same outcomes (such as esteem from the leader), and if traits (such as charisma) drive leadership behavior, then little variation in followers' outcomes is expected.

Burns and the Differences among Groups

Burns (1978) defines leadership as leaders inducing followers to act for certain goals that represent the values and motivations—the wants and needs, the aspirations and expectations—of both leaders and followers. Further, two distinct types of leadership are identified: transactional and transforming. Transactional leadership occurs when one person takes the initiative in making contact with the other person for the purpose of an exchange of valued things. The commodities exchanged could either be tangible or psychological in nature. Each party recognizes the other as a person, yet they have no enduring higher purpose beyond that of self-interest. Thus, the relationship is transitory in nature.

Transforming leaders, on the other hand, assist groups to move from one stage of development to a higher one, and in doing so, create significant societal change. Transactional leadership is a precondition for transforming leadership, as the relationship begins centered on self and then the focus shifts to the environment. Although Burns does not directly articulate a hypothesized level of analysis, it is possible to infer two distinct levels of analyses from his writings.

First, Burns seems to imply the dyad level of analysis. "Leaders and followers are engaged in a common enterprise; they are dependent on each other, their fortunes rise and fall together, they share the results of planned change together." This implies that leaders and followers are mutually dependent, one of the hallmarks of an exchange relationship (Hansbrough and Dansereau 1995). Burns also notes that leaders react to the anticipated motivations of followers, as followers react to the expected leadership actions. Finally, he describes the leader-follower dynamic as characterized by a ceaseless flow and counter flow (Burns 1978:440). This "give and take" also appears similar to an exchange relationship. Thus, the dyad level of analysis may be inferred. At what level, however, within groups, independent of groups, or between groups?

Burns is not explicit. He seems to imply very strongly, however, that leadership is a function of differences between groups because of the inattention that he gives to differences within a group. Either every frog is going to the jumping contest or none are going. Leaders and followers at all levels of an organization expend their social energies, consciously involved in a joint effort for the same goal (Burns 1978:439), or no one does. Variation, in terms of a group's goals, is primarily a function of the leader's vision. Therefore, relationships between leader and follower are the result of differences between groups and not within them.

According to Burns, a transforming leader recognizes and exploits an existing need of followers. This explains that leaders and followers act interdependently as a group, a major insight that he contributes. However, it neglects much of the rest of leadership theory. For example, if followers have distinct needs and motives, as students do in a class, how does the leader view them as unique individuals within a group sharing some characteristic, in this case a common goal? In short, a theory that specifies that leaders interact with followers as unique individuals is incompatible with a level of analysis that focuses on some characteristic allegedly shared by all the group members for better or for worse—too much stress or not enough personal responsibility (Dansereau, Alutto, and Yammarino 1984).

Modal Values as the Key

For Burns, leadership happens when leaders and followers join together to meet their mutual needs and later embark on real change. Leadership in *Leadership* moves beyond group and individual differences and ends with the common good. Burns concedes, however, that the greatest difficulty for a leader is that of identifying and aligning commonalities between leader and follower hierarchies of motivations. Thus he hints at the need to look at the differences within the group of followers that follow from leadership behavior or followers' characteristics. Once found, leaders adjust their purposes in advance to the motive bases of followers; nothing can substitute for common purpose.

Burns only hints at the importance of these differences; however, they have huge implications for applying to, or interfering with, Burns's theory of the day-to-day practice of leadership. Ironically, another neglected aspect of his theory, modal values, may offer the surest path to the applicability of Burns's work to the everyday situations of leadership. Modal values, such as respect and fairness, may provide a way around the inconsistency between the theory and level of analysis and a means to find commonalities among differences. As Burns notes, such values are not especially controversial.

First, the group, leaders and followers would articulate a modal value such as fairness. This value has the advantage of different meanings depending upon the interpretation of the follower. Some followers might interpret fairness as equality. Therefore, these followers would assume that all followers should receive the same grade for some agreed amount of work. Other followers may prefer equity and grades based on merit, however defined, as well as the amount of work. Thus, the modal value, and some tolerance for ambiguity in its use, becomes a unifying value for the group. Finding this modal value, engaging groups in the discussion of its meaning, and then finding a course of action to express it, is paradoxically transforming work.

Martin Luther King Jr. exemplifies mobilizing a group for transforming change around an ambiguous modal value, while appealing to different levels of group conduct and differences within and among groups. He used the phrase "let freedom ring" extensively in his "I have a dream" speech. As Burns might suggest, the value articulated is not especially controv)sial and probably means different things to different people. Yet it had the potential to unite a diverse group of followers. Similarly, the phrases "we can do better" widely used in President Clinton's 1992 campaign and "compassionate conservatism" in President Bush's 2000 election were vague enough to appeal to individuals with varied agendas. "We can do better" might mean "I can make more money" to some, while others might hear "we can eliminate social problems." If leaders use terms that are sufficiently vague but also tap into followers' modal values, then it may indeed be possible to unify followers, despite differences, within a group. At that point, differences between groups may seem more explicit. Not every frog may go to the jumping contest, but those who do and those who don't will understand the selection process. Not every student will agree with their grade, but they will understand the criteria for establishing differences among groups of students. Such a discussion will also enlighten those in charge—leaders, authorities, frog catchers, and professors—about the differences of needs among group members, such as needs related to stress and personal responsibility, and between the group and some hypothesized group.

References

Bass, B.M. 1990. "From Transactional to Transformational Leadership: Learning to Share the Vision." *Organizational Behavior* 18, 19-31

Burns, J.M. 1978. *Leadership.* New York: Harper & Row.

Cohen, R. L. and J. Greenberg. 1982. "The Justice Concept in Social Psychology." In J. Greenberg and R. L. Cohen (Eds.). *Equity and Justice in Social Behavior.* New York, N.Y.: Academic Press.

Dansereau, F. 1995. "A Dyadic Approach to Leadership: Creating and Nurturing It under Fire." *Leadership Quarterly* 6(4), 479-490.

Dansereau, F., J. A. Alutto, and F. J. Yammarino. 1984. *Theory Testing in Organizational Behavior: The Variant Approach.* Englewood Cliffs, N.J.: Prentice-Hall.

Dansereau, F., G. Graen, and W. J. Haga. 1975. "A Vertical Dyad Linkage Approach to Leadership Within Formal Organizations: A Longitudinal Investigation of the Role Making Process." *Organizational Behavior and Human Performance* 13, 46-78.

Dansereau, F., F. J.Yammarino, S. E. Markham, J. A. Alutto, J. Newman, M. Dumas, S. Nachman, K. Kim, S. Al-Kelabi, S. Lee, and T. Hansbrough. 1995. "Individualized Leadership: A New Multiple Level Approach." *Leadership Quarterly* 6, 413-450.

Graen, G. and J. F. Cashman. 1975. "A Role-Making Model of Leadership in Formal Organizations." In J. G. Hunt and L. L. Larson (Eds). *Leadership Frontiers.* Kent, Ohio: Kent State University Press.

Hollander, E. 1978. *Leadership Dynamics: A Practical Guide to Effective Relations.* New York, N.Y.: Free Press.

Homans, G. C. 1974. *Social Behavior: Its Elementary Form* rev. ed. New York, N.Y.: Harcourt, Brace and World.

Hansbrough, T. and F. Dansereau. 1995. "Leadership and Empowerment: A Social Exchange Perspective." *Human Relations* 48,127-146.

Klein, K. J., F. Dansereau, and R. J. Hall. 1994. "Levels Issues in Theory Development, Data Collection, and Analysis." *Academy of Management Review,* 19, 196-229.

CHAPTER 7
LEADERSHIP AND COMMON PURPOSE
Terry L. Price

Bertrand Russell once said that all of philosophy is a footnote to Plato. Similar claims have been made about the connection between contemporary political philosophy and the late John Rawls, whose 1971 treatise *A Theory of Justice* revived a particularly valuable strand of social and moral thought. My own personal experience gives me reason to think that this latter claim is not unjustified.

When I turned my intellectual attention to this field, exactly twenty years after the publication of *Leadership*, my first point of business was to immerse myself in this seminal text. I have been in the field but a very short time, but I can already see that I am unlikely to stray very far from the contributions Burns makes in this work.

When I began writing a thesis in graduate school, I naively set aside the first chapter to deal with and, I hoped, dismiss the Rawlsian approach. I ended up devoting the entire thesis to his work and calling it "Rawls on Fairness to Conceptions of the Good."

The obvious parallel to Rawls in Leadership Studies is James MacGregor Burns. What I offer in this essay is a commentary that aims to build on one of the main arguments of *Leadership*.

The Common Good

Burns defines leadership "as leaders inducing followers to act for certain goals that represent the values and motivations—the wants and needs, the aspirations and expectations—*of both leaders and followers*" (Burns 1978:19). Leadership works in the service of the interests of group members. Generally stated, this claim is uncontentious enough. In fact, in recent times, some such statement has been understood as central to the very concept of leadership. It is not least of all Burns's inspiration for a newfound focus on follower interests that reflects the genuine progress that *Leadership* makes on moral fronts. Nevertheless, a central difficulty remains. How do we specify the relevant values and motivations?

Clearly, most any attempt to answer this question will give rise to more than enough contention to go around. I should say at the outset that it is not my aim in this paper to offer a specification of the values and motivations in terms of which we might understand genuine human interests. Rather, I want to suggest that there is good reason for disagreement about the nature of our interests and that the reasoning behind our disagreements comes to bear on our understanding of good leadership itself. If I am right, good leadership takes these disagreements seriously. Specifically, it facilitates a process of collective reflection about our values and motivations in order that we might achieve some clarity about genuine human interests and what it would take to meet them.

Appeals to the common good carry a great deal of moral weight in leadership discourse. Accordingly, they make for a good starting point in a discussion of the ends of leadership. These appeals are to be contrasted, for example, with more particularistic appeals associated with self-interest and partisanship. Given the moral impotence of their motivational counterparts, it often turns out that common good declarations are something of an argumentative show-stopper.

Against this kind of justification, one can reply that it is a mistake to think that the common good would be served by a particular strategy, but one certainly cannot offer the retort that an appeal to the common good is itself out of place in the argument. Difficulties arise, however, when we endeavor to give a fuller characterization of the common good. But it is important, I think, that we get this concept straight in our minds. Otherwise, we risk attributing moral force to the common good justifications only because we mistakenly assume that they are something that they are not.

Consider the locution itself: 'The Common Good.' Ambiguities surrounding its constitutive words make even an abstract characterization difficult. 'Common' refers to the *shared* aspect of the conception of the good in question. But in what sense is it shared? Pretty clearly, common good discourse cannot assume that the *conception* of the good is itself shared. It cannot assume, that is, that we all conceive of the good in the same way—as, say, lives committed to a particular religious doctrine (e.g., a life in Christ), to the value of autonomy (i.e., critical reflection and rational evaluation), or to utility maximization (where 'utility' is a stand-in for pleasure, preference satisfaction, or human flourishing). For, if this were the case, then arguments over the common good could not be conflicts over the *value* of a particular conception; rather, they could be reduced to disagreements about how it might be best achieved.

The assumption behind common good justifications must instead be that—despite what people happen to believe about the *value* of a particular conception—particular decisions, actions, or policies do in fact work for the good of the group, society, or world and, moreover, that this is sufficient for their justification. The important point, then, is that sharing a good or having a good in common need not imply that those with this commonality *recognize* what it is that they share. This means that there is no necessary connection between the meaning of 'common' in typical appeals to the common good and the meaning of 'common' associated with the notion of agreement. For, actual agreement on a given conception of the collective good means just that: the parties to the agreement accept this conception.

So, the claim that a particular course of action is in the common good does not automatically carry with it the implication that this conception of the good engages the reason of all parties involved, that all relevant players buy into the conception. Insofar as appeals to the common good slip back and forth between these two senses of 'common,' we are likely to attribute to these justifications greater moral force than they deserve. In other words, in those cases in which common good justifications are not sanctioned by broad agreement, it can turn out that such arguments are only superficially weighty. Herein lays the source of the moral risks associated with common good justifications. Detached from the notion of consent, they are liable to overlook ethical issues of leadership centering on the exercise of power and the use of coercion. If we take 'common' to mean merely that a particular conception of the good *applies* to all relevant parties, not that these parties *agree* on this conception, then we are left with a justification unconstrained by the moral safeguards that consent brings with it.

Epistemic Limits

Contention over the appropriate understanding of the common good is to be expected given the epistemic limits faced by both followers and leaders. These are the barriers to knowledge that we all confront by virtue of being human. Here, the argument starts from two assumptions about the epistemic limits of humans. First, we can be mistaken about matters of fact and about matters of morality. That is, we can be mistaken about the way the world works as well as about the way the world should be. For the purposes of this chapter, we might focus simply upon the ways in which followers and leaders can be mistaken both about the nature of their own interests and the interests of others. These sorts of mistakes come in both factual and moral varieties. We can be mistaken about what people really need as well as about the place of any particular need in the relative hierarchy of needs.

The second assumption about the epistemic limits of humans is that we can we can be mistaken even though we are doing the best that we can with the beliefs that we have. In other words, our mistakes cannot in every case be attributed to our own culpability with respect to the acquisition and maintenance of our beliefs. This second assumption, when applied to our beliefs about the nature of our own interests and the interests of others, implies that we can be *faultlessly* mistaken about the factual and moral status of our interests. These two assumptions, I think, have important implications for standard understandings of leadership and, ultimately, for our conception of good leadership.

In *Leadership*, Burns describes transactional leadership in the following way. "Such leadership occurs," he says, "when one person takes the initiative in making a contact with others for the purpose of an exchange of valued things. The exchange could be economic or political or psychological in nature: a swap of goods or of one good for money; a trading of votes between candidate and citizen or between legislators; hospitality to another person in exchange for willingness to listen to one's troubles" (Burns 1978:19). What is distinctive of any particular instance of transactional leadership, Burns thinks, is that "[the exchange] was not one that binds the leader and follower together in a mutual and continuing pursuit of a higher purpose" (Burns 1978:20) This characterization of transactional leadership marks a morally significant kind of transience. The *relationships* upon which such exchanges are based can be fleeting, thin, and superficial. It is in light of this feature that one might be tempted to say that transactional leadership fails to make a direct contribution to what is richest and most meaningful about human experience.

In addition to the transience of the relationships to which transactional leadership sometimes gives rise, it is characterized by a different—but perhaps related—kind of transience. This is the transience of the interests upon which such exchanges are based. Here, what is of moral significance is that transactional leadership understands our interests simply as given. In other words, this form of leadership respects our desires and preferences, no matter how fleeting, thin, or superficial particular *desires and preferences* might well be. In so doing, transactional leadership ignores the fact that we can be mistaken about what it is that we really need. A simple way to put this point is to say that our interests are not always tracked by our desires and preferences. But, if our interests are not always transparent to us, then we sometimes have reason to question the validity of the epistemic position from which we view our own interests.

This point comes out in standard criticisms of market exchanges. Critics of the market, following Karl Marx, charge that consumers are led to develop and, then, to satisfy desires and preferences that are alienated from their own true interests. It is possible that the market system is ultimately supported by factual mistakes about the connection between acquisitiveness and happiness. Of course, this need not lead us to reject capitalism. Market structures may well be justified because we hold the belief, as did John Stuart Mill, that individuals are generally in the best position to recognize their own good and that they generally have the greatest incentive to respect their own interests.

Although our (perhaps uninformed) desires and preferences guide markets, we often expect more than this from our leaders. That is, we expect—with good reason—that they do more in *particular* cases than simply respect what we say we want. In fact, we justifiably hold our leaders blameworthy when they pander to our baser motivations, e.g., when they appeal to our greed, our racism, or our cowardice. Good leadership thus implies a moral responsibility to look beyond the uninformed preferences and desires of followers.

This way of understanding the moral weaknesses of transactional leadership is consistent with what Burns's offers as a morally superior form of leadership. Transforming leadership occurs, Burns tells us, "when one or more persons *engage* in such a way that leaders and followers raise one another to higher levels of motivation and morality" (Burns 1978:20). This conception of leadership asks what people could be motivated by over and above their occurrent desires and preferences. As Burns puts it, "the transforming leader looks for potential motives in followers, seeks to satisfy higher needs, and engages the full person of the follower" (Burns 1978:4) Transforming leadership has as its "essence...the recognition of *real* need..." (Burns 1978:43, emphasis mine) and takes as its "fundamental act...to induce people to be aware or conscious of what they feel—to feel their *true* needs so strongly, to define their values so meaningfully, that they can be moved to purposeful action" (Burns 1978:44, emphasis mine).

This is what makes transforming leadership decidedly moral: "the ultimate test of moral leadership is its capacity to transcend the claims of the multiplicity of *everyday* wants and needs and expectations" (Burns 1978:46, emphasis mine).

Transforming leadership is certainly a moral improvement on transactional leadership. Transforming leadership acknowledges that followers can be mistaken in their occurrent desires and preferences, and, accordingly, it moves beyond the potentially suspect motivational states of followers. Unfortunately, the same epistemic worries that plague transactional leadership also come to bear on our understandings of transforming leadership. According to the first epistemic assumption above, humans can be mistaken about matters of fact and matters of morality. But, if this is true, then leaders (in addition to followers) can be mistaken about the factual as well as the moral status of our interests. Here, my point is importantly different from the claim that transforming leadership is potentially paternalistic. To criticize a decision, action, or policy on paternalistic grounds is to say that the decision, action, or policy is unjustified despite the fact that it actually serves the best interests of followers. My suggestion contrasts with the paternalistic critique in the following respect: I hold that we cannot assume that transforming leaders have a correct understanding of our interests. They can be mistaken, that is, about what it is that we really need.

Transforming Leadership and the Common Good

In leadership studies, no normative theory of leadership is more closely associated with appeals to the common good than is Burns's account of transforming leadership. As he puts it, "leadership is nothing if not linked to a *common purpose*" (Burns 1978:3). One way to understand Burns's view, then, is to say that transforming leadership works in service of a shared conception of the good. Of course, this conception is initially shared only in the sense that it applies to all relevant parties, not—that is—in the sense that all such players buy into it. Else, there would be little room for the transformational element of the account. If the conception already engages all relevant parties from the standpoint of their individual rationality, then what need would there be to raise them to "higher levels of motivation and morality?" This means, as Joanne Ciulla tells us, that transforming leaders do more than merely "water down their values and moral ideals by consensus" (Ciulla 1998:15). Rather, they understand that an ultimately compelling conception of collective good might well conflict with the current cognitive and volitional states of followers.

This feature of transforming leadership has led some critics to reject it on account of the moral perils to which it gives rise. The worry is that transforming leadership does not create sufficient moral space for the discontent of followers. Specifically, it does not take account of the fact that some followers will remain unmoved by a particular conception of the good because they fail to see its worth. Michael Keeley asks, for example, "If not all social participants have the same goals, if transformational leaders are not able to persuade everyone to voluntarily accept a common vision, what is the likely status of people who prefer their own goals and visions" (Keeley 1998:123)? Keeley concludes that "unless leaders are able to transform everyone and create absolute unanimity of interests (a very special case), transformational leadership produces simply a majority will that represents the interests of the strongest faction" (Keeley 1998:124).

On Keeley's critique, then, transforming leadership insufficiently accommodates potential disagreement among followers. As a consequence, when universal transformation proves unsuccessful, the loser is very likely to be the untransformed minority, not the conception of the good that it rejects. We can draw upon the rich resources of transforming leadership to develop a response to this sort of critique. Thomas Wren, for example, has suggested that transforming leadership ultimately takes as its focus "the supremacy of follower interests" (Wren 1998:163). Accordingly, "[i]f transformational leadership is to seek to attain a common interest among relevant stakeholders, the determination of what that good is must derive from the stakeholders themselves" (Wren 1998:164).

Now, I think that this general line of response is on the right track. Keeley's critique turns primarily upon the fact that common good justifications lend themselves to abuse and, consequently, make us vulnerable to evil purposes and simple negligence or, as he puts it, to "the misdeeds of scoundrels and the frailties of ordinary men and women" (Keeley 1998:118). Keeley's concerns, as it were, are ultimately about leaders whose *intentions* are appropriately characterized as culpable to some degree or other. Thus, a tight *motivational* connection between transforming leadership and the interests of followers would generate at least some theoretical protection against the moral weaknesses of leaders, especially those inclined to act in their own self-interest. However, this line of response does not explicitly attend to the fact that a leader with the *best of intentions* can transform followers in ways that do not respect their good. Even if we assume that transforming leaders are ultimately motivated by a concern for followers, transforming leaders can nevertheless be mistaken about follower interests and, so too, about the common good (Price 2006).

Perhaps leaders with mistaken understandings of our needs aren't transforming after all. Bernard Bass distinguishes between *transformational* and *pseudotransformational* leadership. He tells us that

> Leaders are truly transformational when they increase awareness of what is right, good, important, beautiful; when they help to elevate followers' needs for achievement and self-actualization; when they foster in followers higher moral maturity; and when they move followers to go beyond their self-interest for the good of their group, organization, or society. Pseudotransformational leaders may also motivate and transform their followers, but in doing so they arouse support for special interests at the expense of others rather than what's good for the collectivity (Bass 1998:171).

Bass's distinction assumes, of course, that we *know* (or *can* know) which leaders should be characterized as transformational and which should be characterized as pseudotransformational. The problem, however, is that we are often unable reliably to tell the two apart.

Admittedly, an appeal to formal features of a leader's agenda, e.g., to the exclusivity of her concerns, might well lead us to identify her as pseudotransformational. But such formal criteria will ultimately leave us with too many potentially transformational leaders. After all, Jim Jones's Peoples Temple was committed to an inclusive vision of society. The apparent nobility of one's inclusive and other-regarding aims does not make one immune to factual and moral mistakes. One can be mistaken, for example, about how to achieve what is in fact worth achieving as well as about the actual worth of what it is that one hopes to achieve. This is true regardless of whether (and sometimes *because*) leaders have as their aims "*end* values such as order (or security), liberty, equality, justice, and community..." (Burns 1998:x).

My argument here follows directly from the second epistemic point above, viz., that we can be factually and morally mistaken even though *we are doing the best that we can with the beliefs that we have*. Leaders can be *faultlessly* mistaken, that is, about the factual as well as the moral status of our needs. This implies that apparently transforming leaders with the *best of intentions* can transform followers in ways that do not reflect their true needs. So, not only will we often be unable to distinguish the transformational leaders from the pseudotransformational leaders; it also true the leaders themselves will often be unable to tell whether they are transformational or pseudotransformational! Given that our needs can be opaque to leaders in just this fashion, we have reason to question the validity of the *epistemic* position from which leaders view our needs. The upshot of all of this, then, is that we—as followers—must be wary of the extent to which we give ourselves over fully to others. An equally important conclusion, though, is that we—as leaders—must be wary of the extent to which we allow others to give themselves over fully to us.

Transpositional Leadership and Epistemological Restraint

The epistemic limits that humans face come to bear on our understanding of good leadership. Leadership can go wrong because it runs up against severe epistemic limits, and these limits are distinguishable from the standard moral failings associated with leadership. But, if we can question the epistemic positions from which both followers and leaders view our interests, then we have reason—in some cases at least—to question the moral authority of the *aims* of both followers and leaders. This point is particularly relevant to the study of leadership because leaders, we might say, often work at the "epistemic margins" of society. They frequently work for change and, so, must rely upon knowledge bases that are even more fragmented than are the knowledge bases upon which we rely in our everyday dealings with the world.

What we need, then, is a normative conception of leadership that takes the epistemic limits of humans seriously. Put another way, our conception good leadership must respond to the fact that both followers and leaders can be mistaken about the factual as well as the moral status of our needs. In this section, I offer the beginnings of just such a conception. If I am right, good leadership must be *transpositional* (Sen 1993; Werhane 1999; Hicks and Price 1999; Price 2003). It must move beyond the uni-positional interpretations of our needs that plague our characterizations of transactional and transforming leadership. Nevertheless, rather than displacing what have come to be standard understandings of leadership, transpositional leadership builds upon these conceptions. As we shall see, transpositional leadership may well get at some of the more important aspects of what Burns seems to have in mind for transforming leadership.

Transpositional leadership makes *moral discourse* an integral part of the very practice of good leadership. If particular individuals—whether followers or leaders—can be mistaken about the factual and moral status of our needs, then an adequate understanding of what people really need is contingent upon serious dialogue with those from different and, especially, contrary epistemic positions. Moral discourse about what people really need aims to specify and articulate our genuine interests and of the appropriate means of respecting them.

Of course, moral discourse will not always guarantee progress toward these ends; sometimes it will lead to more confusion. However, transpositional leadership offers an improvement on uni-positional understandings of leadership but not as a failsafe solution to the problem of discerning what people really need. More importantly, perhaps, it less than clear what other options there are to which we might appeal in response to the epistemic limits of leadership. Once we recognize that our own epistemic positions might well be flawed, we—as followers and leaders—can only look to others for help. This means that good leadership requires real *engagement* between leaders and followers. In this sense transpositional leadership has the potential to be truly transforming.

By making *moral discourse* an integral part of the very practice of good leadership, I think the notion of transpositional is roughly consistent with appeals to Ronald Heifetz's notion of *adaptive work* (Heifetz 1994; Couto 2001; Wren 1998:164). According to Heifetz,

> Adaptive work consists of the learning required to address conflicts in the values people hold, or to diminish the gap between the values people stand for and the reality they face. Adaptive work requires a change in values, beliefs, or behavior. The exposure and orchestration of conflict—internal contradictions—within individuals and constituencies provide the leverage for mobilizing people to learn new ways (Heifetz 1994:22).

Where adaptive work differs from transpositional leadership, however, is in the fact that the latter aims to engage leaders and followers not only *within* discrete, identifiable groups, but also *between* groups. For, if our understanding of leadership is to respond to our epistemic limits, then it cannot rely simply upon the epistemic positions of group members. We cannot assume, that is, that the entire group is not entirely mistaken in its understandings of its members' needs. Thus, it seems that transpositional leaders must do more than "exploit conflict and tension within persons' value structures" (Burns 1978:42). For, there are several ways in which inconsistent value sets might be made *consistent* but far fewer ways in which they might be made *correct*.

Transpositional leadership is thus *externalist* in its understanding of our needs. It calls for conversations across sectors. If both followers and leaders can be faultlessly mistaken, then there may well be cases in which both are mistaken about what it is that we really need. My suspicion, however, is that the success of this strategy will greatly depend upon leadership context and, in particular, on the extent to which the parameters of moral discourse are tailored to fit particular contexts. Moral discourse will sometimes run out, that is, unless the dialogue is appropriately constrained. One way to put this point is to say that some contexts will require "epistemological restraint" on the part of the parties to the discussion: they cannot bring all of their beliefs to bear on the subject of disagreement (Nagel 1987).

This is especially true in domains characterized by high degrees of moral, philosophical, and religious diversity. In leadership situations of this sort, it may well be impossible to get "agreement on fundamentals" (Wren 1998:164). where a central component of the fundamentals is a characterization of the conception of the good that justifies decisions, actions, or policies. As a consequence, common good justifications will prove out of place in certain leadership contexts. Follower diversity will bring with it a plethora of full-blown conceptions of the good, many of which will compete radically with one another. In such cases, the challenge will not be to move individuals to higher levels of motivation and morality but to exercise leadership in spite of the fact that followers believe that they are at these higher levels already.

It might be thought that common good justifications are most at home in political contexts. I want to close, however, with the suggestion that this is one context in which they are particularly out of place. Simply stated, the argument is the following. First, given the epistemic limits that humans face, citizens can reasonably disagree about the nature of the good. Answers to the most fundamental questions regarding our good are not transparent to us, which explains the high degree of reasonable disagreement that characterizes modern, democratic political life. John Rawls develops the doctrine of *political liberalism* in response to just this kind of disagreement, which he refers to as "the fact of reasonable pluralism" (Rawls 1993:36).

Second, political legitimacy in the liberal state requires that we "not impose arrangements, institutions, or requirements on other people on grounds that they could reasonably reject" (Nagel 1987:221). In other words, state coercion cannot be justified in terms that citizens could reasonably reject. From these two premises, it follows that citizens should not appeal to common good justifications in political contexts. Since no conception of the good is common enough among citizens *in the right way*, common good justifications in politics violate the liberal principle of political legitimacy. The problem, then, is that no conception of the good can be the subject of the kind of broad agreement that would be necessary to justify coercion grounded upon such a conception.

Admittedly, this argument is at risk of making skeptics out of all of us. If citizens must be committed to a kind of epistemological restraint at the level of political justification, then one might wonder how they can forego such a commitment at other levels and, especially, at the level of individual rationality. Brian Barry, for example, doubts that "certainty from the inside about some view can coherently be combined with the line that it is reasonable for others to reject that same view" (Barry 1995:179). Ultimately, however, I do not think that the argument for epistemological restraint need be interpreted as a skeptical one (Price 2000). Even if we concede that others might reasonably reject the conception of the good to which we are committed, we can explain their rejection in a non-skeptical way.

The explanation appeals to the fact that citizens bring diverse sets of *background beliefs* to bear on evidence in support of their personal commitments to various conceptions of the good. In most cases, their background beliefs will hardly lend themselves to complete specification, let alone to successful transference to non-believers. But, if we can explain reasonable disagreement among citizens by appeal to these difficulties of transference, then the argument for epistemological restraint assumes neither that any particular conception of the collective good might be incorrect nor, more strongly, that there is no common good. In other words, the argument does not ask us to skeptics about the common good. Rather, it asks that we attend to the barriers to transference faced by citizens and, accordingly, constrain our dialogue in political contexts. One casualty of the requisite constraints will be appeals to the common good.

References

Bass, B. 1998. "The Ethics of Transformational Leadership." In *Ethics: The Heart of Leadership* (Ed.), Joanne Ciulla, pp. 169-92. Westport, Conn.: Praeger,

Barry, B. 1995. *Justice as Impartiality*. New York, N.Y.: Oxford University Press.

Burns, J. M. 1978. *Leadership*. New York, N.Y.: Harper & Row.

-----. 1998. "Forward." In *Ethics: The Heart of Leadership* (Ed.), Joanne Ciulla pp. ix-xii. Westport, Conn.: Praeger.

Ciulla, Joanne (Ed.). 1998. *Ethics: The Heart of Leadership*. Westport, Conn.: Praeger

Couto, R. A. 2001. "To Give Their Gifts: The Innovative, Transforming Leadership of Adaptive Work." In *Contemporary Issues in Leadership* 5th ed., (Eds.) William E. Rosenbach and Robert L. Taylor, pp. 43-64. Boulder, Colo.: Westview Press.

Heifetz, R. A. 1994. *Leadership without Easy Answers*. Cambridge, Mass.: Belknap Press.

Hicks, D. and T.L. Price. 1999. "What do People Really Need? An Ethical Challenge for Leaders and Scholars." *Selected Proceedings of the International Leadership Association Annual Meeting 1999* (Atlanta), pp. 43-52.

Keeley, M. 1998. "The Trouble with Transformational Leadership: Toward a Federalist Ethic for Organizations." In *Ethics: The Heart of* Leadership (Ed.), Joanne Ciulla., pp. 111-44. Westport, Conn.: Praeger.

Nagel, T. 1987. "Moral and Political Legitimacy." *Philosophy and Public Affairs* 16, 215-240.

Price, T. 2000. "Epistemological Restraint—Revisited." *Journal of Political Philosophy* 8, 401-407.

-----. 2003. "The Ethics of Authentic Transformational Leadership," *Leadership Quarterly* 14: 67-81.

-----. 2006. *Understanding Ethical Failures in Leadership*. New York: Cambridge University Press.

Rawls, J. 1993. *Political Liberalism*. New York, N.Y.: Columbia University Press.

Sen, A. 1993. "Positional Objectivity." *Philosophy and Public Affairs* 22, 119-130.

Werhane, P. 1999. *Moral Imagination and Management Decision Making*. New York, N.Y.: Oxford University Press.

Wren, J. T. 1998. "James Madison and the Ethics of Transformational Leadership." In *Ethics: The Heart of Leadership,* (Ed.), Joanne Ciulla,. pp. 145-68. Westport, Conn.: Praeger.

CHAPTER 8
LEADERSHIP AND THE *VOX POPULI*
J. Thomas Wren

James MacGregor Burns's *Leadership* is one of those marvelous books with the power to comfort and afflict simultaneously. It has had precisely that impact upon me as I have labored in the vineyards of the study of leadership: comforting me with its substance, analytical power, and moral compass; afflicting me with the central leadership issues it poses so well, yet leaves others tantalizingly unresolved. Much of my research in the field of leadership seeks to pursue the implications of these core issues: the role of values in leadership; the elusive concept and function of the common good; and, perhaps most important, how leadership can be conceived and implemented in a regime of popular sovereignty in such a manner that it responds to popular needs while avoiding popular passion. As I acknowledge my connections to Burns's work and make clear my departures from it, I trust I will also show new possibilities for future research, yielding an enhanced understanding of the place and role of leadership in our political life and of the place of historical studies in understanding leadership.

My first brush with Burns's book was also my first encounter with leadership as a distinct field of study. In the spring of 1992, I had accepted an offer to help initiate the Jepson School of Leadership Studies, the first of its kind. While the possibilities inherent in such a venture were the obvious attraction to taking the position, as a historian deeply rooted in the liberal arts and humanistic traditions, I had substantial reservations about the field I was about to enter. Would the scholarship in this new field prove substantive? What about my concern over the moral and ethical implications of leadership? Fortunately, my new dean suggested that the first book I should consult as I entered the field was *Leadership*.

The Value of History in Leadership Studies

As I began teaching leadership studies, the substance of the *Leadership* text quickly allayed my concerns about shallow or superficial treatments, and the centrality of morality in Burns's depiction of leadership reassured me that its study need not be a managerial wasteland. I also found areas for affliction within the pages of *Leadership*. Burns's statement that "the key to understanding leadership lies in recent findings and concepts in psychology" (Burns 1978:49) troubled me. Perhaps not so much because I disputed the truth of the comment, but because it then began to dawn upon me the magnitude of the task I had set before myself in attempting to understand leadership. Much more troubling was his use of "psychobiography." To be fair, Burns acknowledged the weaknesses in an approach where there is such a "paucity of data" and in which "such portraits. . .tend to be speculative and generalized" (Burns 1978:51). Nevertheless, he relied rather heavily upon such studies for many of the early points he made in the book. As a more traditional historian, I was uneasy with any conclusions based upon psychobiography.

His sophisticated and substantive design integrated the discipline of history into his analysis of leadership, however, and quickly assured me about his use of it. He proposed to "place. . .concepts of political leadership centrally into a theory of historical causation" (Burns 1978:4). Going even further, Burns articulated his "hope to build the foundations of a more general theory of the role of leadership in the processes of historical causation" (Burns 1978:59). This focus upon "historical causation" strikes to the heart of what the discipline of history can bring to the study of leadership. While the insights of psychology and many other disciplines are no doubt central to our understanding of the behavioral elements of the leadership process, the historical perspective offers unique insights into the context and continuities or variations of leadership. Because the process of leadership by necessity is deeply enmeshed in broader currents of intellectual, economic, social, and political change, any attempt to devise a universal theory of the process must incorporate such factors.

The book accomplished, with unprecedented flair and substance, the identification of the essential components of such a theory: power, conflict, values, psychological processes, social interactions, collective purpose, and many others. What is more, Burns does this by drawing deeply from the well of history. He taps the lives of such great men as Wilson, Gandhi, Lenin, Hitler, and Mao in somewhat suspect psychobiographies. However, he also traces brilliantly four centuries of Western history, grappling with the issues of liberty and power, and draws upon a series of historical scenarios to illustrate his typology of leadership.

Leadership, then, does an admirable job in integrating historical narrative into the key conceptual components of the process. It is less successful in explicitly formulating propositions of historical causation, although this may be because Burns never turns his hand to actual theory building in this text. Nonetheless, *Leadership* stands as a monument to others, including myself, who follow the path Burns blazed in uniting historical analysis and the study of leadership.

The History of Values in *Leadership*

It remains to consider how well Burns realized his ambitious use of historical perspective. Attention to a key era in American history—the period of the founding of the American Republic—teases out both the substance and the subtleties of the role of values in leadership. Burns identifies key political end-values as liberty and equality (Burns 1978:43, 46, 429-30). He takes care to delineate between conceptions of "negative" liberty, which "defend[s]. . .private liberty against [governmental power]," and "positive" liberty, which involves "the capacity of the people collectively to expand their liberties through the use of governmental power" (Burns 1978:157). In Burns's historical analysis, the Founding Fathers concerned themselves chiefly with the concerns of negative liberty. It was not until the twentieth century that Americans confronted the ultimate leadership challenge of positive liberty: how to tap "the potential resources of the state in education, housing, health, and employment for developing and maximizing real opportunity for the common man." This, in turn, would lead to a difficult grappling with various formulations of the other key end-value, equality (Burns 1978:142, 163).

Popular sovereignty, the actual implementation of rule by the people, has interested me, and its historical implications for leadership initially drew me to the field of leadership studies. I sought to identify the values that generated the leadership challenges of the early Republic; analyze their origins in the social, political, economic, and intellectual context of the time; and explore the dynamics of the conflicts among these values.

I found two sets of conflicting values that constantly played off each other in often complex ways. The first set was equality and order. Emerging claims to equality posed a distinct threat to the deference that had been the glue holding the traditional authority system together. As a result, significant leadership issues emerged, as traditional elites struggled to maintain influence while "new men" sought entry into the system of influence. Likewise, a second set of conflicting values shaped possible solutions to this leadership challenge. These involved the desired nature of shared interrelationships, i.e., individual or communal. Specifically, implied individualism in Jefferson's rhetoric was at odds with a long and deep tradition of communalism and civic duty drawn from the Republic's founders' classical heritage. Many of the leadership challenges of at least the first fifty years of the Republic derive from such tensions between core values (Wren 1998).

These key values—equality, order, individual gain, and common goal—differ from those posited by Burns. He made simple dichotomous distinctions between equality and "negative" and "positive" liberties to achieve it. These differences stem from the differing focuses of our analyses. My interest has consistently been in the implementation of a regime of popular sovereignty after the Revolution and not the negative liberty that so well describes the Revolutionary era.

Leadership and Popular Sovereignty

While Burns believes, for the most part, that American political values have evolved out of pragmatic experience rather than conscious reflection, he perceives a key role for intellectuals in this process. For Burns, "intellectual leadership" articulates the "conscious purpose drawn from values." Indeed, Burns continues, "The ultimate test of political leadership by intellectuals is the capacity to conceive values or purpose in such a way that ends and means are linked analytically and creatively and that the implications of certain values for political action and government organization are clarified. The test is one of transforming power" (Burns 1978:142, 163).

The new Republic's popular sovereignty offered a test for the transforming power of intellectual leadership. Edmund S. Morgan closes his classic book on early popular sovereignty with that challenge—the shift from leader to leadership and the consequent implications for the changing qualifications of both. The word *leader* is old, but *leadership* was a term that no one seems to have felt a need for as long as the qualities it designates remained an adjunct of social superiority. The decline of deference and the emergence of leadership signaled the beginnings of not only a new rhetoric but also a new mode of social relations and a new way of determining who should stand among the few to govern the many (Morgan 1988:306).

The pragmatic and intellectual challenges of the new democratic order also raised questions about how the process of leadership should operate in a democratic regime. How does the process of leadership make this conflict among values a creative one? How does a polity embrace multiple, conflicting values? And, what are the implications for the process of leadership?

The challenge of rule by the people in the early Republic came from a complex and powerful constellation of economic, social, political, and intellectual developments that coalesced after 1800 and gathered momentum. Because of these developments, the leadership challenges that attend the emergence of democracy came to the fore. Burns recognizes these issues. "Authority did not crumble under the impact of these forces," he said, "but it could not be reestablished on the old foundations, for now it was supposed to be derived from the people and hence ultimately lie in their hands." The initial challenge was that "a new secular basis of authority was needed," because "the citizenry now embodied authority." Equally important, "The people had to be protected against themselves"; that is, the new polity grounded in rule by the people "had to be protected against shifting majorities and volatile popular movements" (Burns 1978:24-5).

Implied in this language was the potential problem of the tyranny of the majority, or, phrased in another form, the need to protect minority rights and liberties in democracy. Burns also identified a less obvious problem. "One of the most troublesome questions for democratic politics is how to provide for or compensate for the unheard voices of the unorganized, inarticulate groups. . .the 'powerless'" (Burns 1978:305).

Unfortunately for the American experience, the transforming leadership Burns thought essential was not forthcoming. As a result, no one has yet articulated "a doctrine suitable for the new age. No new, democratized. . .doctrine arose to salvage the authentic and relevant in [the concept of] authority and link these strengths to a doctrine of leadership that recognized the vital need for qualities of integrity, authenticity, initiative, and moral resolve" (Burns 1978:25). In sum, "The United States simply did not possess a body of social and political thought that could lend adequate direction, substance, and legitimacy to [the problems of democracy].... Few thinkers of that day—and this—seemed motivated or able to develop a comprehensive theory that could supply the intellectual foundations for a theory that would unite purpose, politics, and government" (Burns 1978:165). Burns does acknowledge some more recent efforts in this vein and masterfully details some of the pragmatic historical developments, such as the role of liberalism and the rise of the political parties that have served to ameliorate some of the potential evils of democracy (Burns 1978:164, 167, 311).

James Madison and Leadership Of, By, and For the People

It is not that great minds did not apply themselves to the paradox and dilemmas of popular sovereignty. James Madison represents, in almost ideal form, the transforming "intellectual leader" for whom Burns called in *Leadership*. Recall that in his text, Burns had championed a leadership that "conceive[s] values. . .in such a way that ends and means are linked. . .creatively and...the implications of certain values for political action and government organization are clarified" (Burns 1978:163). Madison fulfilled this role well. He continuously responded to challenges to his core values and maintained a steady stream of correspondence and other writings that articulated the nexus between thought and action. He thus serves as a prototype of the sort of leader Burns seems to call for in the continuing search for leadership that hews to the core values of the polity (Wren 1998). Madison's reflections bring us to the democratic challenge that remains for us to resolve: how do we relate equality, order, individual gain, and the common good in means and ends, similarities and interactive relationships?

Madison had a brace of core values that drove his thought and activity during his lifelong efforts to ensure the proper workings of government by the people. The first of these was his unquenchable faith in popular sovereignty itself. "The ultimate authority," he argued, "wherever the derivative may be found, resides in the people alone." All governments are "but agents and trustees of the people," must be "dependent on the great body of citizens," and "derive all. . .powers directly or indirectly from the great body of the people" (Wren 1997). In addition to popular sovereignty, however, Madison had a parallel commitment—to the preservation of the common good. He held to a conception of the common good characterized by a priority of the general interest over local or individual interests, and a polity devoted to liberty and justice in the form of the protection of individual liberty and rights of property. This, in turn, would lead to an orderly and stable regime. The difficulty was that these core values proved to be often in conflict and were perhaps inherently so. As circumstances were to create challenges to one or the other of Madison's core values, he concocted a series of brilliant adaptations as he labored to devise solutions that addressed the perceived threat. In the process, he plumbed the possibilities inherent in his perception of the appropriate role of the people and their political leaders in a regime of popular sovereignty.

As the experiment of government by the people conjured up challenge after challenge to Madison's conception of the common good, he turned to a sophisticated and ever-changing view of the proper role of leaders and their relationship with the people. In the 1780s, when the excesses of state democracies threatened the common good, Madison limited their role. Their place in the leadership process was to choose virtuous leaders to guide them. He then designed a new polity, the federal government, to ensure that result. In the 1790s, when the danger to the common good came from federal leaders such as Hamilton and his followers, Madison expanded his conception of the role of followers in a popular regime. Now he counted upon properly guided followers to challenge the wrongheaded leaders in power. These tactics led to the development of the first party system and ultimately triumph at the polls for a party opposed to those in power. The ultimate challenge to Madison's perception of the common good proved to be insoluble. The rise of individualistic democracy after 1815 led to the sway of unchecked passions of both leaders and followers. Although Madison remained resolutely creative in the face of this final challenge, his solutions proved unacceptable, and he eventually accepted the broad sweeping democracy of the Jacksonian era as the lesser of evils (Wren 1997).

Throughout his career, Madison struggled with the tension that often existed between his two priorities of the common good and popular sovereignty. He consistently looked to an elite of appropriate leaders to pursue what he defined as the common good. These leaders could be called transforming leaders—men, in this case, who perceived the true interest of followers and lifted them above their more mundane and transitory self-interest.

That had been at the heart of his elitist solution to the problem of majority tyranny in the 1780s, the Constitution. His answer in the 1790s had been to create a more popular polity, to hold elite leaders accountable to the common good. Regrettably, at the end of his career, after 1820, with the overwhelming tide of majoritarian democracy sweeping all before it, Madison despaired of ever finding a lasting solution (Wren 1997; McCoy 1989). It certainly poses the most difficult of the leadership issues implied in a regime of popular sovereignty: to pursue the common good of a polity characterized by diverse and often antithetical interests. What happens when individuals are no longer content to rely upon leaders who "know better" what is in their interests? This, in a sense, was Madison's predicament in the latter stages of his career, and he despaired of an answer.

Leadership and the Role of Leaders in a Democratic Regime

James Madison might have been comforted had his wide circle of correspondents included James MacGregor Burns—the historian Burns, rather than the psychologist one. Burns is anything but reticent about the role individual leaders must play in his desired leadership process. With his transforming leadership, Burns sought to identify a process to achieve the common good, even in a democracy, by raising the followers themselves to new levels of insight and commitment in pursuit of shared interests. In this sense, then, transforming leadership represents an advanced stage of Madisonian leadership, dedicated to the same end—achieving the common good. Even Burns, however, acknowledges the remaining "deep ambiguity and confusion over the place of leadership in political life—at least in democracies where leaders are expected to lead the people while the people are supposed to lead the leaders" (Burns 1978:452-55).

Nevertheless, if true "transforming" leadership occurs, leaders will play a central role. Burns asserts that conflict is at the heart of democratic leadership. If the goal of the process itself is the "expressing, shaping, and curbing of [conflict]," then "leaders, whatever their professions of harmony, do not shun conflict, they confront it and ultimately embody it." Moreover, particularly if the followers are heterogeneous in their makeup, it will be incumbent upon the leader to "embrace competing interests and goals within their constituency" (Burns 1978:37-39). Leaders, therefore, play a key, catalytic role in crafting substantive results from the leadership process.

Burns conceived of the role a leader plays as helping the group or society to achieve what might be deemed the common good. "The essence of leadership in any polity," he argues, "is the recognition of real need, the uncovering and exploiting of contradictions among values and between values and practice, the realizing of values, the reorganization of interests where necessary, and the governance of change." In all of these obligations, the role of the leader is "immense" (Burns 1978:420). This leads Burns to his conception of the "transforming" leader. Such leaders, "more than other leaders, must respond not simply to popular attitudes and beliefs, but to the fundamental wants and needs, aspirations and expectations, values and goals of their existing and potential followers" (Burns 1978:420). Indeed, it is often the duty of the leader to perceive and act upon these fundamental needs of followers. "Leaders can. . .shape and elevate the motives and values and goals of followers through the vital teaching role of leadership." Burns concludes, "This is transforming leadership" (Burns 1978:415).

This rather lengthy summary of the argument Burns articulates in *Leadership* brings us a model for proper leadership in a society based upon rule by the people. It stresses the conflict between and among values. Likewise, Burns appears to retain his commitment to a notion of some form of common good. His conception of the potential role of the leader in a regime of popular sovereignty recalls some of James Madison's work. Yet, problems remain with Burns's work.

Despite two centuries of intellectual leadership, the central questions of popular sovereignty—and their implications for leadership in such a regime—have yet to be adequately articulated and explored. Or perhaps the conflict values of democracy have to be adapted to changed environments, as Madison exemplified. Morgan's masterful study of the concept of popular sovereignty needs to be extended, enlarged, and brought forward through the American experience to the present day precisely because the rule by the people calls for leadership more than leaders.

Back to the Future

The collective wisdom of over two centuries of grappling with issues of popular government provides new possibilities for the future. Future reflection on the leadership implications of rule by the people will benefit from keeping the following enduring questions in mind.

Who are "the people"? This question is much more complex than it might at first appear. Throughout the American experience, the definition of who constitutes "the people" has constantly evolved. It is my contention that there has been what I call a "flywheel of democracy" that has included more of the populace in the definition of the people at every turn. There are no longer three-fifths persons or gender distinctions in voting. At the same time, each new revolution of the wheel has posed its own unique aspects; it is important to analyze each for the lessons it contains for future turns of the wheel.

What is the proper relationship of the people to their leaders? This is another enormously complex issue that can benefit from the insights of historical analysis. We have seen that Burns recognized the "deep ambiguity and confusion over the place of leadership in political life" when "leaders are expected to lead the people while the people are supposed to lead the leaders." (Burns 1978:452-55). Madison conducted the prototype for this inquiry with sophisticated nuances of evolving concepts and their applications (Wren 1997). Carefully tracing such matters through the remainder of the American experience can yield important insights that might prove useful in our continuing efforts to resolve an issue fundamental to democratic practice.

What is the role of the "common good" in rule by the people? The notion of the common good is a problematic issue. Some may question whether such a conception is even relevant in a society as diverse and disparate as ours. To the extent that any common direction is found, such critics argue, it is a function of the pragmatic balancing of conflicting interests (Keeley 1996). James Madison and James MacGregor Burns seem to argue the contrary: that there is such a thing as the common good and that it needs to be the end-value of leadership. The question is of more than academic interest, particularly as it relates to conceptions of leadership. A conception of the process as merely a clearinghouse for conflicting interests yields different prescriptions than if it is viewed as an effort to move the polity toward some envisioned end state. Likewise, the role of the leader takes on significantly different attributes. Again, a careful historical analysis of the American experience in this regard is likely to prove insightful. Again, Madison provides a starting point. What happened to his admittedly elitist conceptions of order and the common good under the deluge of democracy? How have Americans sought to identify and pursue the common good in subsequent years? This, in turn, is likely to call forth a continuing exploration of the role of values in the polity.

How can minority interests be protected in a popular regime? This question emerges immediately from any discussion of the potentially dangerous notion of the common good. The analysis of this issue in the American experience must go beyond the mere tracing of the evolution of constitutional rights and practices. While minority "rights" are increasingly acknowledged in a legalistic sense, it is quite a different story with respect to minority "interests" conceived more broadly. The flywheel of democracy metaphor again becomes relevant here. If the functioning of the American polity is conceived of in terms of an engine of popular rule, that engine has impediments of friction and inefficiency, the same as any other. These, in their various manifestations, need to be explored and, together with the solutions, brought to bear.

How should policy be made in a regime of popular sovereignty? This question, intimately related to those that have gone before, looks to the practical implementation of popular sovereignty. Assuming, for each time period studied, reasonably complete answers can be discerned with respect to the foregoing questions. How did each iteration of rule by the people pragmatically achieve implementation? Again, the answers should provide a rich library of possibilities for our modern leadership challenges.

Conclusion

I began this essay by commenting that James MacGregor Burns's classic book, *Leadership,* had both comforted and afflicted me. In its comforting role, it has provided me with the faith that leadership can indeed be a noble, useful, and practical endeavor. When it has afflicted me, it has done so in the best sense of the term. It has challenged and guided me to puzzle out difficult issues related to leadership. Drawing upon the insights of historical analysis embellishes the best current interdisciplinary scholarship in the field, which includes, of course, the historical accounts of leaders who deal with enduring human dilemmas.

References

Burns, J. M. 1978. *Leadership.* New York, N.Y.: Harper & Row.

Keeley, M. "The Trouble with Transformational Leadership: Toward a Federalist Ethic for Organizations." In J. B. Ciulla (Ed.), *Ethics: The Heart of Leadership,* pp. 131-44. Westport, Conn.: Greenwood Press

McCoy, D. 1989. *The Last of the Fathers: James Madison and the Republican Legacy.* Cambridge, Mass.: Cambridge University Press.

Morgan, E. S. 1988. *Inventing the People: The Rise of Popular Sovereignty in England and America.* New York, N.Y.: W. W. Norton & Company.

Wren, J. T. 1996. "The Historical Background of Values in Leadership." In J. B. Ciulla (Ed.), *Ethics and Leadership.* College Park, Md.: University of Maryland Burns Academy of Leadership. Available at http://www.academy.umd.edu/Publications/klspdocs/jwren_p1.htm

----. 1997. "James Madison and the Adaptive Challenges of Popular Sovereignty: Leaders, the People, and the Common Good." Paper presented before the Annual Meeting of the Social Science History Association (October 17).

----. 1998. "James Madison and the Ethics of Transformational Leadership." In J. B. Ciulla (Ed.), *Ethics: The Heart of Leadership*, pp. 145-68. Westport, Conn.: Greenwood Press.

CHAPTER 9
LEADERSHIP: GENDER EXCLUDED YET EMBRACED
Laurien Alexandre

I came to *Leadership* late in life, as many women do. My first reading of this seminal text took place just as the world crossed into the new millennium. Newly responsible for leading a team of scholar-practitioners in the development of a new doctoral program in leadership and change, I was avidly reading anything I could find in search of interdisciplinary substance and serious critique over organizational form and management technique.

As I became acquainted with leadership studies, *Leadership* appeared like an old friend among strangers. With my New (now old) Left eyes, there was something very comforting about a text that strived for grand theory, moral commitment, and yes, even offered some kind words about the Chinese Cultural Revolution. This was epic and historical, and it cared deeply about social injustice. It spoke from a time before the fragmentation of deconstructionism and before chaos became a theoretical paradigm for just about everything. This was home.

However, there was something else all too familiar about this place called home. Women were missing—our presence not even window-dressing, our numbers too small to reach a proverbial glass ceiling. Whether leadership as reform or revolutionary; transactional or transformational; occurring in groups, parties, or executive suites—with whom does *Leadership* fill its pages? Nikolai Lenin, Mahatma Gandhi, Woodrow Wilson, Mao Tse-tung, Roosevelt—that's Franklin D. and Theodore, not Eleanor. Not one of Burns's case studies or lengthy expositions was about a woman leader, in any country or field of endeavor, at any time.

We had, once again, disappeared. I found this omission to be more than a little curious, given Burns's obvious sympathies with democratic impulses, his inclusive and interdisciplinary approach to leadership, and the decade in which the book was first published.

It was this curious invisibility that sparked my reflections on *Leadership* for what it says, and does not say, about women and gender. The chapter's first section briefly explores the invisibility of women leaders in *Leadership* and the second part explores aspects of *Leadership* that seem highly compatible, albeit unrealized, with gendered theories of leadership. I hope that my approach of constructive critique suggests the value of *Leadership* to scholars and practitioners interested in gender, and, at the same time, raises some concerns about the nature of the invisibility of women and of issues of gender.

Coming of Age with Leadership Challenges

First, however, I need to state my own point of departure, as this affects how I think about *Leadership*. I came of age during the anti-war, anti-imperialist movement of the 1960s and 1970s. The decades' "second-wave feminism" enveloped my undergraduate education and the Frankfurt School framed my graduate studies. My current reflections, grounded in this socio-cultural history, come from a strongly held belief that gender is an essential category of analysis and my experience that women and men should share equally in leading the world to a better place.

I find essentialist assertions that women, by nature, are more compassionate in their leadership styles to be fundamentally suspect and simplistic. I doubt the existence of "female advantage" because of some innate, biological predisposition that makes us more able to lead teams or say "thank you" to fellow workers. I think that women's ways of knowing and being have to do with the societal constructions of gender that define or defy roles, opportunities, identities, and perceptions. If women's leadership styles tend to differ from that of men, which current research does not substantiate, I believe it has more to do with the ways women have had to exercise leadership outside the halls of patriarchal power. Women's ways of leading have much to do with the organizations in which they lead, the societies in which they are raised, and the families to which they are born.

All this is to say that I cringe at much of the pop literature about women and leadership that focuses on women's traits and skills building and that favors individual change rather than a structural one. I much prefer to have the substance of grand theory to challenge than the stereotypes of romanticized essentialism to battle. That said, I am also duly wary of "grand universalized theory," which seems blind to gender or race. This is why I embrace *Leadership*, yet feel somewhat distanced from it. I think many feminists would react similarly.

Coming to Terms with Gender in *Leadership*

With my biases now exposed, let us look at those of *Leadership*. Why the virtual invisibility of women in *Leadership*? Were there no women who had inspired social movements for society's betterment somewhere along the trajectory of humankind? One way to answer the question is simply to accept that women were pretty much absent from the type of leadership positions that Burns considers—elite, positional leaders in the political arena—and, therefore, Burns was merely representing reality rather than constructing a partial "malestream" narrative that made women invisible.

However, that is too easy on two scores: first, the selection's arbitrariness contains contradictions because Burns articulates a place for leadership outside the elite power-holders, and second, the deeply gendered conceptualization of leadership itself. These are not unrelated.

As to the first point, if Burns only looked at presidents and prime ministers, there would be few women to include. In fact, more than half of the women who have ever served as a nation's president or prime minister have done so since 1990 (Adler 1999: 247), two decades after the book's publication. We would be remiss not to note that political leadership continues to elude women domestically and internationally. However, Burns does take readers into the lives and stories of those outside positional state leadership. His massive historical sweep includes scientists, philosophers, and intellectual leaders. The chapter "Intellectual Leadership: Ideas as Moral Power," for example, offers a rich discussion of the philosophers and activists who changed our understanding of human rights and liberty in France, England, and the United States over the course of several centuries. What an opportunity Burns missed to include those who took the theory of equality and connected it to justice for all, who wrote the *Vindication of the Rights of Women*, and who gathered at Seneca Falls. These women participated in an intellectual paradigm shift with great moral leadership and with a force that changed the views on half the species from that time forward. Women were there, but for some reason, Burns did not include them.

Another way for me to understand the omission is to recognize that women are invisible because of the way many fields of study have conceptualized leadership, especially political science, international relations, and history. Even though Burns eschews the masculinized, stereotypic, heroic loner leading the charge against all odds, the book's narrative explicitly emphasizes leaders who were charismatic and highly driven visionaries, characteristics often attributed to the male gender.

I do not believe Burns's partiality stems from a belief that women cannot be leaders. He seems passionate about recognizing the need to eliminate all forms of inequality, gender or otherwise. In fact, clearly, his sympathies are in the right place: "As leadership comes properly to be seen as a process of leaders engaging and mobilizing the human needs and aspirations of followers, women will be more readily recognized as leaders and men will change their own leadership styles" (Burns 1978:50). True. Nevertheless, oddly, he sees it as something in the future, not where he stood writing this history, as if women had not mobilized followers in the past.

Despite the democratic passion expressed throughout *Leadership*'s pages, it stands as an extraordinarily impressive story of great men (and I do not mean that pejoratively) in relationship with inspired followers doing transformational work for a better world. *Leadership,* unfortunately, continues in a long tradition that the "makers of history" are men. This despite the fact that Burns recognizes that leaders are also parents, teachers, and peers. Burns believes we all lead and follow, guide and listen, influence and are influenced in our homes, classrooms, and communities. Nevertheless, while the book defends this assertion in the abstract, *Leadership* does not manifest it in its narrative. Did Burns mean for his "grand theory" to be only about leadership in the public sphere? I do not believe so. However, women are absent from his history of leadership, their social movements for equality and social reform unnoticed, and their struggles as peacemakers overshadowed by men too often leading war.

More important than the invisibility of individual women, gender is a non-existent category in Burns's grand theory, even though it constitutes one of the most basic sources of division and experiences of power and leadership. From my perspective, leadership is embedded in a deeply engrained gender system—in our distribution of power and resources, in our self- and collective perceptions of effective leadership, in our identities as leaders and as followers, and in our expectations of who can lead, of where leadership takes place, and for what purposes.

Women were omitted from most of the classic studies of political theory and history and, consequently, the field of leadership studies inherited a genealogical gender bias. Because these deeply held assumptions are the norm, they often remain unquestioned and unexamined. Feminist organizational scholar Amanda Sinclair proposes "a close but obscured connection between constructs of leadership, traditional assumptions of masculinity, and a particular expression of male heterosexual identity" (Sinclair 1998:1). Such is, I believe, the case at hand. *Leadership* is silent on gender, even as it is deeply embedded in it. The connection is close but obscure.

Is it fair to expect a distinguished 1970s political scientist and historian, trained in the old school, to have brought gender into the leadership story? We clearly cannot expect Burns to have known what we have learned about gender and leadership since that time. Yet, given how much his grand theory welcomes social movements for justice, could we have expected more?

Leadership was published in 1978. It appeared at the tail end of a decade that an inspired generation of scholarship about gender revolutionized. *Sisterhood Is Powerful*, the seminal anthology edited by poet Robin Morgan, was published in 1970. Shulamith Firestone's *The Dialectic of Sex,* published in that same year, offered its extremely effective critique of the patriarchal bias of political theory. *Ms. Magazine* was founded in 1972. *Against Our Will* by Susan Brownmiller was published in 1975. Congress passed the ERA in 1972, although states did not ratify it. The United Nations began the Decade of Women with its 1975 international conference held in Mexico City. Women composed 25 percent of the parliaments in Eastern Europe by 1975 (Freedman 2003:378). Clearly, there was a remarkable generation of theorists, scholars, historians, politicians, and novelists being inspired by the women's movement here and around the world. I suspect Burns himself might consider this a generation of intellectual leadership, one where intellectuals, focused in history's tension points, addressed the nature of power and liberty and transformed models of thinking.

Interestingly, in the same decade, there was also "a healthy increase in books and articles about leadership" (Rost 1991:57). Curiously, the two paths—gender and leadership—did not seem to cross until years later. Of course, there were a few notable exceptions such as Rosabeth Kanter's pioneering *Men and*

Women of the Corporations, which was published in 1977 and dealt with the gender, organizational research, and management literature. Nevertheless, the scholars were relatively few and Joseph Rost notes that it was only in the 1980s that women authors appeared in enough numbers to make an impact on the leadership literature (Rost 1991:44).

The point of this brief historical departure into the decade in which *Leadership* was published is only to make note that there, indeed, was a rich generation of feminist intellectual leadership, which produced imaginative scholarship and vibrant action at the time of Burns's writing. However, most leadership theories to date had not specifically addressed gender. In that way, Burns was no exception. However, his theory is so rich, his expanse so epic, his understanding of social movements so great, his demand for moral leadership so passionate, that I would have expected more.

On a Feminist Friendly *Leadership*

This scholar/academic activist paradox is wrapped within another one. Despite the invisibility of women as leaders in *Leadership*, it is paradoxically a text that feminists can embrace. Even though Burns's theoretical expanse may have missed gender, it certainly addresses many issues that feminist scholars have held close to our concerns. *Leadership*'s interdisciplinary model offers fertile ground for gendered considerations about leadership issues, and it precedes by many years much of the most current thinking on gender and leadership. There is so much to praise.

Obviously, other chapters in this book have explored many of the significant breakthroughs in Burns's leadership theory. However, these few short pages cannot provide a meta-analysis of gender and leadership to apply to Burns's grand theory. Fortunately, such rich material does exist elsewhere (Butterfield and Grinnell 1999:223- 238; Eagly, Karau and Makhijani 1995). I will focus on a few elements of Burns's leadership theory that resonated for me as most congruent with feminist scholarship.

This seminal work defines leadership not as an "it," or as an individual, but as "the reciprocal process of mobilizing, by persons with certain motives and values, various economic, political and other resources, in a context of competition and conflict, in order to realize goals independently or mutually held by both leaders and follows" (Burns 1978:425). For me, this very core definition of leadership provides the essential opening for gender considerations. Why?

For many feminists, leadership is all about relationship. Leadership from Burns forward, in most views, depends heavily on leader-follower interactions, and real leadership means followers' empowerment. This is certainly a definition which gender-sensitive scholarship can embrace. Burns's theory welcomes those who value connection over disconnection and cooperation over competition in building relationship for mutual goals. Burns wants both leaders and followers to grow in this connection, in a relationship characterized by empathy and mutual empowerment. Relational competence is certainly something at which the female gender has been expected to excel. By framing leadership in

the language of relationship, I would argue that Burns's theory is quintessentially welcoming of women, even if he failed to include them.

In addition, the historical and social contexts influence Burns's notions of
leadership strongly. This is extremely important in that it provides an opportunity for gender to be included, because it implies that leadership consists of
learned and learnable behavior and is not something that is simply divined or a
by-product of a set of chromosomes. While it may be, in reality, that one sex is
deemed more capable of a particular type of learning because of certain gender
practices and norms, Burns's placement of leadership within social/historical
circumstances contains an opening for women because it suggests that there is
no ideal universal, timeless personality type for all situations. Situations require
different leadership behavior, and, therefore, there is a place for a mix of gender
attributes and sexes.

At the same time, there are interesting and, I believe, unintended gender
aspects of his typology of leadership. Let me share a few. In his categorizations,
Burns suggests that transactional leaders focus on task accomplishment, teamwork, and relatively short-range goals that require a steady exchange relationship with followers. Transactional leaders do not seem to be particularly exciting
to me and, by their very definition, do not seem great. Interestingly, however,
this is likely where we would find the value of many traditionally identified fe-
male-gender skills, since women, for many reasons, may be more prone to
working with others, to negotiating, and to teamwork. Would this lead us to a
trap—that women could be good managers but not great leaders?

Then there are transformational leaders. They live lives of macro-purpose,
mobilizing others for long-range, mutually empowered, real change. They are
involved in the world of ideas and vision. They make history. I am definitely
drawn to these types of leaders, and, in fact, I would have loved to be one. In the
transformational relationship, leaders and followers transcend self-interest, a
process facilitated by a high level of personal identification, shared basic beliefs,
and a mutuality of interests. It is hard for me to imagine that gender, race, and
class would not have much to say about the mutuality of interests and values and
the viability of these relationships. Recent decades have produced evidence of a
growing gender gap in voting that demonstrates the problematic nature of
leader-follower relationships that do not take into account gender.

Finally, another "unintended" aspect of Burns's typology, which begs for
gender analysis, is the simple question: If all of Burns's leaders are men, then
who are the followers? Women?

Essential to the leadership relationship is the energy of power. Burns de-
fines power "not as property or entity or possession, but as a relationship"
(Burns 1978:15). He recognizes that power permeates all human relationships.
Those who wield power over others are not leaders—they are power-wielders.
Leaders, on the other hand, hold power differently. They share power and they
empower their followers.

Burns acknowledges that power is misunderstood in this country because it
focuses too much on leaders and their resources. Many feminists share this belief that power is misunderstood and would suggest that that misunderstanding is

rooted in a very decidedly male disposition of power, with power being expressed through resources, influences, and control (Brasileiro 1996). So, here again, we find Burns presenting a theory that can be embraced by feminists. In fact, it feels reminiscent to me of the groundbreaking work of organizational theorist Mary Parker Follett (1942), who provided us with an understanding of "power with" as opposed to "power over."

This leads to Burns's unflinching commitment to leadership that uses this relational power for a purpose. Burns is refreshingly clear about this. For Burns, leadership brings real change in the "attitudes, norms, institutions, and behaviors that structure our daily lives" (Burns 1978:414), and through the relationship, leaders can shape, alter, and elevate the motives and values of followers. This is moral leadership to improve lives. I think this, too, is highly compatible with feminists' commitment to equality and justice. Nevertheless, here again, without gender as an element of analysis, I find the theory missing. I think feminists of all stripes would argue that real change is unlikely to be so fundamental and as deep-seated as Burns would like unless, as Judith Lorber says, "the pervasiveness of the social institution of gender and its social construction are made explicit" (Lorber 1996:160).

The final point I want to discuss is Burns's welcome sensitivity to the personal and psychological. Modern developmental theory has helped us all to understand the psychological forces immediately working on or in leaders and the dynamic psychological factors moving persons to new levels of understanding and responding to the cognitive, as well as emotional, needs of followers. I was so heartened to find this political scientist's incorporation of the psychological. It made his theory profoundly human and comforting. In fact, he says, "Psychobiography is an indispensable tool in analyzing the shaping influences on leadership" (Burns 1978:53). For Burns, leadership is a rich process held together with the glue of motivations—hidden and apparent. He understands that leaders need empathy; they need to comprehend and respond to the cognitive and emotional structure of needs and values of followers. He is very clear that some decisions made by leaders and followers fulfill personality functions, such as ego needs, self image, and the like—and are not directly related to the issue. His awareness of the psychological dynamics is truly noteworthy. Here, too, his theory is welcoming of women and begging for gender analysis.

Feminist scholars, since the time of the publishing of *Leadership*, have brought into question the male bias of some of that developmental theory scholarship (Gilligan 1982: Belenky et al. 1986). Recent psychoanalytic understandings of the self have now provided us with additional ways to conceive of Burns's preliminary considerations on home life and its influence on leaders. For example, Burns argues that leadership is "the affair of parents," as well as others. Some feminists might take it even a step further. Amanda Sinclair notes, "Mothers are the first leaders in our lives" (Sinclair 1998:28). If we extend that analysis and incorporate psychoanalytic perspectives, mothers as "first leaders" clearly influences an individual's later dealings with women in power, which can unconsciously evoke ambivalent feelings, extended, of course, to women in leadership roles. Relatedly, since we come to know our fathers later, when our sense of self and capacity to separate is stronger, it is conceivable that we are more forgiving of the self-centeredness of fathers than of mothers, that is, women. In recent years, feminist scholarship has taken critique of family and psychoanalytic understanding of self into rich areas that affect notions of leadership.

Conclusion

I do not want to underestimate the degree to which Burns's approach opened up a panorama for women after years of "great man" worship and masculine trait reification. In his work, I found reassuring basic tenets of a feminist construction of leadership: leadership as a collaborative effort, a relationship engaged in for purposeful intended change, in which power is not control over, but rather the ability to energize others. Burns developed a theoretical model in which one finds the space to look deeply into the psychological, even if the gender lens for that examination is missing. In this work, I found basic tenets of a feminist construction of leadership which have been further developed in decades since. We owe a great debt to Burns.

I am glad that I encountered this seminal work in the midst of a terribly troubled and growingly polarized world that cries out for moral leadership. As an old friend among strangers, it gave me a sense of depth, compassion, and hope. I am also glad I found *Leadership* later in life, when I had the patience for its paradoxical exclusion and embrace.

I believe that reflecting on *Leadership* as I build a doctoral program in leadership and change reminded me of some important lessons to infuse in the training of scholar-practitioners. The first is to engage in critique with gentleness and respect. We have much to learn from the field's fathers... and mothers. The second is to be mindful that our daily scholarship and practice is embedded in our own frames of reference and disciplinary assumptions, and that mindfulness requires us to be reflective of our own biases at all times. Finally, I walk away with perhaps the most difficult lesson—to seek congruence between one's scholarship and one's professional and personal life. A belief in the equality of all humans demands the explicitness of this recognition in one's scholarly endeavors.

References

Adler, N. 1999. "Global Leaders: Women of Influence." In Gary Powell (Ed.), *Handbook of Gender & Work*, pp. 239-262. Thousand Oaks, Ca.: Sage Publications,

Belenky, M. F., B. Clinchy, N. Goldberger, J. Tarule. 1986. *Women's Ways of Knowing: The Development of Self, Voice and Mind.* New York, N.Y.: Basic Books.

Brasileiro, A. M. 1996. *Women's Leadership in a Changing World: Reflecting on Experience in Latin America and the Caribbean.* New York, N.Y.: United Nations Development Fund for Women (UNIFEM).

Burns, J. M. 1978. *Leadership.* New York, N.Y.: Harper & Row.

Butterfield, D. A. and J. Grinnell. 1999. "Re-Viewing Gender, Leadership, and Managerial Behavior: Do Three Decades of Research Tell Us Anything?" In *Handbook of*

Gender & Work (Ed.), Gary Powell. pp. 223-238. Thousand Oaks, Ca.: Sage Publications,

Eagly, A., S. Karau, and M. Makhijani. 1995. "Gender and the Effectiveness of Leaders: A Met-Analysis." *Psychological Bulletin.*117, 125-145.

Follett, Mary Parker. 1942. "Power." In Henry C. Metcalf and L. Urwick (Eds.), *Dynamic Administration: The Collected Papers of Mary Parker Follett.* New York: Harper.

Freedman, E. B. 2003. *No Turning Back: The History of Feminism and the Future of Women.* New York, N.Y.: Ballentine Publishers.

Freeman, S. J. M. 2001. "Women at the Top: You've Come a Long Way Baby." In Gary Powell (Ed.), *Handbook of Gender & Work*, pp. 27-60. Thousand Oaks, Ca.: Sage Publications.

Gilligan, C. 1982. *In A Different Voice.* Cambridge, Mass.: Harvard University Press.

Lorber, J. 1996. "Reflections on Gender, Work, and Leadership." In Peter Temes (Ed.), *Teaching Leadership: Essays in Theory and Practice*, pp. 147-162. New York, N.Y.: Peter Lang Publishing.

Rost, J. C. 1993. *Leadership for the Twenty-first Century.* Westport, Conn.: Praeger.

Sinclair, A. 1998. *Doing Leadership Differently: Gender, Power, and Sexuality.* Victoria, Australia: Melbourne University Press.

CHAPTER 10
A NEW PARADIGM FOR A NEW LEADERSHIP
Margaret Wheatley

I want to be known as someone who provokes people. So I hope you get provoked. I went back to look at *Leadership*, and from the view of who I am now and what I think about, the book felt very dated. It was a product of the questions of a time, many years ago, which are not for me the right questions any longer.

A New Set of Questions

Without discounting the value of the book and its contribution to the study of leadership, I think we have different questions now. Were that book to be written today, it would not be written around the same themes of psychology and leadership. For me, the questions have shifted. Then we were very interested in studying the individual who was a leader and the topics in which that person's individual expression of leadership came forth. Since then, we have moved into a different consciousness.

Let me begin by commenting on "Jim" Burns. I confess, I always called him "James MacGregor" Burns, but in these pages he is called "Jim," so, I will call him that too. Jim Burns worked on *Leadership*. Who knows really how it influenced me. I think I accepted it as the great book that it still is. It definitely introduced me to studies about types of leadership, and particularly the psychology of leadership, which is what I think the book is about.

I actually remember when I became aware of a different consciousness and how odd it seemed. It came when I was introduced to systems thinking in 1973 at New York University (NYU). I can go back in time to who I was and how I thought about the world from that individualistic and psychological perspective. When I do that, I realize that we all have traveled a great cultural distance now that we are thinking in terms of systems. The questions that arise in a systems consciousness of the world differ from the questions that *Leadership* answers.

I realize in my own work that I was not concerned about questions of leadership. I was and remain only concerned about issues of how people are effective, how people can be supported to be effective, and how they come together to work together. This is my particular bias. So, I do not want to know about the psyche. I do not want to know about the psychology—if it is not relevant. Because of the way in which I see the world, I am no longer interested in questions of individual preparedness, personality types, background, and other individual, psychological issues. These are things that I have intentionally let go of and stopped looking at. I now look at what happens when we are together in a world that is exquisitely relational. By that, I mean who is in a place and what are the conditions that allow them to contribute when they come together as citizens or as a group?

There has also been an important shift in thinking about systems from the time I learned about them at NYU. Then it was the world of psycho kinetics, but now we think about living systems, and there are many distinctions in systems thinking. Fritjof Capra's book *The Web of Life* (1996) describes wonderfully both the history of cybernetics and living systems and how each differs from mechanistic systems thinking. For me, these are the exciting areas to explore in leadership right now—how do we understand life?

Two years ago I was in a discussion "Can Organizations Be Considered Living Systems?" That is not the conversation I want to be in. I do not care if organizations are living systems. The people who are in the organizations *are* living systems. So, let us just think together about how we could organize to support the life that each of us is and how we could organize around principles that are derived from understanding how life works in and out of organizations. Whether we are talking about bacteria responding to us or about a person sitting across the table screaming at us in frustration, the question remains: How do we work with life? That question led me to inquire into what forces work in all of us. What are the forces that work in life? And the question of my last book, *A Simpler Way* (1996), is how would the human-organizing endeavor change if we understood how life organizes itself?

Wow, We Have Choice!

It is clear to me, with my science background, that the way life organizes itself is entirely different from the way humans have chosen to organize it, especially in modern day life. We are just beginning to understand this difference. I now realize, "Wow, we have a choice in how we organize to live." We do not have to move into these old patterns of organizing, which involve command and control, structure, and rules and policies as the way to create order. We have a choice. There are other ways of organizing, and that is the exploration that I have taken, especially through biology.

There are two distinct schools of thought in biology, as there are in most disciplines, but in biology they are pretty easy to see. One is still highly mechanistic, looking at the organism as a machine. Burns talks about the factors of leadership occurring in a context of competition and conflict. Well, that is a worldview right there: the world comes into being through competition and conflict. That is the dominant worldview. It is one school, the mechanistic view, and the older view of biology, survival of the fittest. The newer biology is very different, and that is where this exploration—of looking at systems rather than individuals, looking at cooperation rather than competition—begins.

I found in biology a world that knows how to organize itself. It does not need us to organize it. This world has the great capacity to self-organize, and by that I simply mean that this is a world that creates organization, structures, processes, communication pathways, norms, and values. All living systems have the capacity to self-create those things that we have labored so hard to create for them.

It is possible even for a group of people who come together to be a living system with this great self-organizing capability. It is possible for us to organize the kind of structures and norms that will support us, that will create a shared sense of purpose, a vision. But we have grown up, until very recently—I certainly was brought up—in a culture in which structure, norms, vision, identity, and communication pathways are created by someone who knows about it better than I, a boss or an outside expert or a consultant. They create systems, then parachute in and impose themselves on the system that people have already created. Now when I started that sentence, I said, "until *very recently*" we believed that those things like vision, structure, norms, and roles would be designed and then brought in. I actually think this change is very current, and I hope to encourage you not to buy into that older, unchanged system.

I saw an advertisement in *Fortune* magazine that illustrates the idea of imposed rather than self-created systems. It said, "You supply the vision, we'll provide everything else." The ad pictured an inspired leader sitting at an empty conference table. This organization comprises only the leader, his vision, and whoever the "we" is. An aura of vision surrounded this leader. A light shone on his face, even on his hands. Who do you think the "we" is? Who is the "we" who will provide everything else? It is definitely an outsider. Most people think that this is an ad for Accenture or another consulting firm, any of the big six. The "we" of this ad is an office-product company. With the right Post-it notes, this man and his vision will take the company far.

Now, this is just a disgusting ad. But they may have gotten a positive response to it. They had a really bad PR firm who believed in a very old sense of leadership. That firm pulled this image from a century ago, perhaps a little longer. It states the belief that leadership is actually giving to the organization your vision for design, role, and performance criteria. Is it all about imposition?

Imposition may work fine when you think of organizations as machines, as we have done for so long now. That is how machines operate. Machines have no intelligence, no spirit, and no inherent creativity. There's nothing innate. Everything that makes a machine what it is comes from an engineer or a designer. They give the machine a set of directions. The myth is that the machine follows the directions. Of course, we know this is not true. Even machines do not follow directions: the expectations imposed by engineers. They have "glitches" that may mess up your life, such as a computer problem you or I may have right now.

Poetry and Freedom of Life

When we shift the frame of thought and begin to think about organizations as living systems, we move into an entirely different universe. Fritjof Capra, in his formulation of life systems, posits that every living thing has to respond to three questions of pattern: What is the pattern of a living system? What is its process? And what is its structure? He has done a truly grand synthesis of a lot of what is happening in science that has affected my thinking about organization. The pattern of a living system is—here is a great word—*autopoiesis*, which translates to "self-making." What makes something alive is the capacity to create itself. *Poiesis*, as you probably read, is the same word as poetry. If I can make the connection, I am actually asserting that something is alive if it has the capacity to author its own life. This concept speaks to the inalienable freedom that is at the heart of all life. That freedom, the right for self-determination, is a biological concept, not only a political concept. I think that it is a profound convergence of political and biological theory. In this definition of life, you are alive if you have shown the capacity to author your own life, to create yourself. Freedom lies at the heart of life. The process by which we make ourselves, and which Capra describes as cognition, has freedom built into it. The living system retains the right not only to decide what it will notice, but also to decide what to do with what it has noticed.

I think we have gotten into a very difficult place, which is fairly horrendous in some situations, because we are self-organizing around the wrong values. If we are self-organizing around self-interest and materialism, it will lead to what we are living in right now. The real shift has to be what are the values? What is the sense of identity around which we are going to choose to organize? That shift will come if we recognize that we cannot change the patterns that have emerged, these ways of being together. We are not going to change the wrong values of self-interest and independence, if we do not talk on a deep level about what values we are trying to express together. Self-organization among humans is a neutral process. It can result in wonderful systems and atrocious systems, depending on the self that gets organized from the values. I believe that the way to affect change in the large organization, the small organization, and down to the individual is to go down to that subterranean level of what are the values, in a very broad sense, including the meaning that we are trying to bring forth in our lives.

In our desire to find meaning, we may have to be deliberate about how we decide to organize our lives and the meaning we decide to invest in things, deliberate about whether those choices actually contribute to a greater good or to the well-being of others. From a system's perspective, we need to hold issues of sustainability and the nourishment of others in our consciousness all the time. We may have to create behaviors that are supportive of others. We need to keep in mind this fundamental question: Does the meaning that I am investing, by which I am making my choices, contribute to greater sustainability and help for others or is it self-serving? If it is very narrow and self-serving, I believe it leads to destructive systems and to the destruction of the organism.

I could talk to you forever about my way of seeing the world, but you would never give up the right to decide whether you were going to notice anything I say. The parents of teenagers and young adults see things very clearly, but I know teenagers do not notice anything I say. They choose not to notice 95 percent of anything I say. They could have a different conversation about what parents choose to notice and not notice. In fact, adults also have the right to choose.

For me, at this time, I choose to notice the issues and organization that are in our lives together as a social system. People complain all the time that they have communication problems. We do not have communication problems. We have problems about meaningfulness. I say something I think is really meaningful, but you do not think it has any meaning at all, so you choose not to notice it. Let us define this as a communication problem, just to show you a little bit of how this works. Say I am your boss and I think something is critically important for you to know. I prepare a presentation and it represents my interest. I believe that these are concerns we all should share. So I give it to you. You look at it, put it down, and say, "Thank you very much." I see that it has not attracted your attention, and I think I have a problem communicating with you. I think, "Well, I've got to make better presentations." So, I go to PowerPoint, and I get glossies, I get colorful, and I get dramatic. I underline or I put more things in italics. I am trying to communicate more. But if the meaning of what I think is important is not meaningful to you, it does not matter what graphics I am using. This is a failure to find shared significance, not a failure to communicate. If I had known that, then I would not have worried about my communication style.

The way I will reach you is to enter into a conversation with you where we can see if what I think is significant, you can find significant. If we make the connection around significance, then you will work with me. You will get on board and you will be committed. If you fail to make that connection with me, you're going to be passive or resistant to my "significant" efforts. We really need to be in conversation to discover what is significant to both of us, and then we can work together. This comes from understanding that this cognition process of deciding what to notice and deciding how to react to it is what is going on in all of life, not just at the human level. It is going on in everything. Look around. Look outside a window. What you see is life informed by this process of cognition.

Then the connection dissipates; in another way of saying that, nothing lasts forever. All connections and structures come and go. A living system has the capacity to reorganize itself. It has the capacity to create a structure, to let go of it, and to create a new one. This is not a capacity that leaders frequently have. I may be stereotyping now, but listen through the stereotype to the truth. There are far too many leaders who believe that they can find the perfect solution to their organization's problems. The solution looks like some form or another: a strategic plan or performance-assessment system or a new organizational chart. They present that to people in the organization, and people, like everything else alive, never accept it blindly. They react to it. And they react to it in many ways—ignoring it, sabotaging it, or changing it. Those are probably the three main possibilities. We never accept anything in total. Nothing in life accepts direction, nothing. The whole history of evolution is a history of life reacting to changes in circumstances; never just blindly going down the path, but always being open and reacting to changes. But often the leader does not know that and says, "This is the perfect plan for our organization. This is my vision." When people do not accept it—which they are not going to—they get labeled by that leader as resistant, subversive, noncompliant, bad, or passive/aggressive.

Whereas if you took a change effort from a living-system perspective, you would know that the only thing you were going to receive from people was their reaction. This is a shift from the remnants of authoritarianism to a living-system model. The shift takes us away from believing that you, as the leader, have the right answer to realizing that you, as the leader, are going to be in a constant dialogue with people in your organization; a dialogue over what makes sense to them, each of them; and whether there exists some shared significance—some shared sense of what is important to worry about.

Self-making, *autopoiesis*, defines the system as alive or dead. It is the technical definition of life in areas of biology. Self-making involves identity, and identity issues are always, I believe, the most important things to work on. They involve a sense of belonging, of fitting in, of joining together, and yet preserving oneself as part of a dynamics process at play in people over a lifespan. The freedom we have to choose what to notice and how to create ourselves is inalienable. Sometimes we give it away, but it never really disappears. You only need to read in literature or history about the human spirit to know that you cannot take away this freedom. For me, there is no better test of this than Frankl's *Man's Search for Meaning* (1962). It really conveys that the one thing we retain our rights over is our ability to find meaning in situations no matter how horrific the circumstances.

Finding Meaning in Interdependence

This is where it gets really interesting for me. Independence is a myth. You do not act as an independent agent in your life. Paradoxically, the freedom to create one's self and to hold on to one's freedom happens in the context of being aware of your relationship with others. This is something that I do not yet understand completely because I was brought up in America. It is very hard for me to think about myself as a network of relationships, rather than to think of myself as just stopping here at my skin. But it is clear to me that what goes on out there in some little forest is not about survival, it is not about independence, and it is not about one tree "making it" at the expense of another. We have barely begun to look at living systems for their essentially cooperative nature. I will tell you one story that is a glimmer of what is going on out there.

One biologist, Lynn Margulis, has shown that when part of the forest is suffering from a nutritional deficit, a specific little fungus travels through the tree root system to go to that part of the forest that is in need of its nourishment. What is going on here? Well, there is obviously a system of communication. We have not the faintest idea how a living system really communicates with itself, but systems of cooperation obviously exist. There must be some sense of one's role in the whole system. Rather than finding individualism, Margulis said that independence is a political concept not a biological concept. It may be how we in the United States have chosen to organize socially but it is not how nature operations. You cannot look at any pattern of behavior in a living system, other than human, and use independence as a useful frame of reference. You just will not see anything useful.

I find this very difficult to think about. I grew up in the American West, the dramatic setting of our greatest myths of independence—the frontier, the cowboy. But when I was in South Africa last year, I learned this wonderful phrase in Zulu. It is also found in many other languages. The word is *ubuto*. I've been told it is difficult to translate because it is so inclusive. There are two translations I like the best: One is a person is a person only through other people. You can think about your life and your psychic self and how much you believe you are a person, but this is only accomplished by evaluating yourself through other people in your own life. Another translation of *ubuto* I like is: I exist through you and you exist through me. This term helped me to understand that there are places that I can go in the world to really understand that independence is a myth. But the United States is not one of them. This "unnatural," anti-independence social concept is a very awkward expression, not easily assimilated or understood in our language.

This is where I think I need to talk to a tree. I am beginning to start to sound very weird, but just read on. I think self-interest is a human construct. It does not really help me as a biologist to look at something through self-interest because self-interest and others-interest are all part of how an ecosystem seems to make a decision. When we look at ecosystems biologically, we find patterns of cooperation that are so different from what I was taught. Symbiosis describes the behavior of two organisms benefiting each other. Have you seen those pictures of the birds on the backs of rhinos? Those birds are eating the bugs that are on the rhinoceros's skin, and the rhinoceros is getting a facial.

The world organizes around mutually beneficial relationships. It is not a choice between self-interest and others-interest. The world is an arrangement of mutual interest. I do not think altruism is an anomaly. I think it is possible to create and preserve oneself, while accounting for the interest of everything and everyone around you because that is part of your self-interest. We are in an ecosystem; this is a concept I am trying to understand fully. It is a challenge for a human being. And it is my challenge. Trying to get my head around symbiosis and ecosystems is my challenge as a human being. It is difficult to learn and understand our interconnectedness. I recognize the problem of learning this in a world that ignores mutually beneficial relationships.

We do not even teach this concept of symbiosis, and yet it is one of the fundamental concepts of the way the world works. It is fascinating to me that my son, at seventeen, did not know what the word *symbiosis* meant. It is the same as not teaching what the word *democracy* means. How can you understand the world as mutuality and cooperation if you do not have a word for it? It is disturbing that we do not teach symbiosis or have words for the mutuality and co-operation it implies but have words for their antithesis.

Creativity—Learning from Relationships

Capra likes to say that a living system is a learning system. It does not have to go off and figure out how to learn. Other forms of life are incredibly aware all the time and incorporate what they have learned into their being. So, the process of adaptation is a constant process of learning. Life is a process of constantly figuring out what is going to work for you. You are learning all the time.

I worked for a group of educators whose major approach to education was a simple statement: "Children learn." They stopped it at that second word, *learn*. It is not that children learn under the right conditions or with the right teacher or at a certain age. Children are learning all the time. The significance of that statement is not *how* but *what* children learn. They could be learning to get around an honor code. They could be learning how to use the system to their own selfish advantage. They could be learning to be helpful to others. They will never stop learning, never. Learning is synonymous with life. People who have stopped learning feel dead. There is just nothing there, nothing to talk about. There is no vitality.

Structures come and go, that is the dissipative nature of life; as they come and go, we may learn from them. Newness is inevitable. Life is incessantly creative and its newness always shows up. People always surprise me. You surprise yourself, do you not? And when you put together a team of individuals who have not been together before, you are going to be surprised. Sometimes, you are surprised; "Wow! I did not know I had it in me. This is great. Look at how wonderful we are as a team!" And other times you are surprised and say, "I thought we were going to get a lot more done."

It is impossible to look at the creativity of life and not ask, "When and why did creativity become a problem for us?" Life is incessantly creative. Yet, if you think back to age five, what happened the minute you were willing to sit in a chair for a teacher? You were rewarded. There is so much that has to be done in our educational system to help people unlearn what has been taught and has stymied creativity—not independence—creativity. You may be sitting there thinking, "Well, I am not a creative person." That is just evidence of a system that corrupted you. We are all creative. Life is creative.

I realized just how creative life is when scientists started discovering and reporting the number of species that existed on the planet. Twenty years ago, scientists and biologists would say there were probably about five million species on this planet. Several years later, scientists and biologists claimed fifty million species on this planet. I know of at least one scientist who estimates that there are at least one hundred million species on the face of the planet. When the count shifts that dramatically, something interesting is going on: we are becoming more and more aware of the great diversity of life. We are starting to look in places where we have not seen life before, such as at the microbial level, on Mars, and in other places. I believe we will soon become frustrated because the number of species on the planet is growing, and we will never catch up with it. We are seeing more and more life. Counting species is far less important than appreciating the fact that we live in and are a part of a place with incredible diversity and creativity.

Conclusion

So what are the conditions that support creative life in an organization?

Participation. If you really sense the need—the right—for self–determination and freedom to create yourself, then you cannot enter into any organizational process that does not include people and that does not invite them in. We have done the opposite for years. We keep trying to tell people what to do. Yet, if you appreciate a person as a life, then you realize that you cannot take away the freedom to create, to participate in things that matter to them. You cannot stop a person from authoring their own life, even though organizations try. We take the tools of authoring away, and we think people will just follow our plans and directives, but they do not. So I do not choose any kind of organizational change process or any kind of leadership strategy that does not include a choice for increasing levels of inclusion and participation; I take *that* directly from biology.

Learning. Life always reacts; it never obeys. We seem not to believe this principle because we do not put it into practice. Anything you do to a living system it—whether you push it, prod it, investigate it, or direct it—it will always push back, *always*, unless it is dead. So command-and-control leadership is a myth. It does not work.

I have had the privilege of spending a lot of time at the highest levels of the Army and I know that they do not believe in command and control. That is not how they operate. A young captain will tell you, "If I have to force people by my command authority to do something, then I have failed as a leader." They are also an organization that talks about love in a very open way, of loving one another, the kinds of commitment they have for one another, and deep heartfelt emotions. It is the only organization that I have been in where people actually express and honor these commitments and emotions.

What reality? We cannot know the world, except through our perceptions that, even at the material and psychological level, are always and forever the results of who we already are. This sounds incredibly close-minded, but how we have chosen to construct and to create ourselves influences profoundly what we chose to see. This has a very important place in science right now. No two people can see the world exactly the same. No two people will read this chapter in the same way. Each reader will focus on something based on who you are, what is important to you, and what other choices you have made. In other words, what is meaningful to you as a person? You are making your own meaning, and it is going to be different from the meaning of another person.

From a systems perspective, each of us has a unique contribution to make to the whole. This chapter is seen through your eyes only, in the manner that you see it. You have a perception of it. If you do not think for yourself, develop your perception, and express it, then the system—your class, your group—loses your unique contribution to its health. You think for yourself to contribute to the whole of which you are a part. That is a concept that is more likely to be found among indigenous and tribal people than it is among others because of different upbringings. Some of us realize better than others the great paradox of diversity: its historical outcome is a stronger community.

Now, where that has led me as an individual and also as a thinker is that I have become curious about what other people see. Rather than insisting that they see the world the way I do, I have had to develop more curiosity about their view. I am not where I want to be yet. This is a hard. I give up my expert view that I know what is right and wrong and that I know what is real and not real and that you do not. That is the expert voice. I have tried to move into curiosity about others—tell me how you see the world; tell me what was meaningful to you. Out of that, I hope it is possible to construct something that is even more meaningful for us all. You have to be willing to be curious and aware that others are going to see the same event differently than you do. This is not the usual way we operate. We just assume we all see the same thing. Or we assume that I saw it right, and you saw it wrong.

This new principle of reality requires curiosity and a different way of being together. If a living system is not functioning well, the way to make it healthier is to connect it up to more of itself. If I am manufacturing a car and things are not going well, I could probably benefit by talking to a few people who buy the car because they are going to have information that is relevant. If I am sick a lot, I may want to connect up to more of the factors in my life. What are those factors that might be contributing to my frequent illness? Talking to people who are a part of our system is a way of bringing in information to the solution of problems, to re-identify what is important to us. For me, this has been the most profound organizational change in strategy. If this system needs to change, my role as the leader is to create more connection between the varied voices and parts of the system. By getting those together, they will solve the problems themselves. My role is not to give them a solution. My role is to connect the parts that can provide the solution.

Order. Finally, life seeks order, but it uses messes to get there. All the processes of a living system never look predictable or neat except in our diagrams and representations. Life is an incredible, buzzing movement network. If you are trying to manage this and trying to know from moment to moment what is going on, you will feel that life is out of control, because you cannot manage it moment to moment. You can explore it; you can work with it to see what is meaningful; you may eventfully help it move toward its own effectiveness by connecting it up to more of itself. Life will always show up as networks, and networks always look confusing, messy. We really do have to learn to look for order that is not found in neat increments or in absolute and precise measurements. We have to start looking for order as it comes out of messes.

Thinking of people in organizations as living systems and as the requirements for living systems is very different than thinking about organizations as very neatly pre-structured machines of production. If you are going to be a leader of a living system, very different skills are going to be required of you: participation, learning, perceptive realities, curiosity, connectedness, and the ability to find meaningful order in messes.

References

Capra, F. 1997. *The Web of Life: A New Scientific Understanding of Living Systems*. New York: Anchor Books.

Frankel, V. E. 2000. *Man's Search for Meaning*. Boston: Beacon Press.

Margulis, L. 2000. *Symbiotic Planet: A New Look at Evolution*. New York: Basic Books.

Wheatley, M. and M. Kellner-Rogers. 1998. *A Simpler Way*. San Francisco: Berrett-Koehler Publishers.

SECTION III
FINDING LEADERSHIP AFTER *LEADERSHIP*

In Section III we begin to grapple with some of the practical consequences of *Leadership* for the practice and study of leadership. Where do we find the generalizations about leadership that Burns yearns for, mindful of the cautions and caveats of Section II? Is transforming leadership ephemerally theoretical or a concrete reality? What are its models and examples? What are the sources for the development of moral leadership with and without formal authority? The chapters of this section bring us back to the issues of Section I—values, adaptive work, change, causality, and, of course, the contributions of *Leadership* and the challenges remaining for leadership studies. They do so in different contexts—formal organizations, ordinary and informal organizations, civic organizations, and social movements.

Gill Hickman looks to a new form of organization, the successor of bureaucracy and organic organizations. Thus, she gently chides Burns for limiting his considerations of formal organizations to bureaucracy, and, subsequently, for judging them incapable of transforming leadership. These organizations of hope premise their success on their interdependence with external and internal environmental factors. She identifies factors to shape organizations into transforming-leadership environments with social goals.

Larraine Matusak takes a much more populist position. She recalls grappling with leadership development as a program officer of the W. K. Kellogg Foundation. After learning and dispelling a great deal of what she learned, she turns to a rock-solid formulation, "We the People," to express her confidence in ordinary people and circumstances as a starting place for leadership. In her direct and most accessible way, Matusak directs us to self-confidence as a necessary step to fulfill the expectant hope that the Founding Fathers had in us.

Robin Gerber echoes this popular approach and, in elegant prose, recounts her work on Capitol Hill as a lobbyist for a labor union. This experience explained to her why ordinary people do not equate politics with public service. It also assured her of the willingness of ordinary people to take extraordinary action for what they believe to be the right thing—the common good. Her example of the Martins brings to mind the actions of ordinary people to right public wrongs through the political process. Their example continues in Cindy Sheehan, who along with her sister, catalyzed a movement of opposition to the war in

Iraq by her campout in Crawford, Texas, and John Brady Kiesling, the U.S. diplomat in Greece who resigned rather than acquiesce to the ill-founded build-up to Iraq's invasion. Their actions express an engaged citizenry in the political process and our habit of overlooking it. She offers the labor movement, and by analogy, other spheres of public involvement and training for civic participation, as a starting place from which the average citizen will not have to live down to the expectations for political engagement that too many political leaders have of them.

Ronald Walters's contribution examines leadership in social movements and in the actions of ordinary people to lift restrictions on human dignity and civil and human rights. His chapter stresses the importance of historical forces in understanding leadership, in general, and black leadership, in particular. Walters asserts in very clear language that moral leadership must address white privilege and, by extension, other forms of privilege, including interpretations of past forms of subordination of groups and the "authenticity" of their leaders. His chapter weaves together race and class into a concept of community in which the needs of people reside and from which legitimacy is conferred to leaders.

Chapter 15 attempts to synthesize the various points that the contributors make in a theory that integrates *Leadership* with the work of Howard Gardner and Ronald Heifetz. The theory of effective narratives of adaptive work permits us to hold fast to the central insights of *Leadership* and address its shortcomings of operationalizing its central concepts for research and practicing them on a day-by-day basis.

CHAPTER 11
CAN ORGANIZATIONS MEET THE TEST OF TRANSFORM-ING LEADERSHIP?[1]
Gill Robinson Hickman

By coincidence or fate, *Leadership* appeared as I completed my PhD in public administration. In one of my conceptual papers, I raised the question, "What kind of organization will be best suited for a highly turbulent environment?" The literature, at the time, portrayed organizational environments of the future as highly turbulent with self-perpetuating changes. So I began writing papers about a new conceptual framework for organization, which I termed "transformistic organizations," to answer my question. Bennis and Slater (1968), Schon (1971), and Emery and Trist (1971) influenced my work then.

> When I joined Jim as a faculty member of the Jepson School of Leadership Studies, I read his book, *Leadership*. There was an immediate and obvious linkage between my earlier work and his concept of trans-forming leadership.

I envisioned that transformistic organizations would succeed their bureaucratic and organic predecessors. I explained that the environmental context of each of the previous two organizational types had changed from stable, to changing, to turbulent and that a new form of organization would emerge. I developed the characteristics of transformistic organizations in relation to a turbulent environmental context and then identified the administrative behaviors that would facilitate the development and functioning of such organizations in that environment. As with other graduate papers, little happened with mine until the early 1990s, when Jim, now my faculty colleague, encouraged me to return to my work on transformistic organizations.

My subsequent writing in this area takes his definition of transforming leadership from the political context and applies it to formal organizations. Transforming organizational leaders shape collective purpose and developmental

---

[1] Portions of this chapter may also be found in "Leadership and the Social Imperative of Organizations in the 21st Century" (Hickman 1998:559-71).

processes within the organization that adapt to some social changes and promote others. Though leadership scholars have previously adapted Burns's concept and incorporated it in leader-follower relationships (Bass 1985; Bennis and Nanus 1985; Tichy and Devanna 1986; Bass, Avolio, and Goodheim 1987; Bass, Waldman, Avolio, and Bebb 1987), my work attempts to infuse organizations with Burns's imperative to link leadership with "collective purpose and social change" (Burns 1978:3).

Concepts from Public Administration in Leadership

Burns uses a static portrayal of organizations as bureaucracies in his discussion of "Bureaucracy Versus Leadership" and in his chapter on "Executive Leadership." Borrowing from classics in public administration, he suggests that bureaucracies prohibit the type of leadership that brings about real, intended social change. His vision of the characteristics of bureaucratic organizations and their inherent flaws describes bureaucracy as the world of explicitly formulated goals, rules, and procedures that define and regulate the place of its "members," a world of specialization and expertise, in which the roles of individuals are minutely specified and differentiated. In other words, bureaucratic organizations discourage the kind of power that is generated by tapping motivational bases among employees and marshaling personal, as opposed to organizational, resources. Furthermore, they swallow up individuals in the machine, leaving them separated from tools, alienated from work, and ultimately, as Thorstein Veblen contended, trained into incapacity— the organization, anti-human, anti-individualistic, anti-their own real nature, man and woman (Burns 1978:295-98).

Max Weber acknowledged the inherent anomalies of a fully developed bureaucratic organization, and Vincent Ostrom described the limits on leadership imposed by the bureaucratic search for order. "The bureaucratic machine will place the professional bureaucrat in chains, will transform citizens into dependent masses, and will make impotent 'dilettantes' of their 'masters'" (Ostrom 1973:33). These views of organizations as bureaucracies support Burns's contention that formal organizations are not compatible with the goals and purpose of transforming leadership.

Burns overlooks, however, that not all formal organizations are bureaucratic. The apparent shortcomings in bureaucratic organizations facilitated the development of a different organization type, organic. *Leadership* did not include the scholarship on these organic organizations (Burns and Stalker 1961; Katz and Kahn 1966; and Schon 1971) that occur primarily in a "disturbed reactive" environment that requires organizational adaptation to conditions of change. The environment is no longer stable, and the organization must compete with numerous similar organizations. In this environmental context, organizations face unique and unfamiliar problems, which cannot be broken down and distributed among specialists in the hierarchy (Burns and Stalker 1961). There is a continuous redefinition of responsibilities, functions, methods, and power generated through interaction with others participating in common tasks or problems. Individuals do their jobs with the overall knowledge of the organization's purpose and circumstances. Communications in the organization consist of lateral consultation in contrast to vertical command. The boss at the top is no longer all-powerful.

Like the bureaucratic structure, the organic organizational type also contained certain anomalies. This model assumed that growth and change would occur in the environment in a relatively linear pattern. The organic model anticipated changes in operations among "similar others" or competitors. Among others, Emery and Trist (1973) foretold of a new turbulent, uncertain environmental context comprised of dynamic processes arising from the field itself and creating significant variances from the component systems. These fields are so complex, so richly textured, that it is difficult to see how individual systems can, by their own efforts, successfully adapt to them.

These dynamic properties of the environment led me to ask what happens when the rate and forms of change increase to create a turbulent environment. I began to think that in these environments, organizations must adapt and transform on individual, organizational, and societal levels if they are to preserve core values and ethics, remain viable, and improve the overall well-being of society. The theory later incorporated many of the ideas associated with Burns's transforming leadership and fundamentally realigned the roles, missions, and functioning of organizations in volatile environmental contexts (Hickman 1993).

Leadership and followership in transformistic organizations are predicated less on positional authority and more on interdependent work relationships centered on common purposes. Participants are active, multifaceted contributors. Their involvement is based on shared, flexible roles. Leadership and followership are different activities but often played by the same people at different times (Kelley 1988; 1995). Individuals who assume leadership roles have the desire and willingness to lead. They possess sound visioning, interpersonal communications, and organizational skills and abilities. Effective followers form the other equally important component of the equation and are distinguished by their capacities for self-management, strong commitment, and courage.

Each of the three organizational types—bureaucratic, organic, and transformistic—requires a different form of leadership. Table 1 provides a comparison of these organizational types and identifies their accompanying environmental contexts, leadership structures, management and member behavior, and organizational characteristics.

A Social Imperative Emanating from the Environmental Context

Leadership scholars concern themselves with "good" leadership or with what leadership ought to be as opposed to what it really is, as Barbara Kellerman in Chapter 1 so accurately observes. I strongly believe that leadership scholars should concern themselves with both the ideal and what actually is, although I concentrate on a normative perspective for organizational leadership in the context of very real turbulent environments. My conceptual points of departure with Burns combine normative responses and real changes into the social imperative of transformistic organizational leadership.

Table 11-1
Environmental Contexts, Organizational Structures, and Leadership Forms of Organizations

	Bureaucratic	Organic	*Transformistic*
Environmental Contexts	Stable environment. "Placid Clustered": Goals and challenges distributed in somewhat predictable form. Strategies and tactics to reach goals.	Changing environment. "Disturbed Reactive": Interaction of organizations with similar goals. Organization employs operations to deter other organizations or, when necessary, come to terms with competitors.	Uncertain. "Turbulent, Dynamic": Interconnectedness to promote mutually beneficial interactions between and within organizations. Use of ethics and values frameworks for organizational and external participants as aligning mechanisms. Creation of organizational matrices.
Leadership Form Management and Member Behavior	**Authoritarian**	**Transactional**	**Transforming**
	Impersonal and functional	Humanistic and reciprocal	Contributive and substantive
Organizational Characteristics	Hierarchical, well-defined chain of command. System of procedures and rules for dealing with all contingencies relating to work activities. Division of labor based on specialization. Promotion and selection based on technical competence.	Network structure of authority. Broad operational procedures and rules with consensual guidelines being developed within work units. Functional units composed of multiple specializations. Work assignments based on contributive knowledge and specializations.	Shifting, collaborative, leadership structures and authority with inter- and intra-organizational linkages. Decision making and action based on vision, purpose and core values. Shifting goals, priorities, and methods of operation. Transforming or temporary units of participants with multiple skills. Work assignments based on capacity to contribute to team or ability to transform skills for new purposes.

The environment that characterizes these organizations includes intense global concern and competition; intra-organizational relationships and collaboration; a focus on democracy, substantive justice, civic virtues, and the common good; values orientation; empowerment and trust; consensus-oriented policy-making processes; diversity and pluralism in structure and participation; critical dialogue, qualitative language and methodologies; collectivized rewards; and market alignments (Kuhnert 1993; Rost 1991; Clegg 1990; Toffler 1980; Emery and Trist 1973; Bennis and Slater 1968). These elements link people and organizations globally in an environmental context of turbulence, unpredictability, and change. Environments with such dynamic properties foster interdependencies.

The social imperative for organizations is to understand interdependency in this new environment and to link purposely their own efforts for success to the survival and well-being of society. Can organizations be reconfigured so that social change and collective purpose serve profitability and productivity? There are increasing numbers of private-sector organizations that are attempting to pursue these seemingly contradictory requirements of balancing the functions for which they exist and assuming responsibility for working on the problems and the challenges of society. Drucker (1994) describes organizations of the twenty-first century as new, integrating mechanisms. He indicates that public and private organizations form the capacity essential in determining how to balance two apparently contradictory requirements, the primary functions for which specific organizations exist and the social responsibility each has to work on the problems and challenges of the community as a whole. This, Drucker contends, needs to be the joint work of both public and private organizations that are capable of social-sector work. The ability to collaborate with organizations domestically and globally is becoming a new indicator of success in highly dynamic environments. Society not only expects this form of success to produce profitability for those organizations involved, but also expects those organizations to demonstrate responsibility and contribute to the collective good of the society in which they function.

The Give and Take of Business

Several organizational initiatives illustrate this commitment to a dual mission that advances purpose and social change. For example, the Timberland Company, maker of rugged outdoor footwear and clothing, won the Corporate Conscience Award given each year by the Council on Economic Priorities. Timberland injects social commitment into its mission statement, "Each individual can, and must, make a difference in the way we experience life on this planet," by providing its employees with thirty-two hours of paid time off and five company-sponsored events that allow them to volunteer their services to make a difference in society (Will 1995:18). The company committed five years of services and funding to the City Year urban "peace corps." The youth corps members teach children to read, clean up trash-strewn lots, and interact with different segments of the community. Timberland shares its private-sector expertise with City Year, and the youth corps provides Timberland employees with opportunities to do community service. Beyond its social commitment in the United States, the company also has international guidelines for choosing business partners based on its Standards for Social Responsibility.

In South Africa, a group of white male business entrepreneurs joined together at a "walkabout" to create a new nonprofit organization aimed at identifying and developing emerging leaders in black South African communities. Simultaneously, one of the entrepreneurs initiated an institute within his enterprise to develop the capacity of black South African small-business owners to sustain their survival.

Why are such unusual affiliations occurring? Because corporations are coming to understand that their interests and the fates of previously "separate" people are inextricably linked. One popular journal indicates that a number of U.S. entrepreneurs whose companies are both profitable and socially active have been moved to action by several unsettling trends, including "the sharp rise in juvenile crime, the dearth of quality child care, and the plight of unskilled workers who can't get jobs" (Lord 1994:103). These are not issues that immediately affect the bottom-line, but they do stand to affect the future availability of workers, the location of businesses, and the quality of life in urban areas.

A major retirement system offers its contributors the opportunity to invest their retirement earnings in a fund called "social choice." The companies in this fund practice social and/or environmental responsibility in their business actions and choices. Investors have actively embraced this fund and have also received economic returns comparable to other market investments. These examples are representative of organizations that are embracing social imperatives in their mission, while meeting their organizational purpose of profit.

As organizations continue to incorporate these dual missions and capacity-building roles, they encounter challenges. They face the difficulties inherent in building appropriate infrastructures and capacity substantial enough to generate and sustain the ambitious pursuit of organizational purpose, economic viability, and social change. Encountering challenges and even setbacks in these areas does not mean that the pursuit should be abandoned or that it is imprudent. It means that pioneering efforts into this new arena require organizational learning, concerted analysis, refinement, and corrections.

Can such efforts be prudent in a time of fierce global competition, downsizing, layoffs, outsourcing, and lean-and-mean strategizing? Apparently so. A survey of 1,005 corporations, which had recently participated in downsizing, found that only one-third of the companies reported that profits increased as much as they expected after layoffs, and less than one-half said the cuts reduced expenses over time. In fact, four out of five organizations rehired the laid-off managers, and a small minority reported a satisfactory increase in shareholders' return on investment (Downs 1995:11-12). Instead of serving as responses, much less as solutions, to larger, more fundamental changes in a postindustrial environmental context, these tactics turn out to be temporary reactions and are often detrimental to long-term success. Organizations with a social imperative linking their survival to the well-being of society may be better positioned in the long run to maintain their human and economic viability.

We live in an era that demands the pursuit of more enduring visions, purposes, and roles for organizations. The essential element is leadership, the type of leadership that assumes elevated sights and dimensions beyond those set in previous eras. Transformistic organizations require leadership by activists who work internally and externally to bring about human and economic metamorphosis. Within the organization, these agents of change generate visions, mission, goals, and a culture that gives individuals, groups, and the organization itself the capacity to practice its values, serve its purpose, maintain strong economic viability, and serve societal needs.

Externally, transforming leaders are both organizational and "social entrepreneurs" (Waddock and Post 1991) who build interconnectedness for business and societal purposes. Frequently, these leaders are business executives, such as those involved in Cleveland Tomorrow, Hands across America, or the Partnership for a Drug-Free America, who recognize crisis-level social problems characterized by multiplicity and extreme levels of complexity and who mobilize interdependent organizations and individuals to begin working toward new solutions. These highly credible leaders generate the sort of follower commitment that fosters a sense of organizational and collective purpose.

How can organizational leaders develop the type of context that maximizes human capabilities for personal, organizational, and societal good? Organizations first will need to develop an ability to generate and expand human capacity at individual, group, organizational, and societal levels and then forge interconnectedness among these levels.

The Conceptual Framework

The four interdependent transformistic organization elements, in their emergent and idealized form, entail: a dynamic and turbulent environment; the organization as a context for capacity building; transforming leadership that mobilizes, facilitates, and elevates human and organizational developmental processes; and outcomes characterized by maximized human and organizational capabilities and contributions for the individual, organization, and society. Though the elements incorporated in the transformistic framework are interdependent and mutually reinforcing, we discuss them separately for purposes of analysis.

Dynamic and Turbulent Environments. The effects of larger societal challenges, such as new markets in new democracies, changes in family structures, cultural and ethnic diversity, decline in urban environments, and environmental sustainability are becoming intermeshed purposefully and often unexpectedly with organizational functioning. In order to build capacity in organizations, leaders are required to be as attentive to the changes and needs in their external and internal environments. As leaders, they must help determine the relationship between the external environment and the human and structural capacities of their own organization.

> A turbulent field environment has dynamic processes created by changes emanating from the environment. Fairly simple examples of this may be seen in fishing and lumbering, where competitive strategies, based on an assumption that the environment is static, may—through overfishing and overcutting—set off disastrous dynamic processes in the fish and plant population, with the consequent destruction of all the competing social systems. It is easy to see how even more complex dynamic processes are triggered in human populations (Emery and Trist 1973:52-53).

Implications for organizations suggest that traditional methods of forecast-

ing, planning, and strategizing will be less effective, making consequences of
the organization's actions or those of its competitors more unpredictable. Collective strategies among multiple organizations linked by their recognition of
"significant values" can provide a coping mechanism in this context. Emery and
Trist discuss significant values as methods of reducing complexity. They suggest that "values are neither strategies nor tactics and cannot be reduced to
them." As Lewin has pointed out, values have the conceptual character of
"'power fields' and act as guides to behavior" (Emery and Trist 1973:69).

In introducing the use of values, Emery and Trist immediately recognize the
problems of determining which values will be used in organizations and how
they will be used. They suggest that a means for dealing with the complex issue
of values is contained in the design of the social organization. Transformistic
organizations link with like, but competitive, others and develop "some relationship between dissimilar organizations whose fates are basically (and) positively
correlated: that is, relationships that will maximize cooperation while still recognizing that no one organization could take over the role of the other" (Emery
and Trist 1973:76).

The results of Emery and Trist's design principle become a responsive, self-
regulating system with core values and a unifying purpose as the inherent self-
regulating device. The creation of such organizational contexts allows cooperative linkages with similar and dissimilar organizations in a dynamic environmental field. Existence within this environmental context, therefore, requires
changes in concepts of the nature, purpose, and design of organizations; organizational leadership; relationships within and between organizations; expectations concerning human capabilities and contributions in organizations; and inherent outcomes.

Organizational Capacity Building. Within the transformistic framework, organizations are recognized as "contexts" for capacity building. As such, they
focus on human purposes and values as the driving force of the institution. Gains
in economic resources become instruments for concerted human activity. This
organizational focus does not mean that significant service and products cannot
result or that bottom line economic considerations and productivity are mini-
mized. It simply means that organizations become human entities with economic
interests as components of human requirements.

Building the context for organizations, which Wheatley (1994) refers to as
"fields," creates an internal setting that shapes its dynamics.

> The field must reach all corners of the organization, involve everyone, and be
> available everywhere. Vision statements move off the walls and into the corri-
> dors, seeking out every employee and every recess of the organization. We
> need all of us out there, stating, clarifying, discussing, modeling, and filling all
> of the space with the messages we care about. If we do that, fields develop, and
> with them, their wondrous capacity to bring energy into form (Wheatley
> 1994:55-56).

Creation of such a context develops the organization's capacity for "resil-
ience" and "self-transcendence" (Carey 1993), so that the human potential that is

unleashed may be realized beyond the organization for societal transformations in the external environment. When these factors are established, the organization can be positioned to create value and purpose alignments with others in the environment whose fates, in the words of Emery and Trist, are "positively correlated."

Several pragmatic challenges arise for organizations moving toward such contexts: (1) how to create contexts that facilitate the liberation of human potential to maximize personal, organizational, and societal capabilities; (2) how to prepare individuals for and engage them in these new challenges; (3) how to identify, develop, and sustain core values and unifying purposes; and (4) how to align organizational values and purposes with others in the environment and/or meet emergent needs in the environment. There are no simple responses to these challenges. However, the ability to meet them seems to rest more with a process and a set of responsibilities, which is leadership.

Mobilizing and Elevating Organizational Processes of Human Development. Changing and reframing organizations to meet the challenges of a new era require innovative leadership structures. Rost (1991) indicates that there is a definite trend toward shared or collaborative leadership. Collaborative leadership, particularly at today's executive levels, entails the redistribution and sharing of power, authority, and position, all of which have been relatively untested in contemporary organizations. In addition to the executive-leadership-team configurations, leadership might function in arrangements such as dyads, triads, representative team leaders, and many other constructs. The leadership structure, like the organizational structure, will need to be developed by stakeholders to fit the purpose, needs, and values of the enterprise.

Transforming leadership is particularly useful for these needs. When Burns's concept of transforming leadership is employed in the transformistic organizational context, it is imperative that three factors maintain prominence: the focus on leadership as a process; the powerful and mutually reinforcing roles and impact of leaders and followers on one another; and the responsibility of leaders and followers to engage in collective purpose to effect social change while implementing the organization's purpose and remaining economically viable.

When viewed from Emery and Trist's perspective, transforming leadership serves to align human, organizational, and environmental values, capabilities, purposes, and needs. This form of leadership influences participants in the process to remain open to new information and inputs and to move themselves and others toward the capacity for self-transcendence (Carey 1992). It involves advancing beyond self-serving, egocentric purposes to focus on a larger perspective or greater good and to serve genuine human needs.

Vital to the concept of transformistic organizations is the role of transforming leadership in establishing external connectedness with similar and dissimilar others in the environment. John Gardner (1990) identified five skills critical to leaders trying to develop interconnectedness as agreement building, networking, exercising non-jurisdictional power, institution building, and flexibility. As pre-

viously indicated, Waddock and Post (1991) would add the skills of social entrepreneurs who bring together social alliances of multiple actors, on multiple
levels and by multiple means, to solve extremely complex societal problems.
Given the complexity of this dynamic environmental field and its accelerated
rate of change, leaders must use the collective sense of organizational values,
identity, purpose, and capabilities as their guide in determining with whom to
connect, for what purposes, and to what end. Collaboration and cooperation
among organizations globally and domestically are becoming new indicators of
success. Society expects this form of success not only to produce profitability
for those involved, but also to prove an organization's ability to exercise social
responsibility in the process.

Maximized Human and Organizational Capabilities and Contributions. The
output of transformistic organizations exceeds products, services, or profits,
though these should indeed result. The real outcomes are qualitative changes in
the well-being of society. Transformation of human capabilities within organizations that change society at large could be tantamount to a new social movement
for the twenty-first century. The comment by Edward Simon, president of Her-
man Miller, that "business is the only institution that has a chance. . . to fundamentally improve the injustice that exists in the world" may generally apply
more directly to interconnected organizations in the next century. Though I believe these capabilities exist within the organizations of various sectors now,
Simon's point illustrates a progression to the new thinking among organizational
leaders, the kind of thinking that will make the transition to transformistic organizations a viable possibility in the twenty-first century.

One of the major roles of leadership in transformistic organizations is to
engage participants in the work of identifying, developing, and employing values. Values serve as the organization's essence, stability, and guide for action.
Still, the question is, which values should be used for the work of organizations
and their alignment with others? In an attempt to develop the beginning of a
global set of values, Kidder (1994) sought the perspectives of twenty-four diverse leaders and influential individuals from around the world. The values identified included love, truthfulness, fairness/justice, freedom, unity, tolerance, responsibility, and respect for life. Even in the unlikely event that these values
become accepted universally, only the reality of their implementation will give
them real meaning.

Heifetz (1994) provides several significant insights concerning the implementation of values. First, he indicates that leadership mobilizes people to do the
"adaptive work" required to address or lessen the gap between value conflicts
among individuals. Second, values are shaped and refined when people must
deploy them in the face of real problems. Third, success is influenced by the
openness of participants to diverse and even competing value perspectives, as
well as their willingness to use creative tensions and conflict to generate new
knowledge, approaches, and outcomes. He urges that leadership tackle the tough
problems by allowing values to evolve without an imperialistic perspective, but
rather by engaging participants in the examination and incorporation of values

from different cultures and organizations.

Collective values provide a foundation for forming the organization's unifying purpose, which represents the substance to which organizational participants are willing to commit. This purpose provides meaning for the organization and in the lives of its participants (Wheatley 1994). The pursuit of unifying or collective purposes requires an elevation of motives and values. Burns asserts that in the pursuit of collective purposes, "whatever the separate interests persons might hold, they are presently or potentially united in the pursuit of 'higher' goals, the realization of which is tested by the achievement of significant change that represents the collective or pooled interests of leaders and followers" (Burns 1978:425-26).

Using foundational values and a unifying purpose, leaders and organizational participants can derive a shared formulation of organizational vision, culture, change efforts, relationships, and external interactions. These factors constitute the identity of an organization and position it to relate and contribute to its environment.

Liberating Human Potential and Increasing Capacity

In transformistic organizations, engagement of the full person involves liberating human potential and his or her capabilities to change. Transforming leadership facilitates this capacity by promoting personal and emotional stability and maturity among organizational participants. Promotion of human development stems from the establishment of a culture, context, or field that supports advancement of self-knowledge, enhanced self-esteem, and emotional and physical wellness. In addition, the development of whole-person relationships is encouraged to include recognition and regard for the uniqueness and diversity of individuals and the interrelated personal, professional, and relational aspects of their lives. In accordance with this is another of transforming leadership's facilitations: the development of the culture and resources for continual learning that empowers individuals to grow, create, and change themselves, their organization, and the environment.

The existence of these interrelated conditions provides organizational participants with the capabilities to respond to complex issues and the needs that arise in rapidly changing dynamic environments. The process that organizations must employ to gain this capacity, this adeptness to learning, has been described in terms of organizational participants, who "must become able not only to transform our institutions in response to changing situations and requirements, but must invent and develop institutions which are 'learning systems' or systems capable of bringing about their own continuous transformations" (Schon 1971:30).

Senge (1990) later refers to this process as generative learning, which enhances the capacity of organizational participants to create. He states that five essential elements must develop as an ensemble to create a fundamental learning organization:

- Personal mastery: continually clarifying and deepening personal vision, focusing energies, developing patience, and seeing reality objectively.

- Mental models: changing ingrained assumptions, generalizations, pictures and images of how the world works.
- Shared vision: unearthing shared "pictures of the future" that foster genuine commitment.
- Team learning: aligning and developing the capacity of a team to create the results its members truly desire.
- Systems thinking: integrating all the elements by fusing them into a coherent body of theory and practice (Senge 1990).

Heifetz (1994) offers another dimension of generative learning with his own work on adaptive work as collective learning that is stimulated during the process of leaders and followers working through hard problems together.

The forms of learning described by Schon, Senge, and Heifetz require organizational participants to undergo continual examination, synthesis, and integration from various disciplines, perspectives, and cultures, a concept that is conceptually sound but difficult to practice. These processes must be built into the organization through deliberately planned opportunities for dialogue, technology used to enhance creativity and problem solving (Passmore 1988), and diligence exercised by leaders and participants in the organization.

Conclusion

The dynamic properties of the environment have delivered us a challenging social imperative, which is to prepare and position our organizations to generate unprecedented advances for society and to resolve highly complex human and environmental problems. The transformistic-organization framework can serve to stimulate organizational movement toward the liberation of human potential in an effort to meet these unprecedented challenges. In this context, transforming leadership itself evolves and becomes multifaceted. In doing so, its shifts are based on several factors: the influences of changes and requirements from the environment; the quality of adaptive work engaged in by followers with leaders; the level, quality and complexity of collaboration within and across organizational boundaries; the ability to use technological capabilities to link participants and change environmental circumstances; and the deployment of economic and material resources for collective purposes.

References

Bass, B. M. 1985. *Leadership and Performance beyond Expectations.* New York: Free Press.

Bass, B. M., B. J. Avolio, and L. Goodheim. 1987. "Biography and the Assessment of Transformational Leadership at the World-Class Level." *Journal of Management* 13, 7-19.

Bass, B. M., D. A. Waldman, B. J. Avolio, and M. Bebb 1987. "Transformational Leadership and the Falling Dominoes Effect." *Group & Organization Studies* 12, 73-87.

Bennis, W. and B. Nanus, 1985. *Leaders: Strategies for Taking Charge.* New York: Harper Collins Publishers, Inc.

Bennis, W. and P. Slater. 1968. *The Temporary Society.* New York: Harper Colophon.

Burns. J. M. 1978. *Leadership.* New York: Harper and Row.

Burns, T. and G.M. Stalker. 1961. *The Management of Innovation.* Chicago: Quadrangle Books.

Carey, M.R. 1992. "Transformational Leadership and the Fundamental Option for Self-Transcendence. *Leadership Quarterly* 3(3), 217-36.

Clegg, S.R. 1990. *Modern Organizations: Organizational Studies in the Postmodern World.* London: Sage Publishers.

Downs, A. 1995. *Corporate Executives: The Ugly Truth about Layoffs—How Corporate Greed is Shattering Lives, Companies, and Communities.* New York: AMACOM.

Drucker, P.F. 1994. "The Age of Social Transformation." *The Atlantic Monthly* 274, 3, 53-56ff.

Emery, F. E. and E. L. Trist. 1973. *Towards a Social Ecology.* New York: Plenum.

Gardner, J. W. 1990. *On Leadership.* New York: Free Press.

Heifetz, R. A. 1994. *Leadership Without Easy Answers.* Cambridge, Mass.: Belknap Press.

Hickman, G. R. 1993. "Toward Transformistic Organizations." Paper presented at the annual meeting of the American Political Science Association, Washington, D.C.

----. Ed. 1998. *Leading Organizations: Perspectives for a New Era.* Thousand Oaks, Ca.: Sage Publications.

Katz, D. and R. I. Kahn. 1966. *The Social Psychology of Organizations.* New York: Wiley.

Kelley, R. 1988. "In Praise of Followers." *Harvard Business Review,* 66(6), 141-48.

----. 1995. "In Praise of Followers." In J.T. Wren (Ed.), *The Leader's Companion: Insight into Leadership Through the Ages,* pp. 193-204. New York: Free Press.

Kidder, R.M. 1994. *Shared Values for a Troubled World: Conversations with Men and Women of Conscience.* San Francisco: Jossey-Bass.

Kuhnert, K. W. 1993. "Leadership Theory in Postmodern Organizations." In R. T. Golembiewski (Ed.), *Handbook of Organizational Behavior,* pp. 189-202. New York: Marcel Decker.

Lord, M. 1994. "Making a Difference and Money Too: Entrepreneurs are Finding Rewarding Remedies for Social Ills." *U.S. News & World Report* (October 31).

Ostrom, V. 1973. *The Intellectual Crisis in American Public Administration.* University, Alabama: University of Alabama Press.

Passmore, W. A. 1988. *Designing Effective Organizations: The Sociotechnical Systems Perspective.* New York: Wiley Publishers.

Rost, J. C. 1991. *Leadership for the Twenty-First Century.* New York: Praeger Publishers.

Schon, D. A. 1971. *Beyond the Stable State.* New York: Norton Publishers.

Senge, P. M. 1990. *The Fifth Discipline: The Art and Practice of the Learning Organization.* New York: Doubleday/Currency.

Tichy, N. and Devanna, M. 1986. *Transformational Leadership.* New York: John Wiley Publishers.

Toffler, A. 1980. *The Third Wave.* New York: William Morrow.

Waddock, S.A. and Post, J.E. 1991. "Social Entrepreneurs and Catalytic Change." *Public Administration Review* 51, 393-401.

Wheatley, M. J. 1994. *Leadership and the New Science: Learning about Organizations from an Orderly Universe.* San Francisco: Berrett-Koehler.

Will, R. 1995. "Corporations with a Conscience." *Business and Society Review* 95, 17-20.

CHAPTER 12

THE LEADERSHIP OF ORDINARY PEOPLE
Larraine Matusak

My first encounter with the book *Leadership* was in 1983. I had accepted a position at the W. K. Kellogg Foundation to direct and design a leadership-development program for professionals in the early years of their careers. I had been serving in leadership roles for quite a few years, as dean and then as president of a state college in New Jersey, before I accepted this position at Kellogg. I readily admit, however, that I had given little thought to the theory or definition of leadership. As is the case with most positional leaders, I was too busy trying to be a leader. Time for reflection on the scholarly study of theories of leadership was a luxury I could not afford, which is why James MacGregor Burns's work means so much to me. I celebrate this opportunity to discuss the growing field of leadership studies, as we continue to expound on a conversation Burns inspired in earnest with *Leadership*.

Leadership probably has contributed more energy to the development of a theory and framework for the scholarly study of leadership than any other book written to date. It has inspired many scholars to delve more deeply into the topic and carve out their own niches within which they reinforce or disagree with Burns's conceptual framework. I consider myself in this company.

Required Reading and a Growing Definition

After one year with the Kellogg National Fellowship program, I became acutely aware that the design of the program had some major deficiencies. To begin with, the program dedicated little time to developing an understanding of leadership's theoretical framework and even less to its practical applications. The program used the convening power of a large foundation to bring bright, young professionals into contact with outstanding public officials and leaders. The assumption was that if we could provide the fellows access to these great minds, then somehow, by observation or by osmosis, they too would begin to grow and develop intellectually and practically into comparable great leaders.

Well, the fellows met and interacted with international heads of state, national leaders in the fields of education, healthcare, and agriculture. Yet, the understanding of leadership was not coming through in the fellows' words or in their actions.

This probably was the first time that I began to think of leadership as a subject, a topic, a body of knowledge, something to study and analyze, and something to teach, learn, and practice. The first book that I read on the subject was John Gardner's *On Leadership*, an excellent, well written, but very politically oriented book. Then a historian friend of mine recommended *Leadership*. I was warned that while it too was historical and political, Burns was making a first attempt to construct a theoretical framework for leadership.

The rest is history for me. I read the book and insisted that all of the fellows read it, because I became very interested in the concept of an interdisciplinary approach to the study of leadership and, in particular, to transformational leadership. Burns gives an amazing, comprehensive analysis of the leadership of historical and political figures, past and present. He makes some penetrating observations about the implications of this leadership on the future of our democracy. He also makes some very strong statements about leadership being far more pervasive than generally recognized. In fact, he states that although leadership occurs in presidential mansions and parliamentary assemblies, it is far more widely and powerfully practiced by parents, teachers, preachers, and other activists. For all his vigorously voiced support for the idea that leadership is far more than a title or position, though, Burns gives no practical examples to which community grassroots leaders might relate.

You might say that this opening in *Leadership* became the launching pad for my own intense interest in the subject of leadership. I began my search for all types of scholars, data, and information that were stretching and moving the concepts of leadership in a more comprehensive direction. I discovered that there were immense reservoirs of data and analysis, but there was no central concept of leadership woven from all disciplines into a comprehensive body of knowledge for leadership. Nor could I find any literature that expanded on the conceptualized pervasiveness of leadership. It was discouraging.

"We the People"

Then, like a Phoenix rising out of the ashes, I realized what my mission in this field of leadership had to be. First, my position in a major foundation gave me responsibility for a leadership-development program and for all grant making in leadership. I convinced our team that in our grant-making efforts it would be essential to find a group, an organization, or an association that would share a passion for the development of a comprehensive theory of leadership, one that would cross all disciplines and interest itself with practical applications of leadership to reach all sectors of society. Next, I was determined to write a book that would take the best thinking available by leadership scholars, put it into a language other than that of political science or business, and cite examples of untitled individuals who had proven themselves to be leaders. I wanted to reach the citizens of communities all over America to help them rediscover what our forefathers meant when they said, "We the People." I saw this, and finding a way to convince positional leaders that they must become leaders of leaders, as my responsibility. I hoped to direct their time toward nurturing other leaders, because I believed, and continue to believe, that effective leadership for the future is all about creative collaboration, about creating a shared sense of purpose. People need meaningful purpose to perform to their full potential.

To prove my point, I reviewed and analyzed more than 280 leadership books. I discovered that a full 87 percent dealt with the corporate sector and used the language and examples of successful or failing executives. Nine percent addressed the political sector and used the usual historical examples. A mere 2 or 3 percent examined the nonprofit sector, and I found only two books that addressed community leaders and community leadership in a constructive, relevant way. By implication then, we are professing to society and teaching our young people that one must be an executive or a politician to be a leader, that one must have the title of CEO or senator to be a leader. Once again, I was challenged by the question, what ever happened to the Constitution's premise, "We the People?"

The Kellogg Foundation has supported many projects addressing the intellectual foundations of leadership and leadership development. The most important may be the project that has brought scholars of leadership together to debate, dialogue, and collaboratively write about new ideas in leadership (Kellogg Leadership Studies www). My own work, *Finding Your Voice* (1999), translates the scholarly knowledge of my colleagues into practical material, useful to all of us who live in a democratic society. This book emphasizes the idea that leadership is a process, not merely a title or position; that it is relational; that it can be taught to anyone who wishes to learn; and that it is a collaborative effort. My book is one small attempt to construct a social architecture to generate intellectual capital and encourage incredibly diverse, creative, bright people to work together and successfully create positive social change for a new century. Accomplishing this will demand the recognition of a new form of leadership, one that is both shared and collaborative.

Collaborative Purpose

A basic premise of collaborative leadership lies in recognizing that no one person has the solutions to the multifaceted problems a group or organization must solve. In this context, leadership requires a set of principles that will empower all members to act and to employ a process that allows collective wisdom to surface. These principles must be based on an understanding that people have the knowledge and creativity to respond to the problems they face. They also must encourage the development of communities and organizations supporting collective action based in shared vision, ownership, and mutual values.

For years, scholars have been trying to define or even describe the nature of leadership. Not surprisingly, Burns's *Leadership* eloquently expounds on this need for clarity of definition. Today, there are scholars who suggest that collaborative leadership will be the most successful approach in the next century and that there is a need to refocus our study and research on the purpose rather than the definition of leadership. They also contend that there are core principles that nurture the interaction and learning so essential to collaborative leadership.

Recognizing the context of our rapidly changing times, we certainly can make some assumptions about the purpose of collaborative leadership in the next century. Optimally, it may very well serve to:

- create a supportive environment where people can thrive, grow, and live in peace with one another;
- promote harmony with nature and thereby provide sustainability for future generations; and
- create a community of reciprocal care and shared responsibility, one in which every person matters and each person's welfare and dignity are respected and supported by everyone involved.

Obviously, these assumptions will require changes in the practice of leadership. They will require in-depth study and scholarly research to address the purpose, the principles, and the practice of a collaborative approach.

Clearing Barriers

One of the most difficult things for human beings to do is to release old patterns of thinking, to move beyond deeply embedded mental boundaries. Too frequently, we allow ourselves to become victims of preconceived notions or of what other people think of us. This leads us to fear change, to fear failure, and to lack the will to develop our potential for leadership. We lose sight of those factors most crucial to promoting successful leadership: commitment, a passion to make a difference, a vision for achieving positive change, and the courage to take action. Perhaps this last element is the source of our greatest struggle. We all dream of being successful and of making a difference, but more frequently than not, we allow ourselves to succumb to the gnawing fear of failure or ridicule that paralyzes us and keeps us from taking action. Preconceived notions about what others may judge to be our ability to succeed or fail are deeply ingrained in our minds and hearts. Subtle messages, real or imagined, come at us all our lives. More times than not, these are based on where we were born and raised, the color of our skin, the socioeconomic level of our family, whether we went to college or not, which college we attended, and sometimes on things as simple-minded and surprising as our gender and how we look. Distorted thinking often results in a self-made mental and social prison.

There is a wonderful parable in the book *Even Eagles Need a Push,* which speaks to this debilitating mindset. A man found a deserted nest with an eagle's egg. He put the egg in the nest of a barnyard hen. The eaglet hatched with the brood of chicks and grew up with them. All his life the eagle did what the barnyard chicks did, thinking he was a barnyard chick. He scratched the earth for worms and insects; he clucked and cackled. He would thrash his wings and fly a few feet into the air. Years passed and the eagle grew very old. One day he saw a magnificent bird above him in the cloudless sky. It glided in graceful majesty among the powerful wind currents, with scarcely a beat of its strong, golden wings. The eagle looked up in awe. "Who's that?" he asked. "That's the eagle, the king of the birds," said his neighbor. "He belongs to the sky. We belong to the earth; we are chickens." So the eagle lived and died a chicken, for that's what he thought he was (McNally 1994:3).

This disturbing parable dramatically describes the results of false mental models and distorted thinking. It illustrates a tragic failure to discover hidden talent, a fear to take a calculated risk. On the other hand, it serves as a poignant shove, embarrassing us enough to force some decisions. We can decide to discard our mental roadblocks. At every opportunity, we should examine them, expose them for what they are, take ownership of them, and then knowingly choose to discard them. Gradually overcoming these mental roadblocks starts us thinking more clearly about who we are and what the possibilities are for what we wish to do and be. Our arrival at this understanding tells us, clearly, that we have the power to choose how to accomplish our goal of citizen leadership.

Conclusion—Recognizing the Power Within

I continue to work toward these same goals. I believe in "We the People." I believe that positive change comes when society reaps the benefits and contributions from all of its citizens, institutions, and organizations. In this regard, change for effective leadership involves both transitions in behavior, as well as in mindset. In the collaborative transforming-leadership model, leaders become learners, and learners must assume the responsibility for leadership whenever their talents are required. This process is activated by the creation of learning communities in which members are encouraged to take risks and each individual is respected, recognized as a potential leader, and encouraged to release old patterns of thinking that stall growth and maturity.

You might say that reading Burns's *Leadership* helped me discern my passion for the subsequent years of my career. I no longer agree with everything espoused in that awesome book, but then, neither does he! Beginning with his book, though, I have learned a great deal about world historical and political leadership. I also have learned a great deal about the need for a conceptual framework for the study of leadership. I now choose to invest my time and energy in what the future demands, which I believe is the study, research, and practical applications of collaborative/shared leadership and its purpose and principles. How do we prepare people to practice this form of leadership, and what forms of education might prove most effective? A sustainable future depends on finding that answer among "We the People."

References

Kellogg Leadership Studies Project. www.academy.umd.edu/publications/klspdocs/.

Matusak, R. 1997. *Finding Your Voice: Learning to Lead...Anywhere You Want to Make a Difference.* San Francisco, Ca.: Jossey-Bass Publishers.

McNally, D. 1994. *Even Eagles Need a Push: Learning to Soar in a Changing World.* New York, N.Y.: Dell Publishing.

CHAPTER 13
LEADERSHIP AND A PLACE CALLED HOPE
Robin Gerber

I was a longtime leadership observer-in-ignorance when I landed on Capitol Hill, one of the most intense leadership environments in the world. I viewed without understanding, observed without analyzing, experienced without reflecting. I was, I now realize, subliminally processing theories, subtly—even to myself—assessing the personalities, interrelationships, and values that surrounded me as a lobbyist in Washington, D.C., for the Carpenters' Union and, to a degree, for all of us as citizens.

Questing for Political Hope

Working in the midst of political leaders and more recently with leadership scholars, including Burns, I cannot help but notice the striking contrast in leadership consciousness between the former and the latter. Analyzing the dynamic social, psychological, and contextual bases of their leadership is not on the agenda of your average member of Congress. They have little time to reflect on "end-values" and "modal values." The pace of governing is exhaustive; demands are unrelenting and in constant conflict.

> It was not until I met Georgia Sorenson, became a Senior Fellow at the University of Maryland's Academy of Leadership, and paged with recognition and wonder through *Leadership* by James MacGregor Burns that I began to articulate my experience as a practitioner of the art, expedience, and drama of transactions and transformations.

Constituents wait for appointments, while members of Congress conduct hearings and committee meetings, and vote on the floor. Who and what has priority? Missing meetings with constituents or their representatives may lead to angry voters back home. Missing committee meetings may mean losing opportunities to shape legislation. Missing floor votes can leave a member's voting record open to negative attacks from an opposing candidate in the future. Members of Congress have little time to ponder complex legislative questions, much less their role as leaders. Those of us "petition(ing) the government for a redress of grievances," my First Amendment mantle of preference as a lobbyist, were too enmeshed in the interplay of governance to expend mental energy on questions of leadership.

The Carpenters Union charged me with representing five hundred thousand working carpenters, millwrights, loggers, and mill workers, and a few thousand organized stragglers in unrelated occupations. I traveled throughout the country, addressed meetings attended by hundreds of union members, and listened to their concerns. Lobbying was the translation of those concerns into the special brand of advocacy that exists on Capitol Hill. Advocacy meant creating a flow of communication that kept our union members actively engaged in the lobbying effort. Advocacy also meant negotiating the complicated, often secretive processes that result in lawmaking in Washington.

On Capitol Hill, I worked in a web that tangled the politically powerful, their supplicants, parasites, and other players in a world detached from common experience, while profoundly influencing that experience. I reevaluated the meaning of primal human experiences, including friendship, loyalty, and trust, as well as the personal values of honesty and fairness.

On the Hill, calling acquaintances "friends" can be advantageous, as can the reverse. Loyalty is a commodity enlarged or contracted by its cost. Republicans demonstrated this fact when they abandoned their former heroes and patrons, first House Speaker Newt Gingrich and later Majority Whip Tom DeLay, to secure their own reelections. We saw Congressional Democrats' trust for President Clinton steadily erode over his term in office. One of the most dramatic political failures of trust occurred when several of Speaker Gingrich's trusted allies planned and later aborted his ousting. Trust is simply in short supply.

Values that we exalt in the culture with little debate lack clarity in our national legislative domain. Applying a code of honesty or fairness becomes ambiguous and complicated. If there is one thing probes and prosecutors, special counsels, and inquiring committees have taught us, it is that ethical line drawing is a messy business.

Against this backdrop of character and relationships, Congress moves through the business of taxing and spending, defending and protecting. Government up close is the political equivalent of the television show *ER*. The crashing forces of Congress and the executive branch put policy on a stretcher and slice it open to expose raw, pulsing struggles for power.

Working on the Hill, I could clearly see the modern dialectic of the aging American democratic experiment: our government is a system beyond saving and a miracle still unfolding. Adherents to the first argument are easily found. They are the pundits left, right, and center, the faceless unfavorables in relentless polls about how our government is doing, political leaders who torch their own house, and other naysayers with the notoriety to capture public attention. Camp followers on the miraculous side are harder to find.

Conjuring leaders with the moral purpose and values to bring the nation to a higher understanding of democratic mission and process is difficult at this time. We look for leaders who will struggle with the failings of government, even as they steer toward the fulfillment of our greatest aspirations as a nation. What we see instead are senators who pontificate and pine over the loss of campaign-finance innocence by day and revel in $1,000-per-plate fund-raisers of their own making by night. Our White House is a fictitious home and, in reality, a shop of political whore mongering. A Democratic president and his vice president find comfort in splitting legal hairs and exalting the ends over the means as they skirt with new and barely legal fund-raising techniques. A Republican vice president refashions the energy policies of the country with the advice of industry representatives almost exclusively, including large contributors; a Republican president describes his political base as the "haves" and the "have mores."

Transactions are rampant, often renegade. Yet transformations are rare. Can the better natures of transactional and transforming leadership exist in our political miasma? Can we muster the political hope to renew our political life? For politicians and others willing to be more conscious of the imperatives and responsibilities of leadership, the answer must be yes. After many years, during which much in government has changed but perhaps more has not, *Leadership* still offers the promise of its title. We can renew our political hope through our struggle to understand what Jim Burns sets out to explain.

Dialectical Politics

Democratic process is constantly revealing contradictions in our system of government. We have opposing parties who are supposed to craft legislation upon which a majority can agree. We have partisans, not only divided by party, but increasingly further divided by region and a devotion to special interests and the sense that reelection is a go-it-alone project. Ideology, practical politics, and party loyalty exert competing pressures. The result seems chaotic, unfocused, and unfettered to the demands of citizens.

We seize these contradictions as undeniable evidence of the failure of American politics. Why does not Congress get more done? Why cannot the executive and legislative branches work cooperatively, find ways to compromise, or at least be civil? In *Leadership*, Burns reminds us that dissension is an essential element of political growth, "the dynamo of political action." Burns invites students of leadership to embrace tension and the struggle of ideas as vital elements of leadership's full potential.

The most basic dissent confronting our leaders today is the widespread belief that politics and public service are mutually exclusive. That government is a troublemaker, but democracy is inviolate. That Congress is a thieving bunch, but the member of Congress who represents us is a worthy soul. Our political leaders are keenly aware of this, but are they responding as our times demand? The popular aspiration of patriotism is indoctrinated from childhood. We learn to believe in government, to be proud and respectful of the nation's democratic legacy. These beliefs are riven by the strife of scandals and attacks that characterize our government as wasteful and ineffectual. Does this conflict operate as the key democratizer of leadership? Are our leaders expanding the "field of combat, reach(ing) out for more followers," searching for allies? Of utmost importance, is this conflict "broaden(ing) and strengthen(ing) values," as Burns's focus on dissensus predicts? At a moment of perilous political decline, leadership must find the way to a greater appreciation and understanding of our democratic system.

Rule by Which People?

I spent a decade talking directly with wage-earning construction workers and their families and advocating for their concerns with the federal government. As part of the larger labor movement in the United States, I often saw polling from other unions—service and industrial workers, teachers, and state and local employees. These people believed in democracy. Few were searching for a new form of government or harking back to socialism or communism. They were searching for leaders they could trust with the burden and honor of representation. Many were keen followers of government.

The story of a taping of Speaker Gingrich's cellular phone conversations dramatically illustrated how astute ordinary citizens could be about their government. John and Alice Martin were driving to Jacksonville shortly before Christmas in 1996 when they accidentally intercepted a cellular phone call on their police scanner. They recognized the voices on the conference call as "real politicians." Knowing of the probe into Gingrich's ethics, they decided to tape the conversation they felt was a part of history. They ended up handing the tape over to the House Ethics Committee.

An important lesson for leaders was lost between the short waves and tall accusations that accompanied the tape's revelation. The Martins are high school-educated, middle-class wage earners. John does maintenance work at a public school. Alice is a teacher's aide. They vote in every election. They volunteer for political activity, as do their children. They work to organize their friends and neighbors to be politically active and aware. The Martins are not bowling alone. They are, however, paying more attention to government than most leaders presume ordinary citizens do. Remember, the Martins recognized the voices of Congress members. Living far from the halls of power, they nonetheless kept abreast of the probe of the speaker of the House and so realized the significance of the conversation they heard. Believing in their government, they tried to do what was right with the information they obtained.

Few political leaders recognize or are willing to acknowledge that an engaged citizenry, such as the Martins, exists. Fewer still can muster the hope and energy to engage the people sitting on the political margins. This ambivalence toward the polity by the political elite is a long-standing contradiction of the American democratic movement. Commenting from his ambassadorship in France on James Madison's updates from the Philadelphia convention, Thomas Jefferson expressed discomfort with election of the House of Representatives by the people. "I think a House chosen by them will be very illy qualified to legislate for the Union, for foreign nations, etc.," Jefferson fretted. He agreed to popular representation only because of his firm belief that the power to levy taxes should only be imposed by representatives directly chosen by the people.

Perhaps it is ambivalence toward the wisdom of citizens that explains present-day leaders' low expectations for renewing citizens' involvement in government. Our self-appointed public parents—national politicians and officials, current and former; media pundits; and academics—seek to enliven the democracy in baby steps. Community service, reinvigorating civic organizations, and voting must build democracy again, they tell us. Laudable goals in palatable bites for a citizenry viewed from on high as paralyzed and in serious need of gradual rehabilitation. *Leadership* reminds us that "leaders engage with followers, but from higher levels of morality; in the enmeshing of goals and values both leaders and followers are raised to more principled levels of judgment....this kind of elevating leadership asks sacrifices *from* followers rather than merely promising them goods" (Burns 1978:455).

In practical terms, this means reviving citizens who have lost faith in the notion that they can be governed well and that they can *be* the government. As much attention as Burns gives to Franklin Roosevelt, it was Eleanor Roosevelt who brought a heart to government programs of the New Deal and a human face of the ordinary people facing the hard times of the Depression and World War II. In the post-war era, she lifted her sights for all of us and forged an international commitment to human rights. Her work on the United Nations' Universal Declaration of Human Rights set a standard of political life that extends beyond governments and their interests. It calls all of us to a universal human standard (Gerber 2000). We need a new class of citizen legislators, and we are them.

Nevertheless, most of the great unelected do not believe they are electable. Another of our political contradictions rests in the vision of rule by the people in a time when "the people" have no sense that they can rule. We have traveled so far from the cultural myth that anyone can be president, much less a city council member, that most citizens have no vision of themselves running for, let alone winning, public office. This perception of them-and-us government, of a professional class of politicians to which few can or want to aspire, creates a revisionist social reality.

In the rich truth of our history, laborers, teachers, carpenters, and stay-at-home parents have won elective public office. Of course, many still are elected on the local level, fewer nationally. Yet our civic disdain, nurtured and fed by stories of political evil, rejects an empowering history of citizens within and in charge of their government. The media, through which we receive most of our political information, practice the politics of caricature. It is an art that enlarges small truths into the ridiculous, magnifying greed, dishonesty, and hypocrisy until we can find no trace of the true portrait of leadership. It is as if our political leaders have only clay feet, no head or heart.

Joe Legislator

Burns likes to play a "parlor game" that involves naming great leaders of the past twenty years, leading to the conclusion that we are caught in a historical moment of leadership deprivation. Whom can we name today to stand with the likes of Franklin Roosevelt, Gandhi, or Martin Luther King Jr.? It is a misleading result that, by the rules of the game, our times fail the test of producing great leaders. We are looking in the wrong places and making false comparisons. In a time when democracy is approaching literal construction, when initiatives and referenda are paving the way to direct representation through computer modems, great leaders may bear no more resemblance to those of the past than a ballot does to a disk drive.

In 1997, the Nobel Peace Prize was given to an unsung woman, Jody Williams, who started the International Campaign to Ban Landmines. She did it from her home in Vermont, sending her message across the Internet. Thousands rallied to the cause, took action, applied pressure, and achieved results, albeit not in the United States. The Nobel Prize served to focus attention on the kind of ordinary leader who is usually neglected by the rough draft of history we call news. In the state of Maine, Dale McCormick, a carpenter, started a model program to train women on welfare to do construction work. She wanted to do more, to direct the power of government toward the needs she had seen firsthand. McCormick won a seat in the state House and now serves as the state treasurer.

We are fast approaching the era when ordinary stories of leadership, by politicians or others, will be instantly notorious. Members of Congress are getting comfortable with websites and the Internet. The White House has put papers, speeches, and press releases on line. We are just beginning to explore the democratizing possibilities of progressive information technology. When they routinely tie the Internet into home television sets and campaigns take to using modems more than mail, what brave new world of politics will we see?

Songs of Political Leadership

Leaders can build on the conflict between our love of democracy and our loathing of government. They can help bridge the gulf that greets citizens who think of stepping into the halls of government. Leaders must look afresh at those who consent to be governed not as a passive, faceless mass to be polled and prodded, but as those who will lead in the future. If leaders will look with the new vision of open minds, the evidence of political prosperity for the country will start turning up everywhere.

In the late 1990s, in an unprecedented move, the AFL-CIO invited every union member they could identify who holds political office in the United States to a conference in Washington, D.C. These political leaders showed an interest in networking with others like themselves and gaining new ideas for change. The meeting was an extension of newfound political activism at all levels in the American labor movement.

A year or so earlier, the AFL-CIO, the umbrella organization for a federation of more than ninety labor unions, spent $35 million to publicize labor's message. The widely reported financial investment in media and mailings obscured news of the extensive grassroots political organizing among union members. The AFL-CIO had grassroots committees in seventy-five congressional districts; they received 17,404 pledge cards from union activists; they trained local political coordinators; and they tested a pilot program to elect union members to political office in three different states.

The labor movement's continuing political efforts need to be matched by political leaders who view leadership as a collective enterprise. This amounts to the handgun in Burns's "Armament of Leadership." The current links between political leaders and movements are pecuniary and temporal. Social movements of workers, environmentalists, women, and minorities all give money and campaign support during elections with little trace of any further connection to politicians and parties. As Burns argued, "The absence in the United States of a major party firmly based in a social movement has impaired the linkage between Americans and their leaders, especially the President."

One way to reconcile the cultural conflict, the paralyzing dialectic that splits democratic values from practice, is to create grandly inclusive politics. We have resolved our founding prejudices that vested the vote in a narrow polity. With the slow steps of decades, we granted all Americans the right to select those who would govern. Now, leaders must insist that all do govern. Not every child has to grow up thinking he can be president, but every child should grow up determined to serve in government at some point in his life.

Is this an unrealistic goal? Pie-in-the-sky patriotism? Consider that many states, including Maryland, require high school students to complete specified community service hours before graduation. It is a short step from volunteering in the community to serving in public office. Most political leaders have served in many community capacities from PTA president to signature-gatherer on a petition drive. Who is encouraging our volunteering young people to take the next step for their communities? Burns tells us that leaders have a special role as activators, initiators, and mobilizers. They must build passion for governing, or we will inch closer to a political void.

Town councils, state legislators, school boards, and county commissions across the country have many more seats than Congress has. In an era of power devolution from the federal government to the states, these positions are gaining importance. President Clinton signed the most sweeping reform of New Deal legislation in sixty years. Welfare reform will put states firmly in control of millions of dollars in assistance to the poor. A legislative transformation of that magnitude should be matched by a transformation in the practice of politics. Lynn Woolsey was a welfare mother who now serves in the House of Representatives. Will leadership accept the role of bringing forward more people like her?

Like Paul Bunyan, Horatio Alger, and Sojourner Truth, ordinary political leaders of today should become the subjects of tales that communicate civic values to us and to our children. As Burns reminds us, a century ago little boys wanted to grow up to be the scintillating pleader, defender, and wit who held the rapt attention of his fellow legislators and the fashionable ladies in the visitors' gallery. He echoes the lyrics of a song of social movements that sings of freedom as:

> A hard won thing,
> You've got to work for it, fight for it. . .
> And every generation's got to win it again.

Pass it on to your children, mother,
Pass it on to your children, father.

What aspirations for democratic participation are we passing on today? Who are
the role models of political leadership for our children?

Our Political Odyssey

In political training for the union, I reminded activists that politicians had three
priorities—get reelected, get reelected, and get reelected. That was a cynical
message, reflecting the distorted priorities of power in American government.
Politicians the world over are not all cast from the same mold, though. Like ex-
plorers stumbling upon a previously unknown civilization, the leaders of the
Czech Republic's Velvet Revolution astonished American journalists. When
asked if the radical changes they were making would not be a problem for their
reelection, the Czechs were puzzled. They focused the priority of their new
power on fundamentally changing a forlorn country. The thought of their own
political future simply had not crossed their minds.

As *Leadership* tells us, a person girded with moral purpose, whether leader
or follower, is a tiny principality of power. Like a quixotic traveler making her
own map, I searched and found such dominions in the U.S. Congress. There
were and are congresswomen and –men, who will vote against party and president to stop an onerous welfare law from passing; who will defy a brilliant and
powerful leader for their belief in a smaller, less intrusive government, despite
the consequences for those who need public services; and who will vote for a tax
bill to taunts from the opposition party, even when they are certain to be de-
feated in the next election for doing so. Our challenge is to elect more leaders of
substance and fewer with shallow purpose.

I came to Capitol Hill in 1985 to lobby for the United Brotherhood of Carpenters and Joiners of America. I was a labor lawyer and I had experience on the
Hill, as do many lobbyists. I worked for subcommittees in the House of Representatives that dealt with labor issues. Shortly after I arrived, they indicted the
representative who hired me. *Leadership* was just beginning to influence the
world when one of the most well-regarded and beloved leaders in the House was
caught in a fraud dubbed "Abscam." Frank Thompson, known as Thompy to
most, left the Hill in shame. A month into my tenure on the Hill, I had learned a
few lessons about political leadership: those entrusted with the power of leadership may violate that trust and cruelly disappoint those who believed in them.

As a young, new arrival on Capitol Hill, I considered the member of Congress I worked for to be the government. The Abscam scandal reframed my
view of government from that time on. The scandal exposed the underside of
Burns's transactional leadership. In Abscam, members took money for influence, and by doing so, exposed the shrunken shape of representation that had
evolved on Capitol Hill. The Democrats had held a majority in the House for
more than a quarter century when I arrived on the Hill. This political stasis ex-
aggerated the Democrats' sense of power. The majority members of the House
and Senate sat atop a strict and complicated hierarchy of power. Everything
from parking spaces, to furniture, office space, budgets, and positions on com-

mittees was carefully and closely controlled. Legitimate transactions were the order of the day, and illegal transactions still were the stuff of active rumors. Subject only to their own rules, the Congress was a cauldron of bubbling trades. Quid did not always immediately follow quo. Unspoken understandings became hard currency.

Transactional demands became more apparent to lobbyists like me. Our union spent $1.5 million in federal political contributions in every two-year election cycle. Money and union volunteers sent to work in campaigns were powerful tools to open a conversation with members of Congress. Endless fundraising receptions offered opportunities to talk with members. Organized outings and trips created venues to build relationships. Small, private gatherings, office meetings, and briefings were all part of a network open only to those who could trade in the currency of politics: money and votes. Of course, given the revelation of White House coffees and sleepovers in the Clinton administration, and the Bush administration's politics of "insider trading," my experiences with the ordinary trade-offs of Washington political life seem tame.

To citizens, the seemingly constant access and influence, bought and sold, shrouds political acts of principle when they do occur. Congress as an institution is circling its wagons. In the fall of 1997, the House Ethics Committee changed its rules for bringing an ethics charge. Citizens, who formerly could bring a charge after proving that three members of Congress had refused to do so, now are shut out entirely. Only members of Congress can bring ethics charges against their own and the parties called a truce shortly after taking that power to themselves. The ordinary citizen is apparently unwanted in the everyday machinations of political life on the Hill. Other than as numbers on poll and focus-group reports, where do those with the power to elect our political leaders exist in the national political realm?

We have focused enormous energy on taking the money out of politics but far less on bringing citizens into political life. Working in a social movement, I tried to bridge the gap workers felt as they tried to understand the workings of government. They wanted more information and less interpretation. More communication about issues of concern to members encouraged their increased involvement in politics. Working people were willing to travel the roads of politics, volunteering in campaigns, meeting with elected officials, sometimes running for office themselves, but they wanted a map. They could master what they understood, but governing was unintelligible. Political leaders played an exclusive game, often in the secret confines of rules committees or with procedural machinations.

Recent exposure of the underside of questionable, if legal, practices in Washington helps drive a larger focus on the fundamentals of democracy. States are reviewing and revising campaign finance and election laws. Alexis de Tocqueville's travels are being relived. *Civil society* has become the catch phrase for renewing the citizen-centered part of the process we call government. This political odyssey is no less fraught with temptations and deception than when Homer wrote about leadership. Failure and redemption, bad choices and renewed commitment, and the quintessentially human desire to eschew complacency in favor of challenge remain guideposts to our expectations for political leadership.

Conclusion

In his hopeful introduction to *Leadership*, Burns put political leadership at the heart of the world as it could be. As promised, he showed that "political leadership depends on a long chain of biological and social processes, of interaction with structures of political opportunity and closures, of interplay between the calls of moral principles and the recognized necessities of power." He believes that "in placing these concepts of political leadership centrally into a theory of historical causation, we will reaffirm the possibilities of human volition and of common standards of justice in the conduct of peoples' affairs" (Burns 1978:3-4).

In turning to *Leadership*, as I often do for explanation and inspiration, I know I am traveling with another optimist of the human spirit. Perhaps that is a prerequisite to an endeavor as daring as explaining leadership. If there is a place called "hope" in politics, it resides in the visionary possibilities for leadership that Burns presents in his groundbreaking, path-making book.

References

Burns, J. M. 1978. *Leadership.* New York, N.Y.: Harper & Row, Publishers.
Gerber, R. 2000. Leadership the Eleanor Roosevelt Way: Timeless Lessons from the First Lady of Courage. New York, N.Y.: De Capo Press.

CHAPTER 14
LEADERSHIP FROM THE BOTTOM UP
By Ronald Walters

Leadership was more than a revelation for me. It contained a veritable feast of ideas, many of which were consistent with my past study of the processes of social change. In his work, Burns agreed with Gunnar Myrdal (1944) that the issue of race in America was a great moral issue and portrayed the civil rights movement as a great moral struggle that was "the most dramatic test in modern democracies of the power of leaders to elevate followers and of followers to sustain leaders" (Burns 1978:455). Burns wrote with a sweep of history that captured the leadership dimension of the great revolutions of our time, consistent with many of the more focused studies of revolutionary movements (Bell 1973; Brinton 1960; Cruse 1968; Fanon 1968; Memi 1965). These works were important studies of organizational dynamics in an environment

In 1978, I returned to the Department of Political Science at Howard University from a three-year interim appointment as Director of Social Science Research at the University. I wanted to offer a course on black leadership organizations and movements. In 1979, I began to look for course material and found Jim Burns's book, *Leadership*.

of high mobilization. They addressed the radical changes that the peoples of color in Asia, Africa, or Latin America were leading, and captured the resistance motif and the "centrifugal" action of the civil rights, Black Power, and pan-African movements and other domestic American social movements of the 1960s.

Leaders and Movements

Burns's ideas supported my intuitive understanding of leadership garnered from my own activist past that began in the civil rights movement. In 1958 I led what was perhaps the first of the modern sit-ins in my hometown of Wichita, Kansas. I attended Fisk University in Nashville, Tennessee, during the height of the sit-ins elsewhere and the early stirrings of the civil rights movement. People such as John Lewis, Dianne Nash, and others were classmates of mine; I was a witness to their committed actions. When I came to graduate school in 1963 at American

University in Washington, D.C., I became active in social-change groups in the city throughout the 1960s and 1970s. As I became a professional academic, the civil rights movement started to emphasize black community control and development that germinated activity in the field of electoral politics.

This pattern of academic work and activism followed me to my first job at Syracuse University where, as an assistant professor in the Maxwell School, I founded a community organization, Coalition for Quality Education, with which to work. In addition, in 1969 when I went to Brandeis University to chair its first Afro-American Studies Department, I joined the Boston anti-apartheid movement. In 1971 I became chair of the Political Science Department at Howard and continued my activism as an organizer for several different organizations. So, after twenty years of activism and study, I came to leadership and *Leadership*.

I recognized that there needed to be far more attention given to the academic study of black leadership as a critical dimension to the success of the social movements of the 1960s and 1970s. We needed to move beyond the stereotypical attention unto the activities of Dr. Martin Luther King Jr., as an individual, and the heads of the other civil rights organizations. The literature of my field, political science, shed no light on this hidden dimension of leadership. The entire field of sociology barely recognized it at the time. Theories of "resource mobilization" were just beginning to be fashionable. As a result, my approach to political issues became far more eclectic. I began to attend meetings of the American Sociological Association and the newly formed Caucus of Black Sociologists, where I encountered the ideas of Aldon Morris (1986) and Doug McAdams (1982).

Their emphasis on the historical context led me logically to assume that part of the reason for the emergence of certain individuals during these movements was the importance of the historical period as a context within which many "heroic" operated. Indeed, Burns implies such a view in the opening pages of his work. He mentions that he grew up in the era when the "titans" of leadership were on the scene (Burns 1978:1-2). Later, he indicates that "heroic leaders" appear to be, not only those who enjoy popular favor of the masses, but extraordinary individuals who often appear in the midst of crises.

For him, the crisis in leadership in a heroic age, manifested by people all over the world, emerges from the need for moral leadership to address a gap in need fulfillment. Aaron Wildavsky pointed out the problem for a leader when great demands exceed great support (Wildavsky 1989:97). I do not view this as a gap in the personal dimension of leadership, except insofar as individuals must arise to meet the challenge of need fulfillment. These gaps define the situation in which a group must be led to achieve certain needs it demands be addressed, such as the voter registration by leaders, such as white registrars, whom they may not support. These theoretical ideas of both Burns and Wildavsky appear to define not only the context of black leadership, but its intensity as well.

Although there was not much in Burns's book about black movements, his elucidation of the role of leaders gave me a useful framework for approaching a dynamic issue that seemed to account for some of the successes. These ideas were important in the publication of my first article on black leadership in the late 1970s. In it, I attempted to account for the "shift" in strategy of black organizational leaders from civil rights tactics and strategies to the arenas of political legislatures and bureaucratic agencies and the relationship between the two in producing values for black communities (Walters 1980). The Reagan era that followed the 1970s, however, presented a new crisis from an African-American standpoint. This further attracted me to search for a greater understanding of the most salient dynamics that would yield a leadership response to the drastic changes occurring in both national politics and public policy. My second work on black leadership, published in 1985, dealt with many of these themes in a series of essays in the *Urban League Review*.

Then, in 1993 while planning the commemoration of the 1963 March on Washington, some youths on the planning committee approached me with the complaint that the character of their participation had become an issue. Their complaint resulted in a special role for them in the commemoration. I attempted to further their interests in leadership with funding from the Dwight E. Eisenhower Leadership Program of the Department of Education and began the Leadership Education and Development (LEAD) Program at Howard University. We had many interesting discussions of the concepts contained in Burns's work illustrating both transactional and transforming leadership in the black community.

The program selected thirty participants and put them through a first-semester curriculum in leadership studies that featured both readings and case-study presentations by well-known leaders. This led to a second-semester placement with a leader, in a variety of fields; a mentor relationship rather than the traditional "intern" experience. Ultimately, my aim was to train a new cadre of young leaders, to utilize the interactions with other black leadership clearly, and to build a model for further research and training. Unfortunately, the Eisenhower Leadership Program in the Department of Education lasted only two years (1994-1996). My experience in the program, including meeting with other program directors, exposed me to the bewildering variety of approaches to the study and practice of leadership that existed uneasily under the umbrella of "leadership studies." Another program director, Georgia Sorenson, helped me to distinguish between some of these approaches and the moral dimension of leadership. I now had a greater desire to both enhance the study of African-American leadership and to understand where it intersected with other varieties.

Leadership during Crisis and Change

The civil rights movement was not only an important action era for social change; it was a laboratory for the study of the elements of leadership in the process of change activities, such as the use of charisma and ideology. Both flowed through Martin Luther King Jr., but the power of the movement did not emanate from the charisma and ideology of King.

In a discussion of Burns's characterization of ideological leadership, Peter Temes uses King's leadership as an example of one that was "almost entirely philosophical" (Temes 1996:74). However, King's leadership was activist ori-

ented. It stimulated social actions aimed at applying pressure on reluctant officials to bring about change. Thus, although Temes considers the text of King's
"Letter from the Birmingham Jail" as his primary reference for this statement,
he should also remember that King wrote it while in jail! Temes's work resem-
bles the normal academic treatment of the civil rights movement and others like
it. They rarely consider black leadership to possess a serious infrastructure comprised of thinkers, strategists, organizers, and resource providers—elements
upon which King depended and which further contextualize his leadership and
the leadership of other movement leaders like him.

This leadership literature also overlooks that ideology can provide leadership in two ways. Ideology may come from above, enforced by military might,
as in Burns's example of the Communist Revolution, the writings of Chairman
Mao, and the great Chinese Cultural Revolution. The other way is for ideology
to emerge from the bottom, for conditions to manifest themselves such that a
group of people is ready for leadership and for the emergence of a set of concepts that define their reality in terms that they understand and can embrace.
King provided ideological leadership from the bottom up because, in Temes's
marvelous phrase, the ideas King utilized "[rode] on the souls of the people"
(Temes 1996:80). King's charisma and the impact of his ideology were the
"readiness" of people to receive his message and to act upon it. They did so, by
virtue of the perceived legitimacy of the message, in light of their own experiences, and by the force of his presentation. These were the keys to the "activat-
ing function" of King's leadership.

The Activating Function

Although Burns does not make copious references to the black political movements or other styles of black leadership, he provides substantial theoretical
grounding for a vision of the formation of social movements. For example, he
suggests that when people are ready for leadership, it may take the form of ini-
tiation of action and/or activation of latent sentiment. He depicts leaders as activators who help the masses become aware of their conditions, that something
can or should be done about it, and that they will have to do it. Such was the
status of many Southern pre-civil rights blacks. He then goes on to discuss the
consequence of this awareness in terms of a "logical chain of actions" (Burns
1978:268).

King describes this process eloquently with respect to his view that crisis
and conflict are embedded in the relations between blacks and whites. The conflict is latent because of the "objective conditions" of racial dominance and subordination that has historically structured it. Thus, the role of the leader is to
employ the instruments to activate it, to bring it to light so that it can be resolved
(Temes 1996:85). John Brown Childs suggests that the role of the activator is
typical of what he calls "vanguard" groups whose task it is to "lift the people out
of the stage of unconscious dormant energy and to give them an awareness of
their own strength by directing them how to act. The sleeping masses cannot

undertake such an act themselves. Instead, their awakening must be accomplished by a group outside the state of immobilizing them" (Childs 1989:3).

So leaders activate followers based on the nature of the latent conflict. However, followers have to be ready to be activated. If they are prepared, then Burns refers to these as "activated followers" (Burns 1978:130). In the interactive process between leader and followers, leaders employ what Burns calls the "kindling power" to ignite the fires of commitment and mobilization to a cause. He believes that followers exist in diverse degrees of latency and potential incitement; they hold beliefs, attitudes, needs, and values of varying intensity. This part of Burns's analysis describes the quality of King's leadership power (Burns 1978:137).

King was an exceptional leader who had the "kindling power," but the aroused power of his followers was as significant to his success as any other element. Indeed, we might attribute the character of the recent movement era of black history and its fertile ground for the emergence of leaders and organizations of all sorts more to the objective cause-activated status of followers rather than to any other elements.

Jim Burns and the Search for "Good" Leaders

Burns gives significant and meaningful attention to "good" leadership, moral leadership and the values leaders attempt to activate. The morality of the black struggle for justice, and thus the values of its leadership, have been bound up in the quest for the achievement of a role in American society equal with other citizens through the elimination of racism and the enhancement of the resource base of the black community. The kernel of that morality contains the certain knowledge that slavery entailed the degradation of black humanity and that America has not yet made just recompense for that heinous historical act and the post-slavery subordination of blacks as well. This knowledge constitutes the moral basis upon which black leadership pursues the demand of just recompense and justice. Much of the content of black-white leadership tension of the moment is an issue of whether or not that claim will continue to have currency in the political system.

Leadership includes the insurgency of those who would challenge civil authority and established social practices with demands for inclusion and a fairer distribution of social resources. Temes's view of King's moral insurgency was that:

- good and evil exist [as reflected in the way in which the racial-opportunity structure is configured];
- the peace that suppresses the conflict of good and evil is harmful; and,
- therefore, the peace, institutions, and practices that suppress the conflict of good and evil must be challenged in order that the good may triumph over evil (Temes 1996:75).

This idea has supported the legitimacy of public policy in its view that racial discrimination—exclusion and subordination—was evil and that racial integration and equality were good. Therefore, measures of peaceful conflict that promoted remedies that resulted in promoting the good were justified.

Burns correctly engages in a search for good leadership based upon the values leaders prioritize. There is no objective standard of good leadership other than values. The values that comprise good leadership are also culturally relative and are divined from the perspective of the various groups often engaged in a contest, each protesting to have morality on their side. Hitler undoubtedly thought that he was doing "good" for the German people in a twisted way.

Nowhere is this better seen than in the current struggle over affirmative action. Conservative ideologists view as "immoral" any racial preferences whatsoever. They do not eschew white privilege and the attendant preferences that comprise their dominance in society. They believe they are right, as in righteous, and that the "immorality" of affirmative action constitutes a sufficient justification to eliminate it. They stridently oppose those who believe that because of past and present racial subordination, there needs to be some racial amelioration to achieve equality in fact.

What is "good" may be the dominant consensus about social values, which is to say that power often determines what is "good" and "right." The swing in the moral attitude of the American people away from civil rights and affirmative action cannot be justified logically on the grounds that the promotion of civil rights today is "bad" because it has caused an imbalance in the power between the races. Nevertheless, this is the perception. The attack on civil rights and other race-based social policies has occurred in political settings that constitute an imposition of values by the majority and amounts to a new round of racial subordination. Where in this reactive setting is the residual quality of the moral claim of blacks to social justice? It is in politics beginning with people who value social equality forming a consensus around values and then projecting them into the political system through leadership.

Leadership as Insurgency

Most of the leadership projects in the black community have aimed toward change of the status of blacks. They seek changes in public accommodations, education, voting, housing, welfare, or economic development that increase the relative share of public resources for the black community. These change efforts require a substantial focus on the mobilization of power. Thus, leaders have often emerged who helped to increase that power quotient in demonstrable ways, most often through the organization of people power in the absence of civil and public resources. "Good" black leaders then are those who have struggled, in whatever arena was available to them, for resources with which the black community might progress. This has often meant that the "good" black leader was a person who would struggle for change.

My own orientation to leadership studies rests on this "insurgent" model. It takes into consideration such factors as:

- the setting: the leadership of the black community and, thus, the cultural dimension of leadership studies,
- the challenge: the social system within that leadership is set as well as the race and class dimensions which formulate the leadership program, and

• the content: the propensity for black leadership projects to stress the necessity
of change.

The nature of the change sought by black leadership varies with the challenges
of each age. Although my initial change orientation contained a substantial appreciation for radical and revolutionary change situations and strategies, Harold
Cruse convinced me that the size of the black community and its status and its
resources mean different forms of change:

> The Negro movement at this moment is not a revolutionary movement because
> it has no present means or program to alter the structural forms of American in-
> stitutions. It is pure political romanticism, at this point, to call the Negro
> movement the 'Negro revolution.' It is more properly called the 'Negro rebel-
> lion' against the American racial status quo (Cruse 1968:101).

Indeed, the Negro movement is a rebellion against the status quo in every
conceivable arena of American life, using a variety of permissibly legal tactics.
Cruse, however, is not altogether correct. It was not "pure political romanticism"
which gave the media and black leaders the vision of a revolutionary change in
the nature of their status through the use of these tactics. Nevertheless, he is correct in that the goals of the rebellion were consistent with the desire for inclusion
into the social, political, and economic order; embracing the philosophical and
constitutional vision of the American Founding Fathers explains the consensus
in the views of a host of leaders of disparate ideologies, such as Malcolm X,
Roy Wilkins, Martin Luther King Jr., Minister Farrakhan, and Jesse Jackson. Of
course, there have been more radical leaders who have advocated more revolutionary goals, such as George Jackson, Huey Newton, Angela Davis, or Elijah
Muhammad. Although important as occasional historical barometers of the
depths of black alienation, these more radical goals have not been accepted by
the mainstream of the black community. A desire for inclusion bound the locus
of change. Although the tactics and strategies at times looked revolutionary, in
the end, they were designed to be consistent with inclusion.

The Issue of Authenticity

The dominant political system contains the resources important to the elevation
of the black community, thus its leaders always had to be aware of the dominant
values of the social system, which set the ideological context and conduct of
major political institutions. Most non-white cultural groups are located in the
subordinate strata of the class structure. The system also defines the resources
available to the dominant majority and the subordinate minority groups, as well
as prospects for change in the distribution of these resources.

Blacks are a comparatively resource-disadvantaged community because of
the racial antagonisms visited upon them through the prism of the black/white
relations that originated in the social system of slavery. This system provided
the bedrock for many of the modern behavioral manifestations of the
black/white social relationship and maintains racial stereotypes and patterns of
institutional outcomes that have strongly negative racial implications.

Thus, racism influences the distribution of benefits for blacks and both the structural and racial definitions of black life. It defines the possibilities of leadership. To put it bluntly, whites often determine the limits of black leadership and thereby are more powerful symbolic leaders of the black community in terms of the distribution of national benefits.

The context of a larger nation of communities and a racially stratified society raises the irony of "leadership" by relatively less powerful groups, an irony even greater because of the vast differences in both the absolute and proportional dimensions of power in American society between blacks and whites. Census data from 1990 suggests that whether one measures economic power in terms of wealth (10:1), or income (10:6), or Fortune 500 firms (500:1); or political power in terms of the number of elected officials (97:3); or virtually any other power ratio that one would want to examine, leadership would appear to be a function of white power and not for the underclass (Bennett 1995).

In its confrontation with the political system, the black community has had to mobilize pressure that forced the system to consider its demands. In doing so, it has established an important model of legal theory and administrative practice, important to the empowerment of both other non-white groups seeking to enter society and all Americans who have a form of serious disadvantage.

The fundamental matter of resources raises the question of the contours, limits, and possibilities of black leadership, even the question of who is considered a legitimate black leader. For example, previous public opinion polls have consistently showed that among blacks, Jesse Jackson ranked first as a black leader (Gallup Poll 1993). Yet in its November 1997 issue, *Vanity Fair* identified sixty-five top leaders and Jackson was not among them. Ironically, the same month, he became the special emissary to Africa of the president and of the secretary of state and led a demonstration of thousands of people in Sacramento, California, against the affirmative-action stance of the political leaders in that state. Obviously, the editors of *Vanity Fair* had every right to draw up their own list of world leaders. They included blacks such as Colin Powell, Minister Louis Farrakhan, and Nelson Mandela, and even though they did not pretend to speak for any group other than their own magazine, their class/race perspective appears in the exclusion of a black leader whom the black community recognizes.

The *Vanity Fair* lists suggest how whites often manufacture black leadership, not malignly, but according to their own needs and perspectives. Whatever the intent, the consequences of white choices of black leaders often distort or change the legitimate context of leadership as it flows from the racial or ethnic group in question. Does it suffice to ask, as one television talk show host asked ex-basketball great Kareem Abdul-Jabar, about the educational needs of black children (WTGG-TV 1997)? Perhaps, at that moment, Jabar's opinion might motivate a youth to pay closer attention to his or her studies. However, celebrity must be distinguished from leadership. Celebrity gives individuals public visibility, one of the ingredients important to exercising leadership. However, it does not confer all the other characteristics that are necessary to move communities of people toward civic goals.

In that light, Colin Powell illustrates the standard that a black person must achieve in American society to be considered capable of leading all races in the nation. Powell emerged in the fall of 1995 in the minds of many Americans as a possible candidate for president. From that moment, most Republicans viewed him as a leading candidate for national office. What leadership qualities does he possess that make him appear to be acceptable to most of the white population at the same time that he is substantially not as acceptable to blacks? He earned his reputation outside of government and thus escaped the negative opinion of government held by many Americans. He is a military man with proven fidelity to his county; he is a charismatic figure in appearance; he has adopted moderate views on social issues, with the exception of affirmative action; and whites view him as "raceless."

Blacks, on the other hand, appear to have concluded that many of the same qualities cast doubt upon his legitimacy to perform as a "black leader." He served in the Reagan administration, renowned for its attack on issues and programs considered important to blacks; he directed the Gulf War and the invasion of the black countries of Grenada and Panama, acts considered to be unpopular by blacks; he has declared himself to be a Republican when Republicanism meant attacks on social programs; and as secretary of state he has served point for the inherent contradictions of President George W. Bush's international relations. Colin Powell is not yet considered to be a "black leader" by most African-Americans, a fact which does not disqualify him in the future.

Because of his prominence and his color, Powell and other white-approved leaders present a danger of providing "safe" substitutes for black leaders with authentic ties to their community, political roles, and unsettling demands for the political system. Ultimately, what makes Powell or anyone else an authentic leader of blacks is not skin color but cultural grounding. Whether or not black leadership is determined by color or culture, authentic black leadership must begin with its definition by blacks themselves (Walters and Smith 1999).

Temes suggests that King's successful leadership depended upon his intimate knowledge of the needs of black people and his association with them and their culture. From this Temes extrapolates the general postulate: "To teach students to be leaders, then, we must help them cultivate a serious understanding of ordinary people as they live their lives today" (Temes 1996:76). "Bottom-up" leadership begins with the demands of a community for its needs of survival, and development of these demands constitutes the essential challenges that leadership addresses (Walters 1999). Perhaps one of Burns's major failings is a less-than-explicit elaboration of the concept of community as the basis of leadership and the dimensions of community to which leadership is directed (Burns 1978:131). This is important because all social change projects involve some aspect of community rehabilitation and maintenance.

Bottom-Up Organization

Locating the community as the source of leadership does not resolve the issue of what sector of the community leadership should emerge for it to be the most authentic. Harold Cruse observed during the height of the civil rights movement that it was led by "bourgeoisie Negroes" and if the revolutionary wing of the movement did not create its own ideology and methodology, it would render the "revolutionary" potential of the movement a myth. The bourgeois element would emerge as the defining element of the entire movement (Cruse 1968:189).

Now, many groups are engaged in an attempt to revitalize the civic culture of cities that have suffered from neglect. The rehabilitation movements spawned by this effort have sought to mobilize citizens to engage each other as a necessary prelude to the successful encounter with the issues that are pertinent to the enhancement in the quality of life of their community. No progressive advance in civic culture can take place without a change in the status of those at the bottom that permits them to join a democratic civic culture in a truly corporate enterprise. What often substitutes for such change is the appropriation of representatives from the bottom into projects of rehabilitation that reinforce the status quo, with little meaningful resource transfer.

It is entirely possible for new "development" or the "revival of civic culture" to take place in a context of racial and class exclusion. The traditional leadership structures of many of the older urban areas has been exclusive, and although many of the older cities have passed into the hands of black political leadership, the white business establishment has either fled or made an uneasy rapprochement with its black political counterpart. It may be that the newer, growing "edge cities" and counties to which the black middle class has migrated are the incubators of new experiments in democratic leadership (Pierce and Johnson 1997).

At a national level, the issue of "the bottom" was the perspective of the 1984 and 1988 Jesse Jackson presidential campaigns. It spoke to the class position, not only of blacks, but also of other disadvantaged cultural groups in general and illustrated how dynamic leadership for social change must be postured in the electoral arena. The Jackson campaign was, from the beginning, a movement devoted to raising questions and devising solutions for the bottom half of society. As such, it was an untraditional effort and destined to fail as a reform movement in American politics. The Democratic party and its leadership did accept some of the issue proposals of the two Jackson campaigns, such as the rejection of South African apartheid, the use of pension funds for social development projects, elimination of the trade deficit, retraining of American workers, the War on Drugs, and the like (Walters 1990). However, the party's faithful firmly rejected his claim to the power that might have made possible the actualization of some of these issues. In recent times, the traditional candidates for president have appealed to the class interests of the rich and the middle class, the aberration being the Johnson campaign of 1964 that occurred in the midst of the civil rights movement.

Class Interests and the Bottom-Up Perspective

The bottom-up perspective must eventually confront the problem of class interest since many blacks have become part of the middle class because of individual initiatives and the successes of the civil rights/Black Power movements. Their new roles bring them within major institutions that serve the interests of the nation as a whole. Their dilemma is whether and how much to emphasize, from their new vantage point, the continuing quest for change in the black community and the morality which supports it, by expending the emotional and other personal resources in an environment within which they are vulnerable. This is evident in the personal crises which confront many blacks about mounting a charge of racism for perceived maltreatment of themselves or other minorities within institutions; decisions of whether to support decisions made by black leaders such as leaving work to participate in the Million Man March or the Million Woman March; validating the views of black public spokespersons in the context of interracial situations; and using their personal resources to support black causes or patterns of consumption. These and many other decisions confront the new black middle class as they manifest the tension in their new class position while confronting the existing vitality of the old ways of challenging injustice.

Therefore, much of the internal politics of the black community concerns the appropriate strategy to address existing problems. An emerging strain declares that the pursuit of economic power is the new phase of the civil rights movement. The leadership of the NAACP has emphasized this phase by its *reciprocity* campaign directed at the hotel industry and at other corporations that do business in the black community. Long a part of the arsenal of black leadership strategy, the idea of reciprocity stirred up "Don't Buy Where You Can't Work" campaigns mounted by the NAACP in many cities in the 1940s and 1950s. Since the 1960s, it was the basis of Jesse Jackson's Operation Breadbasket and the "Fair Share" agreements with corporations propounded by the SCLC, the NAACP, and other civil rights organizations. In the early 1970s this theme of economic development became the watchword of the Joint Center for Political and Economic Studies as it sought to usher in a new generation of black elected officials and focus them on an agenda for change. As the conservative era continues and racism persists, a significant question of resources and tactics confronts black leadership: to fight against the backward-looking issues of racism or to mount forward-looking projects and campaigns of change.

Multicultural Leadership

Although the process of identifying "authentic" black leadership originates within the black community, whites have an enormous role in legitimizing black leadership. Black leaders have to work within the confines of white-dominated institutions to transmit black interests. To the extent that these institutions confer status upon black leaders and recognize their racial authority and role, this "biracial" source of legitimacy enhances the function of black leaders in the tasks they perform.

Several of Burns's concepts extend and sharpen the discussion about content, context, and legitimacy of leadership. They help us understand in detail the fundamental dynamics of black leadership as political mobilization of the black

community in community organization and electoral politics. Rather than allowing the weight of the leadership literature to be decisive, however, our task will
be to let the experience of blacks determine the shape of analytical models of
leadership. This blend of experience and scholarship should serve as a critique
of the existing leadership literature and add certain richness to it from the perspective of a cultural community.

The need for culturally linked leadership frameworks is all the more important in light of the challenge facing this country. Leaders of color will come to
play a more important role not only in the lives of their constituent cultural
groups, but also in the lives of all Americans. Leadership is one of the last preserves of privilege in the construction of a new democratic society. It reflects the
power position and social status of the dominant group. There is a very real
sense in which white-skin privilege creates a "bottomness" for all people of
color in America, which often makes their class positions conflate into a subordinate status, depending upon the issue. We need to prepare for the diversity of a
new leadership structure in both the private and public arenas. President Clinton
attempted to engage the public in preparing the changing context of race relations in response to the changing demographics with the creation of a national
discussion about race.

There are two broad categories where the leaders of diverse groups of white
and non-whites may work together where their interests might harmonize. Qual-
ity-of-life issues, such as transportation, government services, housing, environmental quality, and consumer protection, affect the residual group of whites
in the urban areas and the expanding suburbanization of blacks, Hispanics, and
Asians. Second, some issues, such as affirmative action, have a strong race- or
ethnic-valued character and may forge coalitions among people of color with
similar interests in social-justice issues as they face the white majority group.

The necessity to create a power grid that has the capacity to sustain a system of moral values and resources requires multiracial and multiethnic leadership coalitions. Leadership is a function of group integrity. For coalitional leadership groups to function well, group members must respect this integrity. Without it, coalitions are generally shallow affairs and exist on a horizontal level,
lacking real substance. When leadership comes from deep roots planted in cultural communities, each of the sets of interests in the organizations represented
has the possibility of genuinely transforming leadership.

Yet there is a very real sense in which white-skin privilege creates a "bottomness" for all people of color in America, often making their class positions
conflate into a subordinate status. The need for political coalition among cultural
groups at the bottom of society to achieve social justice fits into the paradigm of
a leadership that is authentic in being culturally linked. That is to say, to the extent that blacks, Hispanics, Native Americans, and Asians construct political
coalitions to fight racism, they will be more effective if they are comprised of
authentic leaders. Bottom-up projects, such as the elimination of poverty, access
to the labor force, the viability of voting rights, access to health services and
decent housing, and many others, create opportunities for coalitions as these
groups become an even greater proportion of the American population. In the

terms of James MacGregor Burns, moral leadership is required to assume the task of pursuing the social justice agenda reflected above.

Conclusion

The question raised above with the respect to the *Vanity Fair* decisions is whether or not blacks who operate predominantly within the context of white institutions and interests may be considered to be "black leaders." Here I would manifest substantial doubt, and any contrary assertion would be not only the issue of whether or not a black person considers himself or herself to be a representative of black interest, but the degree to which that person is grounded or associated in the legitimacy system of the black community in any critical fashion at all.

For the foreseeable future, I believe that it is important to attempt to understand in greater detail the fundamental dynamics of black leadership in the fields of community organization, electoral politics, bureaucratic politics, and others relevant to the black community. The objective would be to design reflective models of theorized behavior which might yield more results for research and practical testing. In this work, the utilization of a "transforming" or "transformational" (a distinction yet to be decided) leadership concept will be useful; but rather than allow the weight of the leadership literature to be decisive, the task will be to let the real experience of blacks determine the shape of the models. As such, this experience would ultimately serve as a critique of the existing leadership literature and add a certain richness to it from the perspective of a cultural community.

References

Bell, D. 1973. *Resistance and Revolution*. Boston, Mass.: Houghton Mifflin.
Bennett, C. E. 1995. "The Black Population in the United States: March 1994 and 1993." Bureau of the Census, U.S. Department of Commerce (January).
Brinton, C. 1960. *Anatomy of Revolution*. New York, N.Y.: Vintage Book.
Burns, J. M. 1978. *Leadership*. New York, N.Y.: Harper and Row.
Childs, J. B. 1989. *Leadership, Conflict, and Cooperation in Afro-American Social Thought*. Philadelphia, Penn.: Temple University Press.
Cruse, H. 1968. *Rebellion or Revolution*. New York, N.Y.: William Morrow.
Fanon, F. 1968. *The Wretched of the Earth*. New York, N.Y.: Grove Press.
Gallup Poll. 1993. *CNN/USA Today* (August).
Hagopian, M. N. 1974. *The Phenomenon of Revolution*. New York, N.Y.: Dodd and Mead.
McAdams, D. 1982. *Political Process and the Development of Black Insurgency*. Chicago, Ill.: University of Chicago.
Memi, A. 1965. *The Colonizer and the Colonized*. Boston, Mass.: Beacon Pres.
Morris, A. D. 1986. The Origins of the Civil Rights Movement: Black Communities Organizing for Change. New York, N.Y.: The Free Press.
Peirce, N. and C. Johnson. 1997. *Boundary Crossers: Community Leadership for a Global Age*. College Park, Md.: University of Maryland, Burns Academy of Leadership.

Temes, P. 1996. *Teaching Leadership: Essays in Theory and Practice*. New York, N.Y.: Peter Lang.

Urban League Review. 1985. Tenth Anniversary Edition, 9:1 (Summer).

Walters, R. 1980. "The Challenge of Black Leadership: An Analysis of the Problem of Strategy Shift." *Urban League Review*, 5(1), 77-88.

-----. 1990. "The Issue Politics of the Jesse Jackson Campaign for President in 1984." In L. Morris (Ed.), *The Social and Political Implications of the 1984, Jesse Jackson Presidential Campaign,* pp. 15-48. New York, N.Y.: Praeger.

-----. 1993. "The Sit-in Movement in the Mid-West." Paper presented at the conference, "African Americans in the Mid-West." Center for Great Plains Stories, University of Nebraska at Lincoln (Spring).

----. 1999. "A Paradigm of the Practice of Black Leadership." In R. Walters and R. Smith (Eds.), *Black Leadership: Theory, Research and Praxis*, Albany, N.Y.: SUNY Press.

---- and R. Smith, (Eds). 1999. *Black Leadership: Theory, Research and Praxis*. Albany, N.Y.: SUNY Press.

Wildavsky, A. 1989. "A Cultural Theory of Leadership." In B. D. Jones.(Ed.), *Leadership and Politics: New Perspectives in Political Science*. Lawrence, Ks.: University of Kansas Press.

WTGG-TV. 1997. Washington, D.C. (November 2).

CHAPTER 15
LEADERSHIP AS EFFECTIVE NARRATIVES OF ADAPTIVE WORK
Richard A. Couto

The contributors have done their parts to explain what they see in the future of the research, study, and practice of leadership from the vantage point of James MacGregor Burns's now classic *Leadership*. Throughout the past fourteen chapters, they have raised some of the many questions his book leaves unanswered. This chapter combines their work with that of Howard Gardner and Emma Laskin (1995) on narratives and Ronald Heifetz (1994) on adaptive work to construct and test a theory that may permit us new understanding for the study and practice of leadership.

I knew about James MacGregor Burns before I learned of his work on leadership. His scholarly honors and awards made him an academic celebrity. To my chagrin, at our first meeting I found myself disagreeing with him about the amount and caliber of leadership in the United States. As we talked, we discovered that we were looking in different places. He searched in vain for national political leadership that continued the progressive agenda of the New Deal. I found an abundance of effective leadership for social justice at the local level (Couto 1995). This first exchange, like those that followed, challenged and stimulated my thinking.

My first impression of *Leadership*, most of which I read on a long car ride taking my daughter back for her second semester of college, remains with me: a thoughtful, intelligent compendium of knowledge focused on a single topic and an outstanding intellectual feat.

Narratives and Leadership

We begin our theory building with the work of Gardner and Laskin (1995) and their conception of leadership as embodied narratives across domains and within them. Domains range from small and homogenous groups, such as leadership scholars and family members, to large, undifferentiated, and heterogeneous groups, such as a nation and a family of nations. In between these domains comes a domain with organizations and formal groups of people, with structures of authority and shared values and experiences that differentiate them from other groups, such as corporate stockholders or religious denominations.

Narratives, in Gardner and Laskin's work, vary from the visionary to the ordinary, with an intermediary category of innovative narratives. They vary according to the degree of new ideas and values they impart and the attendant changes in attitudes and behaviors they suggest, with visionary narratives asking the most and ordinary narratives the least. Narratives are more than words. They include actions and other embodiments of values. Achilles's actions as well as Homer's epic poem recounting them are both narratives; the latter immortalizing the former. Their narratives' insight, that even the seeming invincible may have a vulnerable spot, remains pertinent for both the seemingly invincible and those who face such a person.

Gardner and Laskin examine leaders who use narratives to cross the borders of domains, from one set of groups to another broader set. These leaders attempt, deliberately and intentionally, to shape narratives for adherents in larger and larger domains to influence the thoughts, values, and actions of more and more people. By this measure, Homer's narrative was leadership just as much as Achilles's, and perhaps more so. As Ron Walters points out, in a parallel manner, Martin Luther King Jr. was not the narrative but the narrator of the story of thousands of heroic efforts of African Americans and the poor to sustain dreams of human worth and dignity. The manner in which he identified with those narratives gave his telling of them an authenticity and his leadership legitimacy. The venues, or domains, in which he told them, permitted people unaware of those heroic efforts to relate their own values to them. King shaped narratives for adherents in larger and larger domains to influence the thoughts, values, and actions of more and more people. His "I have a dream" speech on the steps of the Lincoln Memorial brought these narratives to the nation's center stage.

Before the narratives of visionary leadership, with their radical and unfamiliar values of human bonds and relationships, appear on center stage, they begin with a small and homogeneous group. This is the domain of religious figures, such as Moses, Jesus, Mohammed, Mary Baker Eddy; great social-movement leaders such as Gandhi and King; and those who share their vision. This is the realm of the penultimate transforming leadership, in Burns's terms, of "real, significant change" (Burns 1978:425) or, in operational terms, the challenge to some caste-like restriction on a group.

Figure 15-1 arranges the degrees of change of ordinary, innovative, and visionary leadership with the domains in which change may take place. It portrays the origins of visionary and innovative narratives in small domains and relatively homogenous groups, such as Gandhi's *ashram*, before they move to large heterogeneous groups and take on a march to the sea with thousands of people from myriad backgrounds.

Transforming Leadership Down from Mount Rushmore

For Burns, Gandhi serves as an example of transforming leadership and for

Gardner and Laskin, Gandhi provides an example of visionary leadership. Both Burns's book and Gardner and Laskin's book clearly paint on a huge canvas; perhaps too huge for most of us, given Gandhi's international role in decolonization and social change on a national level. Most of us, in contrast, are like Ronald Heifetz's students and look to leadership studies for insights to improve our practice of leadership on a day-to-day basis in ordinary venues.

In his chapter, Heifetz cautions that not all leadership is visionary and transforming; he calls for humility about the scale of change even the most extraordinary leader may conduct. On the other hand, by his concept of adaptive work, he brings leadership within the reach of those in positions and without positions of authority. The different levels and forms of adaptive work permit us to reduce the scale or domain of transforming leadership. When someone draws attention to the contradiction of a group's values or the gap between its values and practices and mobilizes its members to address them, that person exercises leadership regardless of domain, position, or authority. That gap might be as large as caste-like restrictions or as narrow as the need for support groups to aid people with chemical dependencies.

Adaptive work, at the level of neighborhood, precinct, school, or workplace, brings transforming leadership within our reach. It may imply narratives of new human possibilities, as visionary and transforming leadership do, but, more often they are less dramatic and more subtle narratives, such as calling attention to sexist remarks in a meeting. These latter narratives may cross no large domains and call for fairly modest change, but they are rooted in a visionary narrative of gender equality. Thus, we imagine cameos of otherwise ordinary people imparting visionary and transforming narratives by their actions—people like Lois Gibbs, the Love Canal resident who fought the consequences of dumping toxic materials in her neighborhood in Niagara Falls, New York, and later in other places across the United States. These cameos of extraordinary leadership are certainly the messages that Larraine Matusak and Robin Gerber give us when they call attention to the capacity for leadership in all people. Matusak, in particular, supports our contention when she offers a perspective on transforming leadership as overcoming old patterns of thinking and confronting the narratives in our head, much in the manner that Peter Senge (1990) did.

A student offers a particularly vibrant example of transforming leadership within us and the choice among conflicting narratives. She tells the story of her first day of college. Divorced and a single mom, she decided to go to college after a successful but unfulfilling ten years in interior design. Just as so many women of her generation, her college plans had been discouraged by her high school guidance counselor; better to prepare for work as a secretary and avoid the risk of failing in college, they advised. The only thing different was that she had attended a Catholic high school. Her dread persisted even after admission and registration.

> The night before the first day of class, I prayed for a snowstorm so the university would close for the day, for several days; apparently, it was my day to begin because when I woke up that January morning, the roads were clear and dry. The drive to the university was excruciating, the nuns were in the backseat of the car chanting, "You can't do this, you can't do this." My hands gripped the steering wheel and my mind raced as I was trying to think of ways I could get out of

beginning my college career. I finally decided that if I could not find a metered parking space, I would have to go home. I felt confident I would not find one and the nuns continued their chants, just as if they were saying their rosaries.

Also in the car with her, however, was the echo of her seventh-grade daughter's narrative of congratulations and confidence upon her mom's acceptance into college.

The innovative-visionary narratives of adaptive work go on at the most local level, within us. Even there they encounter conflicting and corroborative narratives. These moments of transformation may not remove or reduce the caste-like restrictions of a group, but they may be acts of liberation for an individual in a group with caste-like or other restrictions—such as the homeowners in Love Canal or those of us raised on low expectations—that others impose on us and we impose on ourselves. Such modest narratives of adaptive work may never reach a broad audience and may be shared only in range of very small domains: the intrapersonal; one-on-one leader and follower relationships, such as Edwin Hollander discusses; among a slowly growing number of residents of a community, as in Heifetz's example in Chapter 3 of Maggie and Lois and their battle against alcoholism in her tribe; or among people within the transformistic organization that Gill Hickman envisions.

Adaptive work expresses an innovative or visionary narrative depending upon the values and the practices that make the dimensions of the gap. Because we are primarily concerned with modest forms of leadership, however, we will focus on a range of innovative narratives about adaptive work. These innovative narratives may have their origins in visionary narratives, but as the latter move across domains they become more and more familiar to more and more people, with less and less demand on them for radical change, and finally reach the simpler and simpler reductionist narratives in the minds of large numbers of people in a diffuse and general public. The narratives of innovative leadership have limits: not too visionary so as to lose an audience for its narratives, but not so ordinary that its narratives completely lose all semblance of their explicit message of the need for some degree of adaptive work. We will focus on this move from one group of adherents to another, this segment of innovative narratives, and this balance of the visionary and the ordinary.

Ordinary leadership's narratives, the last in Gardner and Laskin's analysis, impart no new sense of human relationships and no sense of the need for the adaptive work that Heifetz stresses. These elementary narratives, the currency of ordinary leadership, are deposited in our minds before we even start school, Gardner and Laskin maintain. They remain with us in our basic frameworks of what the world is supposed to be like and the rudimentary elements of right and wrong. Thus, the most visionary of persons also has a tide of ordinary narratives and feels the powerful pull of their meanings at least in their subconscious. Ordinary narratives reinforce existing practices and may prevent their change.

Burns warned about the dichotomies in his work, and establishing a trichotomy of visionary, innovative, and ordinary narratives does not improve matters a great deal. Let us take his advice and establish a spectrum among these forms of narratives. Innovative leadership may have links to the narratives of ordinary leadership by bringing new attention, or a "fresh twist," to a familiar but ignored story, reasserting traditional and familiar values, and instituting change on behalf of those values. We will call these narratives *innovative-ordinary* and represent them in Figure 15-1 as the space that blends innovative and ordinary narratives.

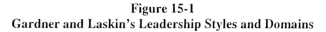

Figure 15-1
Gardner and Laskin's Leadership Styles and Domains

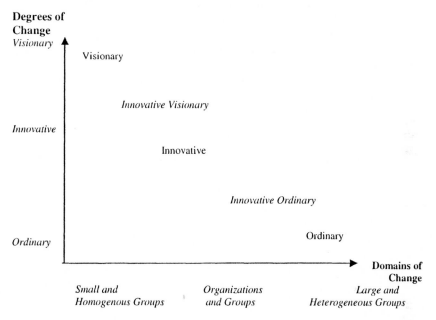

Margaret Thatcher and Ronald Reagan, as examples of leadership with innovative-ordinary narratives, did much to reinvigorate the values of market economies, personal responsibility, and limited government in the 1980s. As innovative leaders, Reagan and Thatcher told ordinary stories extraordinarily well. They "put forth a simple nostalgic message in which they personally believed, one that they could articulate persuasively" (Gardner and Laskin 1994:235) and "reactivated beliefs and values that had been dormant...for many years" (Gardner and Laskin 1994:241). As Gardner and Laskin say of Thatcher, with equal applicability to Reagan, she saw "the world in stark black-and-white terms and could not tolerate ambiguity or subtlety" (Gardner and Laskin 1994:237). They appealed to the simpler times of ordinary narratives and innovated by relating stories of human possibilities and ordinary values and practices.

Other innovative leaders relate stories of new human possibilities and less familiar values in an effort, for example, to mitigate the failures of market economies, to promote social responsibility, and to advocate for expanded government programs of social welfare. These innovative stories and truths, depicted in the area between visionary and innovative leadership, tell of groups

marginalized by the current distribution of social, economic, and political resources (Gardner and Laskin 1994:223) and the possibility of removing their
caste-like restrictions. We will call this leadership *innovative-visionary* and
place it in the area between visionary and innovative in Figure 15-1

In describing Eleanor Roosevelt, for example, Gardner and Laskin explain
that in her roles as first lady and representative to the United Nations, Roosevelt
would "call attention to the role of women in politics, the need for progressive
politics, and the obligation to help the disenfranchised; but she spoke as well
about newly emerged issues of disarmament, poverty, and hunger throughout the
world" (Gardner and Laskin 1995:198). The old familiar values and practices
would not do, and she fashioned and championed new innovative narratives of
social responsibility and empowerment, such as the United Nations Universal
Declaration of Human Rights. Burns, responding to criticism of the androcentric
nature of *Leadership* such as Laurien Alexandre offered, describes Eleanor Roosevelt as a transforming leader in a later and more engendered work (Burns
2003).

A Theory of Effective Narratives of Adaptive Work

Gardner and Laskin assert that in order to influence people and stimulate
change, direct leadership must cross domains and win adherents by appealing to
increasingly basic and fundamental concepts common to larger and larger
groups. While this may be necessary to conduct change, it does not explain
when it is sufficient. Their work begs the question: Why do some narratives
succeed and others do not? This question provides us the material for theory
building.

We may start with the material that our contributors supply. Tom Wren
points out that over time James Madison had three narratives of the resolution of
the tension of popular sovereignty and leadership. Burns looks back at his own
work and suggests three areas of change he would make to it. Laurien Alexandre
argues persuasively that in the current time of gender consciousness, Burns's
1978 narrative of leadership has serious shortcomings that were less evident at
the time of the book's publication. Margaret Wheatley finds Burns's 1978 work
dated because of its emphasis on psychology and its omission of systems. Evi-
dently, the appeal and relevance of a narrative may increase and decrease with
time.

Time as a factor of the appeal and relevance of a narrative begs another
question: Why? Why do some narratives make sense and seem reasonable at one
time but not another? Why do their appeal and relevance vary? Change, implicit
in the concept of time, may be the answer. Adam Yarmolinsky stressed change
as a constant backdrop to leadership. Ronald Walters, in discussing the changing
demands of black leadership, implied that the changes sought by a group may
change with the changes wrought by others, events, or their own success. Here
we suggest that changes over time provide fertile or rocky soil for a narrative.
Indeed, Thatcher and Reagan were innovative and successful only because the
innovative-visionary narratives of their predecessors had become ordinary and

apparently had run their course. In this vein, Walters singles out Doug McAdams's work (1982) to explain that the success of the narrative of social movements depends on a constellation of other changes in political and social conditions; the migration of African Americans to the urban North and their service in World War II, for example, contributed unique factors and increased possibility for success of the visionary narratives of racial equality in the 1950s and 1960s. Change creates the need for adaptive work, the central aspect of leadership in Ronald Heifetz's estimation. In Heifetz's story, time and change made one woman's visionary work of alcohol rehabilitation—a vision that included meeting "with the spirits and the ancestors" and the confidence that "one day our people will come"—into an innovative narrative of adaptive work.

Of course, change permits people a choice among narratives about the nature of adaptive work and the need to address or avoid it. A condition in which Wheatley rejoiced, we have a choice in the realities to which we ascribe. Leadership defined as the effort to influence the thoughts and actions of others entails conflicting with competing narratives and corroborating the leader's own narratives with supporting narratives about the choices that people have about the adaptive work facing a group. Thatcher and Reagan had strong beliefs in their narratives and could quickly silence competing narratives about choices with the assertions "There is no alternative!" and the more genial "There you go again!" respectively. Other leaders succeeded Thatcher and Reagan, bringing different choices of innovative narratives that appealed to another set of familiar values, such as the "third way" of Tony Blair and "a kinder, gentler nation" of George H. W. Bush.

Several contributors touched on this aspect of conflicting and corroborating narratives. Larraine Matusak invokes a familiar and supporting narrative of "We the People!" to compete with the narratives of lethargy. Robin Gerber explains the powerful narratives of citizen apathy sent out by political leaders and then offers the conflicting narrative of the value that ordinary citizens place on civic duty with corroborative narratives. Gill Hickman clearly pointed out the contending narratives of organizations—bureaucratic, organic, and transformistic— as she espoused the possibilities of the latter and the narratives of change in organizational environments to corroborate her own narrative. Terry Price places competing narratives and values at the center of his model of transpositional leadership. Wren helps us loop at least the matter of conflicting narratives back to Burns. In particular, Wren suggests that heterogeneous groups, i.e., larger domains, require leaders to "embrace competing interests and goals within their constituency (Burns 1978:37-39)." Wren concludes that leaders play a catalytic role in the leadership process, which is consistent with our emerging theory of leadership working within a context that includes competing narratives. The values embedded in old and familiar stories continue even in the company of new ones to conflict and corroborate with them regarding the form or necessity of adaptive work.

This suggests that around any narrative, change, conflict, and corroboration orbit in a field that defines a narrative's relevance. The orbits of these elements are shaped by the narratives, but the necessity and sufficiency of the narrative depends upon the three elements—change, conflict, and collaboration—orbiting around it. We draw here from both Margaret Wheatley's and Adam Yarmolinsky's suggestions of systems', interdependence, interrelatedness, reflexive, and, albeit implicit, quantum mechanics. Figure 15-2 offers a crude illustration of this quantum element of leadership with change, conflict, and collaboration orbiting in a field of energy around a narrative.

Figure 15-2
A Quantum of Leadership

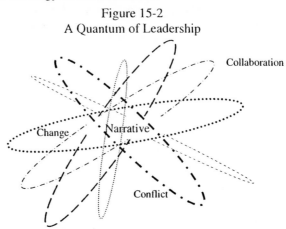

Time and change explain why some narratives succeed and others do not. However, they do not explain why some conflicting narratives appeal to one group and not another at the same time; Colin Powell's narratives appeal to white audiences more than African-American audiences and Jesse Jackson's narratives have just the opposite effect, in Ron Walter's estimation. Walters suggests an answer: the roots of a person's embodied narrative in a community contribute to the authenticity and legitimacy of that person's leadership. As an embodied narrative on African-American leadership, such as Powell's or that of his successor Condoleezza Rice, crosses domains, some groups cling to the narratives that relate to their own experiences with race.

Our contributors help us fill in some missing elements of Gardner and Laskin's theory—time, change, our own experiences, and conflicting and corroborative, interdependent, reflexive, and interrelated narratives. These factors, and probably more, help us to explain why some narratives succeed at one time and place and among some groups and others do not. Figure 15-3 portrays an area of effective narrative that extends from visionary, through innovative-visionary, to innovative-ordinary narratives. As depicted in Figure 15-3, the path of effective narrative suggests the manner in which a visionary narrative finds increased adherents by reducing the degree of change entailed and making new or ignored narratives and values compatible with some old or prominent ones.

From Grandiosity to a Nexus of Narratives

Our contributors' insights have helped us to address missing elements of Gardner and Laskin's work. Can they go further to help us apply that work to Burns and *Leadership?* Can we get any further in understanding and practicing leadership with these insights? Or is our theory yet another to throw on the hopelessly academic and impracticable heap? We will address the first two questions to support the most favorable answer to the last one. We will address these questions by reversing the test of scientific discovery that Georgia Sorenson relayed to us from Thomas Kuhn. Rather than asking others to assimilate this work with theirs, we will attempt the "reconstruction of proper theory and the re-evaluation of prior fact" in order to see how much of the work of our contributors and of *Leadership* our theory can assimilate.

Figure 15-3
The Pathway of Effective Narratives of Adaptive Work

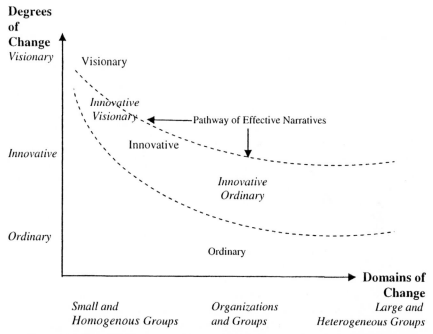

Let us begin with Figure 15-3's suggestion that innovative-ordinary narratives have a larger area, and hence, more narratives and a better prospect of success than narratives of innovative-visionary leadership. This is certainly in keeping with both Yarmolinsky and Heifetz and their emphasis on humility about how much change is possible. It also suggests that the prospects of innovative-ordinary leadership increase because it has the easier task of conducting change. These narratives ask people to take on discarded but familiar behaviors and attitudes and not untested and unfamiliar ones. Lifting ordinary stories and familiar values into the realm of innovative would appear easier than the task of bringing dramatic, new visionary stories closer to the realm of the ordinary—the task that innovative-visionary leadership faces.

For example, Jesus, as a visionary leader, deliberately contrasted the narrative of an eye for an eye with a radically new one of turning the other cheek. But in everyday experience, it seems far easier to accommodate this visionary narrative of love for one's enemies—probably the most historically accurate account of any of Jesus's narratives (Funk et al. 1993:143)—to the ordinary narratives and values of violent revenge—which serve war, capital punishment, and other forms of everyday aggression—than to win Christian adherents to a call for the adaptive work of reducing violence. Max Weber (1958 rpt) spent much of one his most famous essays doing just that. He rejected the Christian ethic of the Sermon on the Mount as appropriate for political leadership because of the latter's distinguishing characteristic, a monopoly on the legitimate use of violence.

The profound changes that accompany visionary narratives send us scurrying for counter narratives—Jesus did chase the money changers out of the Temple in a fit of anger—to attenuate them to more ordinary narratives and less change. Anger and violence have their own narratives embedded in the ordinary narratives and values of many cultures. They may combine the adaptive work entailed in the radically peaceful visionary narrative of the Sermon on the Mount and other visionary narratives of human bonds with ordinary narratives legitimating violent force. The radical changes of visionary leadership place it and related forms of transforming leadership out of reach of all but a few leaders, just as our contributors suggest and we noted before. Now, however, transforming leadership is limited not only by its grandiosity but also by the insulation we have from it, which competing narratives provide. .

Transforming leadership remains a more likely possibility for innovative leadership that can bring ordinary and ignored stories of marginalized groups into the mainstream of social discourse about values. Walters portrays Martin Luther King Jr.'s innovative, or transforming, role in precisely this manner. Alexandre describes how the ignored narratives of women have gained more visibility since the 1960s. These changes indicate some degree of success in the adaptive work of improving the status of some groups in light of our values of human equality.

The pathway of effective narratives, illustrated in Figure 15-3, moves from a narrow band up at the visionary point to the broadest band at ordinary and thus permits us a range of change from the most dramatic to the most ordinary. Given this, is the pathway limited to leadership of persons of power and position? Can it link the path of effective narratives to Hollander's pioneering work stressing relationships? Or to Tiffany Hansbrough's concern with levels of analysis? It can.

Hansbrough describes differences that stem from a professor's preferences rather than individual assessments or from competition within the group. Clearly, leadership may create distinctions among students, frogs, or followers. Our theory of effective narratives tells us that this story of differences is but one version of the origin of difference. Unless students and professors share the values of the narrative of distinction, they fall back on the old and familiar narrative of power of authority. At any level of analysis, part of the teacher-student interaction is the stock of stories each has—in conflict and support of each other—

about power and authority. These narratives mediate the relationship of leaders and followers, the central focus of Hollander's work. Thus, the path of effective narrative applies to discussions between spouses, between a boss and a worker, and among a small group; it also applies to election strategies at the local, state, or national level.

Hollander makes communication within and among groups central to the idiosyncrasy credit attributed to leadership. He thus brings to followers a more active role in leadership. Wheatley does the same with explicit attention to a system of relationships in which the success of communication depends on finding shared significance. Terry Price also gives communication sustained attention. His concept of transpositional leadership suggests conflicting narratives, as our theory does, and the need, as well as the possibility, of burrowing into our own narratives, or in Price's case—arguments—to uncover their epistemic limits. In terms of our theory, this reflexive adaptive work requires us to recall our own or our group's narratives about misinformed narratives and changed narratives in the past. This reflection on narratives permits individuals to move beyond group think and the conflict of narratives to critical insights and corroborative narratives. In turn, this change in action and attitudes better enables moral discourse on adaptive work between and within groups. It is the positive side of leadership with doubt, or as Heifetz puts it, "the doubt."

This attention to communication touches on the importance of modal values and transactional leadership at any level of discourse; neglected parts of Burns's work as ordinary narratives. Because narratives are embodied, those speaking of end-values such as equality, liberty, justice, etc., have a better chance of succeeding if they and their narrators display the modal values of widely shared ordinary narratives, such as honesty, accountability, trustworthiness, courage, responsibility, etc. Our theory suggests that one cannot reach the end-values of transforming or innovative-visionary leadership without roots in modal values and ordinary narratives. The narrative of forgiveness of one's enemies that Jesus offered would have even less appeal if we had only his example of chasing the money changers from the temple and not of his love of the poor and marginalized members of his society, Samaritans for example.

The Anomalies of Change, Systems, and Values

Our theory of effective narratives of adaptive work permits us to assimilate major parts of the contributions of Alexandre, Gerber, Heifetz, Hickman, Hollander, Hansbrough, Price, and Walters about Burns's work, including modal values and transactional leadership. Some of them and other contributors provide additional tests of assimilation for our theory.

The deference which our contributors have for Burns and his work suggests the manner in which *Leadership* transformed the imagination of scholars studying leadership. That imagination raises new problems with Burns's work; in Kuhn's terms, there are puzzles—questions without answers—and anomalies—persistently unexplainable phenomena. Yarmolinsky suggests one puzzle: change is a constant; you don't need leadership to initiate change, as Burns suggests. "The leader is a mediator," Yarmolinsky points out, "a moderator, someone who adjusts the facts of change and the intransigent facts of organizations and institutions." Wheatley suggests another shortcoming when she offers a perspective of systems of constant change among interrelated and interdependent parts, recognized or not. For example, many African Americans recognized the relatedness of their experiences to the narratives of Martin Luther King Jr., even though he was not aware of each of them. Kellerman has the additional anomalous concern with effective leadership and less with Burns's concern of leadership as a moral exercise. Finally, Heifetz suggests that Burns had not quite wrestled the question of values to the mat—another anomaly for our theory of narrative leadership of adaptive work to address. Accepting Kuhn's and Sorenson's criteria for a theory, ours should further our understanding of these puzzles and anomalies in Burns.

Let us start with Kellerman's anomaly, the neglect of attention to effectiveness—what works?—due to the emphasis of leadership as moral activity. Suppose we posit end-values such as liberty, justice, and equality at the visionary position of Figure 15-3, as both Gardner and Laskin and Burns would advise. Let us set aside the very real conflicts among those values as Price and Wren suggest—we will come back to them—and focus on the path of effective narratives in our model in Figure 15-3—the ability to shape narratives along larger and larger domains to influence the thoughts, values, and actions of more and more people. Kellerman asks, "Does leadership—for liberty, justice, and equality—range from only visionary to ordinary?" "Is leadership solely concerned with only 'good' end-values?" If one espouses restriction, injustice, and inequality, does one remain on the leadership path of effective narratives? Burns says no. In his standard answer to the ubiquitous question, was Hitler a leader? Burns answers, "Hitler once he gained power and crushed all opposition was no leader—he was a tyrant (Burns 1978:2-3). Fair enough: if Hitler, with the help of a few henchmen, imposed a terror of restriction, injustice, inequality, and death, then even by the ancient measure of Aristotle's classification of constitutions (Aristotle III,7), Hitler was a tyrant. Aristotle also would call Hitler a tyrant because he pursued his ends with the complicity of the many at severe cost to others.

But even the authority of Aristotle does not let us off the hook. Burns's test of transforming leadership may be real, significant change in the sense of removing or reducing some caste-like restrictions on a group. But does this preclude transforming leadership that imposes or increases them? We may call it tyranny, but as Kellerman makes clear, and our experience bears her out, tyrants may also be effective in influencing people and gaining adherents to a narrative of change. Figure 15-3 brings the path of effective narrative to a broad end at ordinary narratives. We may place the narratives of tyrants in the stock of ordinary narratives—a serious contradiction of our theory; ordinary narratives are supposed to support the status quo. We may also do as Burns and Gardner and Laskin do and limit our narratives to the "good" ones of inclusion and strengthened human bonds—a serious shortcoming of their work, in light of everyday experience. We may also place the narratives of tyranny and brute force outside of the path of effective narratives and floating in its own environment—a serious shortcoming given our experience. We know that "evil" narratives may mobilize people to conduct atrocities of adaptive work.

Our model needs to be expanded to take into account all these shortcomings. It needs a set of end-values opposite to liberty, equality, and justice and a pathway of effective narratives for them from visionary to ordinary. The expansion suggests that tyrants or "evil" leaders (Kellerman 2005:191-216) are effective in exactly the same manner as other leaders. They shape narratives along larger and larger domains to influence the thoughts, values, and actions of more and more people. They have their own path! Kellerman's concerns with effectiveness bring us to the shadowy side of leadership and to Figure 15-4. We may all be children of God in some narratives, but other narratives, ranging from visionary to ordinary, may portray groups as vermin, cockroaches, enemies of a revolution, or children of the "wrong" God and thus justify violent and inhumane action toward them. Figure 15-4 suggests that the difference between transforming leaders and tyrants is more the values they espouse than the processes of leadership they employ. Innovative-visionary and innovative-ordinary narratives may be invoked to mobilize the adaptive work for different and even opposite values.

Figure 15-4 solves one problem and presents another for our evolving theory. It suggests merged and permeable boundaries in the area of innovative-ordinary leadership containing a mix from both sides of the values divide. How then does Figure 15-4 take into account these conflicting narratives even among those who may share the same values and goals? It does so but permitting us to place a mix of conflicting and corroborative narratives within the realm of innovative narratives. The number of these other narratives increases as the path of effective narratives broadens and merges with a large volume of ordinary narratives at the bottom of its arc. These ordinary narratives have the extraordinary power of shining light on some "good" innovative narratives to show the "evil" of them. This is not to repeat the corruption of the values of "good" narratives by the values of ordinary narratives, which we discussed before. Here we explain the possibility that ordinary narratives may take an innovative narrative from one side of the good/evil divide and place it on the other. Choir members may take different inspiration from the same hymns. John Brown, a divisive figure in American history, resorted to violence as a means of transformation unlike other abolitionists such as members of the Underground Railroad. His transforming vision of the abolition of slavery butted against the ordinary narrative against killing unarmed persons, even if they were pro-slavery.

Let us take Yarmolinsky's attention-capturing statement about abolitionists. "I do not know that the abolitionists were admirable people; admirable as individuals perhaps, but not as leaders." Yarmolinsky places them in the context of other conflicting and corroborating narratives, thus suggesting that there is not one value at stake in any decision of consequence, but several, even in a matter

Figure 15-4
The Pathway of Effective Narratives of Adaptive Work

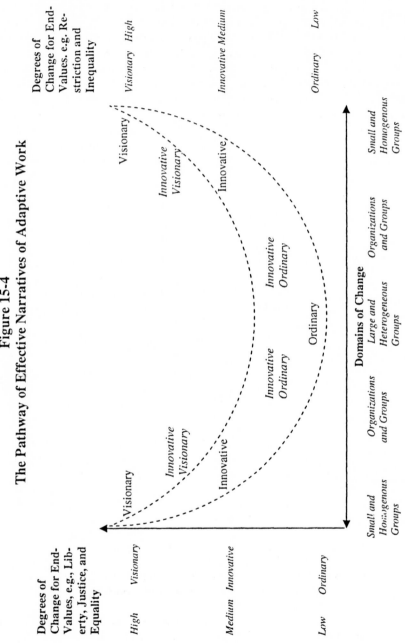

Degrees of Change for End-Values, e.g., Liberty, Justice, and Equality

High   *Visionary*

Medium *Innovative*

Low   *Ordinary*

Degrees of Change for End-Values. e.g. Restriction and Inequality

Visionary   High

Innovative Medium

Ordinary   Low

Visionary

Innovative Visionary

Innovative

Innovative Ordinary

Ordinary

Domains of Change

Small and Homogenous Groups

Organizations and Groups

Large and Heterogeneous Groups

Organizations and Groups

Small and Homogenous Groups

where values seem so clear. The historical record clearly shows that there were differences of kind and degree—conflicting and collaborating, interrelated and interdependent narratives—among and between abolitionists and secessionists before, during, and after the war. The degree of support for the suffrage of the freedmen sparked a modest but unheeded demand for women's suffrage among some female abolitionists. The degree of opposition to suffrage of freedmen ranged from muted narratives about the franchise among them to political terrorism in the form of the Ku Klux Klan; the success of the latter is a much neglected narrative about successful political terrorism in the United States.

These differences of kind and degree among narratives between groups with conflicting values as well as within them suggest three important additional elements to our theory of effective narratives of adaptive work:

- there are several conflicting and collaborating narratives, Yarmolinsky's contribution, that are interrelated and interdependent—Wheatley's point—within a single decision or act of leadership;
- there is conflict and corroboration among the narratives of the groups sharing common goals and values as well as between groups with opposing ones;
- and most narrative conflicts entailing values are not Manichean dramas about black and white, good versus evil, but a grey mix of difficult choices.

Yarmolinsky suggests that leaders of organizations, especially large ones, have to strike a balance among narratives of change and stability. Hollander helps us understand that the leader-and-follower relationship is far more complex than the formal authority of the leader, precisely because followers have their own stock of narratives. Both leaders and followers have a stock of narratives about authority itself upon which each group may draw. Efforts to initiate the transformistic organizations, which Hickman envisions, contain the narratives of bureaucratic and organic organizations as well. Thus, we might envision the leadership process as a large system of narratives with subsystems of narratives which have similar characteristics of the whole system, in much the same way as fractal geometry has taught us to think about systems.

Some of the narratives in conflict and corroboration within organizations or groups relate to the interpretation of their environments and the necessity of adaptive work facing a group. Robin Gerber, for example, points out that John and Alice Martin taped the cellular phone call they intercepted because they understood its context and, therefore, could decide on its importance, which proved to be multifaceted. Ms. Martin recalled her citizen's excitement to hear the voices of "real politicians" but reached for the tape recorder for very personal values.

We're going to have a grandson at the end of January, and we were thinking how neat it would be to play this tape for him and for him to hear the voices of people who we thought were important. That's really all it was going to be—a little tape we put aside, and when he was old enough to hear it, he could hear it.

As the conversation of these "real politicians"—then-Speaker of the House Newt Gingrich and other leading Republicans in the House—continued, the Martins realized the political, in addition to the personal, context of the conversation; the Ethics Committee hearings related to Gingrich's conduct. As lifelong Democrats, another narrative trail, they put the tapes into the hands of the ranking Democrat on the House Ethics Committee, who understood the conversation to be a violation of the speaker's promise not to orchestrate a campaign, which was exactly what the conversation made clear he was doing. When the tapes became public information on the front page of *The New York Times* two days later, Republicans offered their own conflicting narrative of the Martins' criminal behavior—taping a cellular phone call is against the law. Far from a family affair for their grandchild or the civic duty of ordinary citizens, the Martins were now embroiled in a narrative of federal-law violation. Their lawyer expressed confidence in a narrative of innocent intent.

> My hope is that once it's understood that these folks are Mr. and Mrs. John Q. Citizen, who happened to discover something they felt was pertinent to the Ethics Commission and did what I think we want citizens to do, which is take it to the commission responsible for the investigation and say, here, you do what's right, my hope is that those who are responsible for making prosecuting decisions will decide this shouldn't be prosecuted (PBS 1997).

This proved partially true. The Martins were permitted to plead guilty to a lesser change in exchange for their cooperation in the prosecution of the Democrat who leaked the tapes to *The New York Times*. The Martins' leadership took place in a context of changes, apart from any of their own, with interrelated and interdependent, conflicting and corroborative narratives, which they could not possibly have foreseen. These narratives framed the adaptive work to be done— investigate the speaker or punish those who broke the law by taping a conversation that showed the speaker had gone back on his word to the House Ethics Committee! In the hardball political context of Washington, the latter narrative was muted. By 2006, former Speaker Gingrich was offering the nation political commentary and building a platform on competency for a presidential race in 2008 and the Martins' experience was a cautionary tale about citizen action.

There is conflict and corroboration within the groups sharing common goals and values as well as between groups with opposing ones. In the Martins' case, they were swept up in conflicting narratives between Democrats and Republicans in the House. Within each party, however, there were also conflicting narratives. All the Democratic congressional representatives knew about the tapes, but only one of them took action to leak it to the press. Three other Republican leaders conversed with Speaker Gingrich precisely because they had differences in their perspectives that they need to coordinate into one—to get their story straight.

The puzzles and anomalies that our contributors have presented required us to extend our theory of effective narratives of adaptive work to incorporate a mirror image of the initial pathway of effective narratives. We can now take into account the effectiveness of leadership regardless of moral values, Kellerman's concern, and by the same measure shape narratives, deliberately and intentionally, for adherents in larger and larger domains, and thus influence the thoughts, values, and actions of more and more people. Although the model remains very much values centered, it also permits for modesty in leadership, Heifetz's concern, and a smaller scale than transforming change. Finding the pathway of effective narratives applies to international as well as interpersonal differences over the appropriate adaptive work to undertake. We have also introduced a context of change and a web of interrelated and interdependent, conflicting and corroborating narratives, thereby addressing the concerns of Yarmolinsky and Wheatley, respectively.

Values, Inclusion, Initiative, and Creativity

As already noted, most narrative conflicts are not matters of black and white, good versus evil, even if, in trying to win adherents to a particular narrative, leaders demonize those who support a conflicting narrative. Most times, the adaptive work to be decided upon entails one meaning of liberty or another, rather than the stark difference of liberty or repression. This decision exceeds a merely intellectual task and involves a calculation of consequences of who wins, who loses, who is entitled to play, and the balance of the gains and losses. Calculations, and hence, conflicts over the nature of adaptive work will vary depending upon whose interests are at stake and what groups are included.

The Fourteenth Amendment to the U.S. Constitution provides a wonderful example of conflicting narratives based on inclusion of some groups but not others. It also permits us to continue the thread of abolitionist examples. The abolition of slavery set forth in the Thirteenth Amendment eliminated "three-fifths people" in apportioning membership in the House of Representatives. Because freed people were now five-fifths of a person, the states with the largest population of former slaves were now entitled to greater representation in the House.

In practical terms, this meant that former secessionist states would send larger delegations to Congress than before the Civil War and that these states could push for legislation to pay their war debts from the federal treasury. To prevent this, the amendment was written to include freed people more completely into the constitutional guarantees of the United States and exclude from the federal government, for all practical purposes, all people with political experience in the states that seceded. It also prohibited the possibility of paying the debts of the secessionist states from federal funds.

The first clause of the amendment included freed people in the guarantee of equal protection under the law so that they too could not be deprived of life, liberty, and property without "due process." Of course, the narrative of Jim Crow and legal segregation make a mockery of that constitutional guarantee. At the same time, the narrative of due process expanded to include corporations and to apply to situations not foreseen and with literally historic consequences for the country. In a crowning irony, the narrative of equal protection and due process was the grounds upon which the U.S. Supreme Court decided the controversy over the 2000 presidential election in Florida, which included the narratives of tens of thousands of African-American voters denied access to the ballot in that election. The sad and proud history of the narrative of due process makes clear how history may offer the opportunity for new narratives to conflict with or corroborate the original values of the narrative.

These narrative conflicts have narrower bounds than the extremes of tyranny and transforming leadership. One may disagree with the Supreme Court decision in 2000 and the outcome of the election without subscribing to a narrative of tyranny. Price pointed out narrative conflicts may occur over the very same terms; the public good, or in our example, equal protection and due process. If we add Wren's views into the mix, the conflicts within conflicting and collaborating narratives may lead the same person to subscribe to different views, with different implications for action over time, as Madison and the subsequent interpretation of equal protection and due process illustrate. Heifetz explained the different narratives of Sam Gejdenson, an anti-war activist and a congressman representing a district that was home to thousands of jobs dependent upon the continued construction of nuclear submarines.

The conflicts among those sharing common values make it inevitable that some will take action on common goals and values earlier than others. To revert back to the example of the abolitionists, some whites and freed blacks participated in the Underground Railroad, but most did not. In the example of the Martins and the taped narratives, all the Democrats on the Ethics Committee knew about the tapes, but only one of them passed them along. On the other side of that story, one of the four Republican leaders on the call initiated it.

Just as some will take initiative before others, some people are more creative at relating one narrative with another. This includes modal values, communicative skills, imagination, the embodied nature of the narrative, and other factors that help a leader relate an innovative narrative to other narratives and thus win acceptance. Frederick Douglass stands out for this creative capacity in the last half of the nineteenth century. Lincoln creatively wove the narrative of the Civil War with the Declaration of Independence in the Gettysburg address, and King imaginatively linked his "I have a dream" speech to Lincoln's Gettysburg address and "government of the people, by the people, and for the people."

These factors—values, initiative, inclusiveness, and creativity—suggest that an effective narrative is a dynamic system with values at its center. The initiative and inclusiveness that people may take will depend upon the priorities they place among conflicting and collaborating narratives and the values embedded in them. The Martins took their action out of civic duty and perhaps Democratic partisanship. Values will also influence who is included in the purpose of change and the conduct of change. The Martins included Democratic legislators, including one on the House Ethics Committee. The House member included the newspapers in an effort to disseminate the phone conversation for the values of public information, exposure of the speaker's backtracking on his promise in an ethics investigation, or some combination of the two. Finally, Wheatley stresses creativity as a natural part of the life process nurtured by learning and relationships. Perhaps then this part of a dynamic system of narrative depends on a person developing and expressing the full capacities of human life.

A Quantum Model of Effective Narratives of Adaptive Work

Figure 15-5 assembles the elements of narrative—values, initiative, inclusiveness, and creativity—within the orbits of change, conflict, and collaboration to form another model of the quantum of leadership. Instead of narrative in the center of this quantum model, we have its constitutive elements in a dynamic tension and constant motion. Values are at the center of this system, as Burns instructed us. It centers a quantum-like system with the interrelated parts of inclusiveness, initiative, and creativity. Orbiting around this nucleus is another system of interrelated parts of change, conflict, and collaboration. Figure 15-5 also includes two orbits with replications of the factors of the system; systems of change-conflict-collaboration and values, inclusiveness-initiative-creativity within systems with the same factors. Not only is the system in constant change, Yarmolinsky's point, but its parts are interrelated and interdependent, Wheatley's emphasis. This static depiction, frozen in print, crudely approximates a dynamic system and subsystems of interrelated and interdependent parts of conflict, corroboration, initiative, inclusiveness, creativity, and, of course, changes and values.

Figure 15-5
The Quantum of Effective Narratives

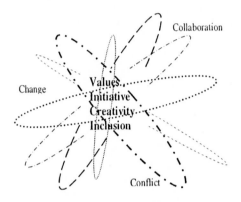

The next step in our model is to combine this quantum of leadership with the path of effective narrative; filling in the entire path with large and small models of the quantum. Likewise, we may fill in the spaces of ineffective narratives with even more quantum narratives of change and values and the field of energy around them. This suggests that the simplest leadership act combines several narratives of changes and values and their interrelated parts. Walters, for example, explained the complexity of leadership legitimacy in terms of shared, or embodied, narratives of a community. White Americans may think of Colin Powell or Condoleezza Rice as black leaders, but Walters assures us that the legitimacy of leadership is far more complicated than skin color and far more rooted in a complex set of narratives within a community.

Powell is an especially notable case. His personal narrative made him the most credible spokesperson for the Bush administration. As such, he was designated to offer its narrative for military action against Iraq before the United Nations. His personal and official narratives were powerfully matched. They convinced much of the U.S. public but that presentation has since become a stain on his record. Oddly, a black man taking the burden for a white man's intentions and falling under it is a recognizable narrative within the black community and could provide him more legitimacy as a black leader within it.

The plethora of quantum narratives highlights the role of creativity in effective leadership. The successful leader chooses those values and changes that best fit the pathway across domains and reach more and more people; this satisfies Kellerman's test for "what works?" Effective leaders do more than merely find adherents, however. They offer simplicity in the midst of the chaos of literary thousands of possibly relevant narratives, each with its own quantum dynamic, even in a dyadic relationship; an argument with a lover offers a good measure of the incredible number of narratives in a one-on-one relationship.

The creative simplicity of effective leadership permits action in the face of innumerable options in complex relationships but, ironically, only after stretching the epistemic limits, Price's term, to incorporate doubt, Heifetz's term. Wheatley's promotion of the new science also entails doubt or uncertainty at its center. By our efforts to probe or measure something, we can never be sure that what we know is the same as the object was before or after. As we know more and more about a particular matter, we can begin to predict the likelihood of an event by a pattern of probability.

Effective leadership makes a convincing argument of the pattern of numerous narratives and the probability of a particular outcome. Of course, leadership is more than prognostication. The prognosticator takes action to convince others of the same pattern and the same probable outcome and to urge them to take action. This task is the same whether applied to leading people from a burning building, recommending a particular item from a menu, or leading a nation into or out of war. Obviously, the stakes differ from one case to another.

This need not be rocket science—although astrophysics is filled with uncertainty and the use of patterns of probability. Any dog owner can tell stories of the uncanny ability of a canine to come to understand a pattern of their owner's actions. Betsy, my deceased dog, knew that shutting off the television late at night could signal the end of the night and a walk under the night sky. She also came to understand that if I put my shoes on, the probability of a walk increased. When I said "leash," she could be certain and would begin a frantic search around the house for her leash to bring to me. Similarly, she came to understand, before I did, the pattern of probability that explained her chances of going in the car with me. I wondered why sometimes she just continued her rest as I approached the door leading to the garage and then at other times went excitedly and impatiently to the door before I could reach it. I came to understand that the time of day, my clothing, and my book bag were elements of a system that came together in certain patterns to signal the probability of my travel to a place, such as work or an appointment, where she could not come along. She also understood, before I did, that other patterns signaled the probability that she was welcomed to accompany me.

Leadership may offer simplicity short of sorting through the complexity of all relevant narratives and their pattern of probability. The U.S. invasion of Iraq suggests the consequences of ignoring relevant narratives and the difference between successful and effective leadership. The first may win adherents to a simple narrative of adaptive work short of the complexity of the competing and collaborative narratives. Effective leadership also offers a simple narrative of adaptive work, but only after finding order in chaos. As Wheatley advises, "We really do have to learn to look for order that is not found in neat increments or in absolute and precise measurements. We have to start looking for order as it comes out of messes."

Another aspect of effective leadership suggests the normative base of values for leadership, a piece started in *Leadership* in Heifetz's estimation. They embody modal values—especially transparency, accountability, responsibility, and honesty—in addressing the nature of adaptive work. The test of an embodied narrative of transforming leadership within any domain and at any level of interaction entails narrators treating all others, regardless of status and prestige, with modal values. Ironically, the measure of transforming leadership as the use of modal values in all relationships provides one normative measure for values in leadership. It preserves Burns's concern with moral leadership without making it moral activity in pursuit of end-values.

The quantum of leadership in the center of the pathway of innovative-visionary and innovative-ordinary narratives and other quanta in and out of the effective pathway permit us to discuss competing narratives within reasonable boundaries of conflicting and corroborating narratives and the nature and degree of adaptive work that each represents. We thus avoid the stark and usually inaccurate contrast of good and evil. Instead, we present the dilemma of innovative leadership of adaptive work as deciding which narratives conflict with or corroborate its own, choosing among relevant and irrelevant collaborating narratives, and then selecting among the elements of the relevant collaborating and conflicting narratives to win more and more adherents to a change of attitude and action. It places less emphasis on a leader shaping the motives and needs of others or elevating them. It places people in relations in which everyone has a stock of narratives which represent resources that shape the motives and needs of and leaders alike and may elevate both of them.

Conclusion

Georgia Sorenson invoked Thomas Kuhn in her discussion of the scholarly importance of *Leadership* and offered one of Kuhn's several formulations of paradigm shifts and the consequence for the field of study in which it occurs. Let us be appropriately candid: if our theory proves useful, it might be called a discovery, but not a revolutionary one, much less a paradigm. Nonetheless, however pretentious it may appear to even ask this question, can our theory pass the test that Kuhn, via Sorenson, set for a theory? Clearly, it comes from the work several people conducted over time. It proposes a shift in the study of leadership away from the traits, style, values, vision, gender, or race of those in position, authority, and power and toward the nexus of their narratives about the nature and degree of adaptive work (Stutts 2006) with those without authority, position, and power. This shift invites an expanded imagination, a new narrative in reflexive terms, about the way to study leadership.

This chapter has assimilated Burns's work and our contributors' ideas in a theory of effective narratives of adaptive work. Whatever its relationship with other scholarship, however, a theory has another test: Is it useful? What is its strategic and tactical utility? How does it explain what people mean when they say that leadership is called for? In terms of our theory, the questions ask whether someone can step forward and, in a universe of narratives, select the most relevant and combine them effectively in a manner to win more and more adherents in the appropriate domains. Leadership in our theory requires knowledge of who the pertinent audiences are and what are their stocks of stories; of the values at the heart of conflicting and corroborating narratives; of the nature and degree of changes that a group faces; and of the adaptive work required to address them. This leadership also remains mindful that leadership is more than a good story that relieves others of their responsibility. It is an innovative narrative of adaptive work that includes mobilizing the appropriate resources, our own and others, to get that work done.

References

Aristotle. www. *Politics. http://classics.mit.edu/Aristotle/politics.3.three.html.* Retrieved February 18, 2006.

Burns, J. M. 1978. *Leadership.* New York, N.Y.: Harper & Row.

----. 2003. *Transforming Leadership: A New Pursuit of Happiness.* New York: Grove Press.

----. and Susan Dunn. 2002. *The Three Roosevelts: Patrician Leaders Who Transformed America.* New York: Grove Press.

Funk, R.W., R.W. Hoover, and the Jesus Seminar. 1993. *The Five Gospels: What Did Jesus Really Say—The Search for the Authentic Words of Jesus.* San Francisco: HarperCollins Publisher.

Heifetz, R. A. 1994. *Leadership without Easy Answers.* Cambridge, Mass.: Belknap Press.

Gardner, H. and E. Laskin. 1995. *Leading Minds: An Anatomy of Leadership.* New York, N.Y.: HarperCollins.

Kellerman, B. 2004. *Bad Leadership: What It Is, How It Happens, Why It Matters.* Cambridge, Mass.: Harvard Business School Press.

McAdams, D. 1982. *Political Process and the Development of Black Insurgency.* Chicago, Ill.: University of Chicago.

PBS. www. 1997. "Speaker Phone." January 14. http://www.pbs.org/newshour/bb/congress/january97/cellular_1-14.html Retrieved from January 28, 2006.

Senge, P. M. 1990. *The Fifth Discipline: The Art & Practice of the Learning Organization.* New York: Doubleday.

Stutts, N. 2006. Personal communication. February 23.

Weber, Max. 1958rpt. "Politics as a Vocation." In *From Max Weber: Essays in Sociology* eds. H.H. Gerth and C. Wright Mills. New York: Oxford University Press, pp. 77-128.

Wheatley, M. and M. Kellner-Rogers. 1998. *A Simpler Way.* San Francisco: Berrett-Koehler Publishers.

CONCLUSION AS PROLOUGE
Richard A. Couto

With the work of theory building and synthesis done, let us return to where we began: Burns's reflections on his own work. After the fifteen chapters of this book, do we have a better vantage point to apply the insights of *Leadership* to the current challenges of the study and practice of leadership, which Burns offers—power, general theory, and fewer dichotomies?

Fewer Dichotomies

The last of Burns's concerns may be the easiest to address. In a quantum, the degree of interrelation and interdependence is such that dichotomies appear only as a snapshot to capture a far more complex reality or an analytical tool with which to examine it. Our theory relates modal values and end-values and transactional and transforming leadership—the champion dichotomies of *Leadership*—and integrates them, making modal values a test of transforming leadership. An effective narrative requires some degree of embodiment or human dimension of the vision or values of the narrative. This includes the role of modal values as the means to achieve end-values. If a narrative is to win adherents across domains, its adherents must embody modal values as well as espouse end-values.

Transforming leadership, in these terms, relates directly to transactional leadership. Transforming leadership offers narratives to move people to extend modal values of honesty, kindness, etc., to other groups of people, or ourselves, with some caste-like restrictions. Access for the physically disabled and group housing, rather than institutionalization, for competent but mentally retarded adults are examples of transforming changes toward end-values of equality and liberty but through the requirement that we act toward members of these groups as if they were like "us" and not alien "others." Of course, there is the shadowy side of this set of narratives as well. Those are the narratives of the alien others and the fear that permits "us" to treat others as "them" without modal vaiues in the name of end-values of security, including protections of our self-image.

Transforming leadership as the extension of modal values applies equally to intrapersonal, interpersonal, group, organizational, and even global domains. When we speak of the global community, we more often mean the technology, travel, and economic interdependencies that bind us in the same manner that coal-mining communities in Appalachia have ties with coal-mining communities in China. Less often do we mean by global community a sense of social justice or responsibility for some modal degree of safety for those who work in the mines and for the economic security and physical comfort of those who live in the coal-mining communities. If and when we speak of a global community, in the sense of the consideration and kindness to one another like that which miners and their families extend to one another, we will have pushed the narrative of moral values and human interrelatedness and interconnections from the domain of workplace and neighborhood to nation and to community of nations. That will make transforming leadership, among other things, a unified and not dichotomized universe of small acts of kindness and other modal values.

Power

In his simple story of a person bent on suicide running into an armed robber, Burns offers us this puzzle: when does someone with the means and intent to harm us physically not have power over us? The case offers the implied narrative, "Do what I say or I will harm you." It assumes that a person will respond to that threat out of fear for their well-being. The other person, however, has written a narrative of their life's end, and this threat simply adds a twist—death by a gunshot rather than drowning. In terms of our theory, we would say that persons with superior forces are powerless to gain compliance of others unless their threat is an effective narrative that coincides with those of others.

The conflict of narratives of threat may play out in dramatic fashion. For example, on September 11, 2001, when some of the passengers on Flight 93 learned that three planes had crashed into the World Trade Center's Twin Towers and into the Pentagon, they had reason to believe—a pattern of probability—that their plane was being hijacked as a fourth missile heading for a crash target in Washington, D.C. They had a new narrative of terrorism that uncoupled compliance to their captors' demands and safety. In the new narrative of terror, their deaths and the deaths of many more people were a given unless they resisted. They did so heroically and tragically.

Classical political science explains power in these situations. A has power over B when A can get B to do something B would not otherwise do (Dahl 1969:80)—hand over our money or comply with hijackers. We are adding here that A's power must include narratives and values that are shared with B. In our two cases, A has the means of physical harm but not power because B no longer values freedom from personal harm or believes that compliance with A is not a means to achieve it.

The ostensible use of violence as power occurs most frequently in the realm of political leadership. The state makes claim to its authority through the monopoly of legitimate violence and exercises it through its police, penal system, and armed forces. The state also arbitrates the appropriate and legitimate forms of coercion between citizens. Those who use violence against the state, assuming more than criminal intent, base their actions on other narratives, such as the corruption or injustice of the state and, hence, the state's illegal and immoral use of violence. War, civil disorder, political terrorism, and other strikes against the state are violent struggles over who will prevail and impose a narrative of justice and moral status upon the other; perhaps this is best summarized in the concise narrative "Might makes right!" Others may take nonviolent action to protest immoral but legal authority that disguises forms of state-sanctioned violence. Human history is replete with examples of groups who have resisted legal subordination, unpunished violence towards them, and an unequal distribution of public resources because of race, ethnicity, gender, age, ability, sexual preference, or some other characteristic. Similarly, groups have taken nonviolent action to protest the state violence of war and capital punishment or forms of state inaction to protect some for the violence of others. A surfeit of modal values in this "Right makes might!" narrative safeguards its moral purpose as well as its nonviolent means (Schell 2003).

In contexts other than the political, A's power over B is the use of authority without violence. If B does not comply with the wishes of A, in most cases, A has the authority to impose sanctions, such as a parent's grounding of a child, placing a negative performance assessment into an employee's personnel file, withholding promotions and pay raises, and perhaps even temporary and proportionate physical coercion within legal parameters.

This expression of authoritative power that preserves coercion finds less favor within the field of leadership studies after the increased emphasis on relationships within the practice of leadership. Sanctions and other manifestation of overt coercive power smack of command-and-control, hierarchical, and needless to say, authoritative or even authoritarian leadership. Leadership studies, correctly, leans toward leadership without the appearance of authority, or better, without invoking the narrative of coercive authority. Thus we talk about shared vision and relationship, informal authority, leadership without authority, etc.

Studies of power within political science (Bachrach and Baratz 1962; Berger and Luckman 1966; Couto 1993; Freire 1972; Edelman 1971; Gaventa 1980; Lukes 1974; Schattschneider 1960; Scott 1990) suggest what leadership studies affirms: formal authority, with the power of coercion, is best exercised when this capacity is not used. They explain, however, that other forms of power may carry on even in the absence of coercion. Thus, it is not a matter of power or no power at play but a matter of what dimensions of power are at play. In its second and third dimensions—which Alexandre, Gerber, and Walters deal with implicitly—power manifests itself as narratives and value-laden premises shaped by the powerful, for the preservation of the status quo, and shared with those whom derive little benefit from them. In these dimensions, coercion—power's first dimension—recedes because narratives about the legitimacy of authority and its sanctions make them unnecessary. In addition to this socialization, the second dimension of power regulates what narratives acquire legitimacy, and the third affects the supply of alternative narratives. These dimensions of power without coercion are familiar to us from the dystopian novels *Animal Farm* and *Brave New World*. They are also familiar to us but far less apparent in culture, including corporate; mores; and in other taken-for-granted situations of social con-

structed inequality. Ronald Walters had these dimensions of power without coercion in mind when he observed that power often determines what is good.

Joseph Schumpeter captured the outlines of the second and third dimensions
of power in pointing out, as did Karl Marx, that humans may have the capacity
to make choices but others shape their "choosing mentalities."

> Mankind is not free to choose....Things economic and social move by their
> own momentum and the ensuing situations compel individuals and groups to
> behave in certain ways whatever they may wish to do—not indeed by destroy-
> ing their freedom of choice but by shaping the choosing mentalities [second
> dimension] by narrowing the list of possibilities from which to choose [third
> dimension] (Schumpeter 1942: 129-30).

Schumpeter uses hyperbole in insisting that humans are not free to choose,
when he means that our freedom is limited to the alternatives that we can imagine and our ability to bring them forward. He extols the entrepreneurs of the
corporate sector precisely because of their imagination and this ability. Similarly, the chapters of this book abound with the celebration of the imagination
and courage of people, including of course Burns, to address adaptive work in
additional sectors to the corporate.

Choosing mentalities may limit our imaginations but they do not eliminate
it. Apparent compliance with narratives of the powerful may simply signal that
imaginative people have calculated that countering a dominant narrative may not
be effective or safe at a particular time. When action upon a set of counter narratives seems unlikely or even dangerous, their holders simply go offstage or *sotto
voce*. In Saddam Hussein's Iraq, for example, many prominent Shiite Muslims
invoked their doctrine of *tu'quia*, which gives a person the right to protect oneself from danger by thinking one thing and saying another or remaining silent to
give the appearance of agreement with the narratives of the powerful.

It is precisely because conflicting narratives endure that effective leadership
of adaptive work is at all possible. The capacity to shape and share narratives
exclusive of or even in conflict with the power of legitimate violence or authoritative sanctions is another form of leadership without authority that entails additional dimensions of power. Eleanor Roosevelt's work on behalf of the Universal Declaration of Human Rights illustrates this leadership with the moral authority to challenge the multidimensional power of narratives of exclusion and
subordination. So does Gandhi's work on behalf of decolonization and a society
divested of caste and religious repression. It is also the adaptive work of parent-
ing and local action such as the steps that Maggie and Lois took to promote the
value of sobriety in their band.

Power is a factor of informal authority and effective narratives of adaptive
work. Not the power of coercion, its first dimension, but in its resistance to the
ordinary narratives of the second and third dimensions of power that shape our
"choosing mentalities." Innovative narratives of leaders with and without authority have the power to shape our awareness of the need for adaptive work, its
appropriate forms, and its feasibility. They regulate conflict in power's first dimension; legitimate conflict in the second dimensions; and preserve hope in the
possibility of an improved state of affairs in power's third dimension. Challeng-

ing power and its effort to shape choosing mentalities, including what is good, becomes the insurgency of leadership about which Walters talks. Its insurgent nature may explain why some forms of leadership may be harmful to one's career or safety.

Burns explains that power is more than physical force and legal authority. Our theory of effective narratives of adaptive work suggests that leadership depends on a shared stock of narratives—including legitimacy authority, the threat of sanction, and the prospect of success—to motivate a person, group, or domain to take some action they might not have take otherwise. Thus we arrive back at "your money or your life." The power in that command to turn over money ultimately depends upon the stock of narratives in the person to whom it is addressed, regardless of the violence or form of authority entailed. Narratives consequently offer a key to understanding the resources of power available to all persons in a leadership relationship, those with and without authority, followers as well as leaders.

A General Theory of Leadership

Burns hoped to develop a general theory of leadership, one that might apply across cultures at any time and in the same place at different times. The very breadth of his analysis makes this difficult, however. He examines intellectual, reform, revolutionary, heroic, opinion, group, party, legislative, and executive leadership(s) and their developmental, social, and psychological origins and finds a bright thread of transforming and transactional leadership that holds them together and distinguishes them. He is far less mindful of context, however, and writes mainly with a concern for political leadership and leadership of broad social movements. Consequently, it is hard to apply his constructs to everyday occasions in our homes, workplace, and communities.

Our theory of effective narrative of adaptive work, on the other hand, may be used to explain leadership and its challenges in all venues—politics, organizations both for-profit and not-for-profit, social movements, etc. Within each of these venues, our theory has micro—even dyadic and intrapersonal—analytical capacity as well as macro. Likewise, our theory applies to all cultures and at different times. Wherever and whenever humans are engaged in trying to influence each other, we may explain their relationship and the process of change through the conflict and corroboration of narratives to support one or more values with precedents of initiative, inclusiveness, and creativity and consequences for one course of action over another. Wherever and whenever humans are engaged in story telling, we may probe those stories for their explicit and implicit, intended or consequential, influence over relationships.

Our theory may provide better understanding of "one of the most observed and least understood phenomena on earth" (Burns 1978:2). It clearly conveys it own limits of explanation. In a dynamic world of constant change, we can never understand all of the narratives conflicting and collaborating for adherence. Exacerbating this epistemic limit, every person undergoes that system of change differently. Thus we have a myriad of narratives in the various public domains multiplied by the number of people, each with a myriad of narratives. We have a chaotic system in which the number of parts, their systematic interrelatedness, and their changing nature surpass any ability to measure. Leadership thus entails uncertainty and the choice among many narratives of adaptive work within a path of effectiveness. It entails acting in the face of doubt. Leadership studies, in turn, entails a calculation, predictive or retrospective, within this complex system riddled with uncertainty of the pattern of probability of effective narratives about adaptive work. It entails a limited narrative of the actions of others based upon their limited knowledge of the narratives among which to choose.

Prologue

In 1978 Burns attempted to reach some generalizations about leadership. He got a discussion going. These pages report some of that discussion. The book's contributors explain the benefit they have derived from *Leadership*, the path they have taken from it, and the paths that lie ahead for others to take. We hope that our words do not end the discussion that *Leadership* started but will help your own efforts to contribute to a better understanding and practice of leadership. We offer not a conclusion to our work but a prologue to your own.

References

Bachrach, P. and Baratz, M. 1962. "The Two Faces of Power." *American Political Science Review,* 56:947-52.

Berger, P.L. and Luckman, T. 1966. *The Social Construction of Reality.* New York: Doubleday and Co.

Couto, R.A. 1993. "Narrative, Free Space, and Political Leadership in Social Movements." *Journal of Politics* 55:57-79.

Couto, R. A. 1995. "Defining a Citizen Leader." In *Leader's Companion: Insights on Leadership Through the Ages* ed. J. Thomas Wren. New York: Free Press.

Dahl, R.A. 1969. "The Concept of Power." In *Political Power: A Reader in Theory and Research* eds. R. Bell, D. M. Edwards, and R. H. Wagner. New York: Free Press.

Edelman, M. 1971. *Politics as Symbolic Action: Mass Arousal and Quiescence.* Chicago: Markham Publishing Co.

Freire, P. 1972. *The Pedagogy of the Oppressed.* New York: Penguin Books.

Gaventa, J. 1980. *Power and Powerlessness: Quiescence and Rebellion in an Appalachian Valley.* Urbana: University of Illinois Press.

Lukes, S. 1974. *Power: A Radical View.* New York: Macmillan.

Schattschneider, E.E. 1960. *The Semi-Sovereign People: A Realist's View of Democracy in America.* New York: Holt, Rinehart and Winston.

Schell, J. 2003. *The Unconquerable World: Power, Nonviolence, and the Will of the People.* New York: Metropolitan Books.

Schumpeter, J.R. 1942. *Capitalism, Socialism, and Democracy.* New York: Haprer & Row Publishers.

Scott, J.C. 1990. *Domination and the Arts of Resistance: Hidden Transcripts.* New Haven, Conn.: Yale University Press.

CONTRIBUTORS

Laurien Alexandre is founding director of Antioch University's Ph.D. in Leadership and Change Program and serves as professor and member of its core faculty. She is also Antioch's vice president for institution-wide programs. She received her Ph.D. in comparative culture from the University of California, Irvine, in 1984. She has long been committed to interdisciplinary inquiry, especially in her teaching and writing on media and international affairs. Her publications include articles on the media for both academic and popular audiences. She has also translated several scholarly books and articles for publication. She served on the editorial board for the *Encyclopedia of Leadership* and contributed several articles to it, including one on Emma Goldman.

James MacGregor Burns is a senior scholar of the Burns Academy of Leadership at the University of Maryland. He received his doctorate from Harvard in political science in 1947 and attended the London School of Economics in 1949. His career has included being a teacher, writer, scholar, and activist. He has won the Pulitzer Prize, the National Book Award, the Woodrow Wilson Prize, and numerous other awards. Professor Burns's theory on transforming leadership is the subject of much scholarship done in the area of leadership studies and has been the basis of more than four hundred doctoral dissertations. He has been president of the New England Political Science Association, the American Political Science Association, and the International Society for Political Psychology. His most recent book, *Transforming Leadership* (Atlantic Monthly Press), marks his continuing contribution to the field.

Richard Couto was a founding faculty member in two leadership programs, the Jepson School of Leadership Studies at the University of Richmond (1991-2001) and Antioch University's Ph.D. program in Leadership and Change. As a member of the editorial board of the *Encyclopedia of Leadership,* he contributed several entries to it, including "Narrative." His Ph.D. work at the University of Kentucky and later work as director of Vanderbilt University's Center for Health Services supported his research and community-development work in Appalachia. His teaching and publications on civil rights, teaching, and community-based organizations have won several national awards. From 1982-85 he was a Kellogg National Fellow and from 1985-88, a Lyndhurst Prize winner.

Robin Gerber is a national commentator and speaker on leadership and the author of *Leadership in the Eleanor Roosevelt Way: Timeless Strategies from the First Lady of Courage* (Penguin/Portfolio, 2002) and *Katharine Graham: The Leadership Journey of an American Icon* (Penguin/Portfolio, October 2005). She is also senior faculty for the Gallup Organization and a senior fellow in Executive Education at the Robert H. Smith School of Business, University of Maryland at College Park. She consults and lectures widely, in addition to serving on the Board of Contributors for the opinion pages of *USA Today* and appearing frequently on national media news programs. Gerber is a contributing author, with James MacGregor Burns and Georgia Sorenson, of *Dead Center: Clin-*

ton-Gore Leadership and the Perils of Moderation (Scribner, 1999). She obtained her law degree at Antioch Law School in Washington, D.C.

Ronald A. Heifetz, the King Hussein bin Talal Lecturer in Public Leadership, is co-founder of the Center for Public Leadership at Harvard University's John F. Kennedy School of Government. Known for his seminal work during the past two decades on the practice and teaching of leadership, his research focuses on how to build adaptive capacity in societies, businesses, and nonprofits. His book *Leadership Without Easy Answers* (Belknap) has been translated into many languages and is currently in its thirteenth printing; he coauthored the bestselling book *Leadership on the Line: Staying Alive through the Dangers of Leading* with Marty Linsky (Harvard Business School Press). Heifetz consults extensively in the United States and abroad. A graduate of Columbia University, Harvard Medical School, and the Kennedy School, Heifetz is a physician and a cellist.

Gill Robinson Hickman is currently a professor of leadership studies at the Jepson School of Leadership Studies, University of Richmond. Her career has involved both academic and administrative appointments. She has been a faculty presenter at the Salzburg Seminar in Salzburg, Austria, and at the University of the Western Cape in South Africa, where she presented a conceptual framework for leadership and transformation in twenty-first century organizations. She is editor of *Leading Organizations: Perspectives for a New Era* and coauthor with Dalton Lee of *Managing Human Resources in the Public Sector: A Shared Responsibility*; portions of her chapter may be found there as well. She received her B.A. from the University of Denver in political science, Masters of public administration from the University of California, and Ph.D. in public administration from the University of Southern California.

Edwin P. Hollander has been City University of New York Distinguished Professor of Psychology at Baruch College and the Graduate Center since 1989, with emeritus status awarded in 1999. Previously he served at SUNY Buffalo as professor of psychology from 1962, founding director of the doctoral program in social/organizational psychology, then provost of social sciences. He has a B.S. in psychology from Case Western Reserve (1948) and an M.A. and Ph.D. (1950, 1952) from Columbia. He taught at Carnegie-Mellon, Washington (St. Louis), and American (D.C.). He was Fulbright professor at Istanbul; NIMH senior fellow at London's Tavistock Institute; and visiting faculty at Wisconsin, Harvard, Oxford, and the Institute of American Studies in Paris. He was a study director at the National Academy of Sciences in D.C. and a naval aviation psychologist at Pensacola in 1951-1954, where he began his leadership studies. Using peer nominations and critical incidents, two techniques his work has furthered, he studied organizational leadership-followership, innovation, and autonomy. His publications include *Leaders, Groups, and Influence* (1964), *Leadership Dynamics* (1978), *Principles and Methods of Social Psychology* (1981, 4th ed.), and numerous chapters, articles, and reviews. His recent honors include awards from the New York Academy of Sciences and the Center for Creative Leadership (CCL) for "outstanding, career-long contributions."

Tiffany Hansbrough directs the Brain Leadership Program at Baldwin-Wallace College. Her program includes a minor in leadership. She was formerly an assistant professor of leadership studies at the Jepson School of Leadership Studies, University of Richmond, and prior to that, visiting assistant professor of Management at Purdue University. She has presented at the Academy of Management Conference and has published articles in *The Leadership Quarterly*. She received her B.A. in psychology from the University of Iowa and her Ph.D. in organizational behavior from the State University of New York at Buffalo.

Barbara Kellerman is research director of the Center for Public Leadership and lecturer in public policy at Harvard University's Kennedy School of Government. She served as the center's executive director from 2000-2003 and as director of the Center for the Advanced Study of Leadership at the Burns Academy of Leadership at the University of Maryland. She has held numerous professorships, including a Fulbright fellowship. Kellerman received her B.A. from Sarah Lawrence College and her M.A., M.Phil., and Ph.D. (1975 in political science) degrees from Yale University. She pioneered the multidisciplinary nature of leadership studies, and her most recent book, *Bad Leadership: What It Is, How It Happens, Why It Matters*, breaks new ground as well. Her political commentary has aired on CBS, NBC, PBS, and CNN and has appeared in the nation's most distinguished newspapers.

Larraine Matusak is a leadership scholar and former program officer at the W. K. Kellogg Foundation, where she directed the Kellogg National Fellowship Program. She also led in the creation of the leadership grant-making area at the foundation. She has served in a wide variety of leadership roles, including as president of Thomas A. Edison State College in New Jersey and dean and founder of the College of Alternative Programs at the University of Evansville, Indiana. Matusak presently consults with numerous organizations, communities, academic institutions, and foundations. Her book *Finding Your Own Voice* exemplifies her plain-spoken trust in the ability of ordinary people to do extraordinary things.

Terry L. Price, associate professor of leadership studies at the Jepson School of Leadership Studies, University of Richmond, specializes in leadership ethics, moral psychology, applied epistemology, and social, political, and legal theory. A philosopher with grounding in politics and psychology, he also studied politics on a John M. Olin Fellowship at the University of Oxford. He wrote the entries for "Ethics," "Philosophy," and "Dirty Hands" for the *Encyclopedia of Leadership*. He is author of *Understanding Ethical Failures in Leadership* and co-editor of *The International Library of Leadership*.

Georgia Sorenson served as a speech writer/consultant on two presidential campaigns. She has been published in professional journals and is a frequent public commentator on social issues in the popular media. As founder, director, and staff member of the Burns Academy of Leadership at the University of Maryland, she has been involved in leadership and civic education in over twenty-eight countries. She received a bachelor's degree in psychology from American University, a master's degree in psychology from Hood College, and her D.Ed. from the University of Maryland at College Park. She is co-editor of *The Encyclopedia of Leadership* and the forthcoming *The Quest for a General Theory of Leadership* (Elgar).

Ronald Walters is a professor in the Afro-American Studies Program, Department of Government and Politics, and a senior fellow at the Burns Academy of Leadership at the University of Maryland. He has combined scholarship and activism his entire life. In 1958, he conducted a sit-in as a high school student in his hometown of Wichita, Kansas. He has served as assistant professor of political science at Syracuse, assistant professor and chairman of Afro-American Studies at Brandeis University, and professor and chairman of the Political Science Department at Howard University. He has also served as visiting professor at Princeton University and as a fellow of the Institute of Politics at the Kennedy School of Government at Harvard University. His recently co-authored *Black Leadership: Theory, Research and Praxis* with Robert Smith. He is a frequent commentator on race and politics in the print and electronic media.

Margaret Wheatley is president of The Berkana Institute, which explores new ideas, processes, and structures that investigate how organizations can develop and sustain their capacity, clarity, and resiliency in these turbulent times. She has been an organizational consultant and researcher since 1973 with an unusually broad variety of organizations on six different continents. Her clients and audiences range from the head of the U.S. Army to twelve-year-old Girl Scouts, from CEOs to small-town ministers. Her first work was as a public school teacher and urban education administrator in New York and a Peace Corps volunteer in Korea. Wheatley's path-breaking book, *Leadership and the New Science,* was first published in 1992 and has since been translated into twelve different languages. She received her doctorate from Harvard University's program in administration and social policy. She holds an M.A. in communications and systems thinking from New York University.

J. Thomas Wren is an associate professor and associate dean in leadership studies at the Jepson School of Leadership Studies, University of Richmond. He received a B.A. in economics and social studies from Denisen University, a J.D. from the University of Virginia, an M.A. in public affairs from George Washington University, and an M.A. and Ph.D. in history from the College of William and Mary. He is an associate editor of the *Journal of Leadership Studies* and has served on the board of the International Leadership Association. He edited *The Leader's Companion: Insights on Leadership Through the Ages* and co-edited *The International Library of Leadership* in addition to authoring several articles in the fields of history and leadership. His primary research interest is the leadership implications of the implementation of popular sovereignty in America. In 1996, he received the Distinguished Educators Award at the University of Richmond.

Adam Yarmolinsky. Sadly, Adam Yarmolinsky died on January 5, 2000, at the age of 77. His contribution comes from a talk delivered at the Jepson School of Leadership Studies, University of Richmond, on April 13, 1998. After his completing undergraduate work at Harvard and obtaining a law degree from Yale, Mr. Yarmolinsky clerked for Justice Stanley Reed in the U.S. Supreme Court. He held responsible positions in the campaign and administration of John F. Kennedy and several subsequent Democratic administrations. Yarmolinsky was a principal architect of the anti-poverty programs of the Great Society and a high-ranking member of the Defense Department from 1961 to 1996. His last post in the Defense Department entailed responsibility for international security affairs. He served on the faculty at Harvard, the University of Massachusetts, and the University of Maryland, Baltimore County. He served as provost at the University of Maryland, Baltimore County, from 1985 to 1993 and continued in the role of Regents Professor of Public Policy up until his death.

INDEX